SECOND EDITION

forbidden drugs

Philip Robson

Consultant Psychiatrist and

Senior Clinical Lecturer

The Warneford Hospital

Oxford, UK

OXFORD

UNIVERSITY PRESS

OXFORD
UNIVERSITY PRESS

Great Clarendon Street, Oxford OX2 6DP
Oxford University Press is a department of the University of Oxford.
It furthers the University's objective of excellence in research, scholarship,
and education by publishing worldwide in

Oxford New York

Auckland Cape Town Dar es Salaam Hong Kong Karachi
Kuala Lumpur Madrid Melbourne Mexico City Nairobi
New Delhi Shanghai Taipei Toronto

With offices in

Argentina Austria Brazil Chile Czech Republic France Greece
Guatemala Hungary Italy Japan South Korea Poland Portugal
Singapore Switzerland Thailand Turkey Ukraine Vietnam

Published in the United States
by Oxford University Press Inc., New York

First Edition published 1994
Second Edition published 1999
Reprinted 2001, 2002, 2005

A catalogue record for this book is available from theBritish Library

Library of Congress Cataloging in Publication Data
Robson, Philip.
Forbidden drugs / by Philip Robson.—2nd ed.
Includes bibliographical references and index.
1. Substance abuse.   2. Psychotropic drugs Popular works.
I. Title.
[DNLM: 1. Substance-Related Disorders.   2. Street Drugs.
3. Substance-Related Disorders—etiology.   WM 270 R667f 1999]
RC564.29.R65   1999   362.29—dc21   99–32331
DNLM/DLC

ISBN 0 19 262955 7

Printed in Great Britain
on acid-free paper by
Biddles Ltd., King's Lynn, Norfolk

forbidden drugs

for Renée, Harry, and Sophie

That humanity at large will
ever be able to dispense
with Artificial Paradises
seems very unlikely
Aldous Huxley

The best of life is
but intoxication
Lord Byron

Every form of addiction
is bad, no matter whether
the narcotic be alcohol
or morphine or idealism
C. G. Jung

I was teetotal
until prohibition
Groucho Marx

preface

to the second edition

A request from a publisher for a second edition, like the ingestion of a recreational drug, is bound to result in a mixture of pleasure and pain. Pleasure, because of the implication that the initial offering was not entirely devoid of merit; pain in contemplating the mountain of unforeseen work that is suddenly conjured up.

The subject matter of the book certainly remains topical. The controversy and concern generated globally by 'the drugs problem' show no sign of abating as we approach the millennium. The British Prime Minister must have echoed the thoughts of many world leaders when he stated in 1998 that this country would be a better place to live ' . . . if we could break once and for all the vicious cycle of drugs and crime which wrecks lives and threatens communities'.

The book is based primarily upon a critical analysis of the relevant scientific literature. It is also shaped by the research I have been involved in over the years exploring various aspects of the human response to drugs, both prescribed and recreational, and by my daily contact with patients and their often anguished families at the drug dependency unit in Oxford. But I was conscious of a wider personal perspective as I wrote the new edition: as a parent of teenage children; as one whose contact with certain friends and acquaintances has ensured familiarity with most forms of recreational drug use in the real world outside the clinic and the laboratory; and as one whose formative student years were spent in the patchouli-laden atmosphere of swinging London during the psychedelic Sixties.

In preparing this second edition I have taken note of the comments of friends, patients, and reviewers, and paid heed to sagacious voices from within Oxford University Press. My purpose remains unchanged: to provide a readable and informative appraisal of recreational drugs and the issues which surround their use, and to blow away some of the cobwebs of myth, prejudice, and hyperbole which envelop them.

The first part of the book explores the reasons why people take drugs and the likely consequences of this; the second examines the nature of the drugs themselves; and in the final section there is a discussion of the meaning of addiction, a review of the various ways of helping people cope with drug-related problems, and an analysis of contemporary drug policy in various countries. The most obvious change is the addition of three new chapters on tobacco, alcohol, and anabolic steroids. I always regretted not including these in the first edition, not least because their omission might perpetuate the illusion that there is some logic in setting them apart from other, less socially acceptable recreational drugs. Nor can they be sensibly excluded on account of the book's title: all three have been forbidden at some time or place.

All the other chapters have been fully revised and updated, and the layout has been improved by the introduction of subtitles throughout. The fairly detailed historical accounts of the various drugs met with some approval, so these have been retained and in some cases slightly expanded. Sections dealing with scientific matters are written in plain English and with no expectation of prior knowledge.

No author could wish for a more agreeable and constructive relationship with a publisher than I have experienced with Oxford University Press. In particular, I would like to thank Alison Langton, without whom the book would never have been conceived; Susan Harrison, who always looks for new angles; Martin Baum, a feisty new editor for the second edition; and, above all, John Harrison, whose amiable and undeviating support, encouragement and wise advice sustained me through both editions.

Oxford   P.R.
April, 1999

preface

to the first edition

I try my best never to talk about drugs at social gatherings. This is because I have learnt from hard experience that if I do forget my golden rule and get drawn on the subject and my wife is not on hand to turn the conversation to safer matters, the discussion invariably becomes heated. On one memorable occasion in Australia, I would undoubtedly have been knocked unconscious had it not been for the diplomatic skills of our hostess.

It is rare to come across anybody who feels neutral or unconcerned about the issues surrounding the forbidden drugs. This is because you don't have to be a user to be profoundly affected by them on a personal level. Parents concerned about what their children are up to; teachers, doctors, lawyers, and other professionals who come into contact with drug use in the course of their work; victims of the spiralling levels of drug-related crime; policy makers, social activists, and libertarians; and almost anyone who ever opens a newspaper.

This sense of personal involvement introduces an emotional tone into any debate which can lead to bombast and speculation taking the place of a calm appraisal of the various dilemmas. 'Stamp out reality' was a typically provocative slogan of the hallucinatory sixties, but it would also seem an apt motto for some of the modern rhetoricians and gurus who support or oppose the 'war on drugs'.

Recent opinion polls have indicated that many North Americans think that illegal drugs represent the nation's number one problem, with the related nightmares of AIDS and crime close behind. We don't yet seem quite so concerned in the United Kingdom, possibly because organized crime is less high-profile, and many of us still do not connect the soaring levels of muggings, car crime, and burglaries with someone's need to feed a drug habit. The bald truth is that tens of thousands of people in Britain are faced with the challenge of raising £100 or so every day of their lives to maintain their supply of heroin or cocaine, with no legal income except a social security cheque worth about £40 a week.

Discovering that they are addicted is sometimes the first inkling that people have of the potency of the drugs they have been ingesting. Only the other day, this account was published in the letters section of a national newspaper:

> 'I made the decision to stop ... in my quest for a healthier
> lifestyle, and [had my last dose] ... last Thursday morning.
> By evening I had a mild headache. On Friday morning I had a
> fierce headache and felt dizzy and sick. I could not go to
> work. Friday evening I was physically sick and the headache
> was worse, with shooting pains in my neck and shoulders.
> Saturday I still had a bad headache, but I wasn't feeling
> sick and pain relief was possible.
>   Today, Sunday, I have a mild headache but I still feel very
> drowsy. I hope I shall continue to feel better tomorrow.'

This writer was describing the consequences of breaking her addiction to coffee and tea. Many people today would either not classify caffeine as a real drug at all or would see it as being of negligible potency. My 11-year-old daughter enjoys a cup of tea most days and nobody reports me to Social Services, yet in 17th-century Britain coffee was regarded very much as cannabis is nowadays: a potent mind-altering chemical which should be treated with respect. Since one only becomes aware of being addicted to something when it ceases to be available, most people remain blissfully unaware that they are indeed hooked – just as many 19th-century Britons and North Americans remained unaware that they were hooked on opium or cocaine since these too were freely available at that time.

Cultural conditioning is very powerful and accounts for much of the glaring inconsistency in attitudes towards familiar and unfamiliar drugs, and it is fascinating to look back and see how these cultural attitudes have fluctuated over the decades. The public perception of cocaine is a case in point: from a harmless tonic and constituent of that refreshing beverage Coca-Cola in the 19th century to a terrifyingly addictive narcotic fit only for debauchees and criminals between the world wars, to being *de rigueur* for everyone who aspired to a Porsche or even just a mobile phone in the Thatcher/Reagan years. The properties of cocaine, although significantly influenced by the way it is used, have remained constant, but the way they are interpreted by 'experts' and the public at large continually changes.

My aim in writing this book has been to set out for the interested reader with no special experience or scientific knowledge what is known about the drugs themselves and why people take them, the meaning of addiction and the treatments that are available for it, and the natural history of drug use. I have also described the current policy on drugs in Britain, and discussed some ideas for reducing drug-related problems in the future. I have not tried too hard to resist expressing some personal opinions along the way and I hope these are consistent with the known facts. This will be for the reader to judge and react appropriately with assent or outrage; the only response that would disappoint would be indifference.

Oxford   P. R.
June 1994

contents

part one

why use drugs?

Most readers will be neither surprised nor disturbed to be reminded that almost every adult in Britain and North America uses drugs every day of their lives in the form of caffeine, alcohol, or tobacco. Although the latter gets a uniformly bad press these days, most parents would probably react calmly to a survey* suggesting that by the age of 16 the vast majority (94%) of their children will have sampled alcohol, two-thirds will describe themselves as regular drinkers, and only one in five will deny ever having been drunk. In sharp contrast to this equanimity, a growing awareness that almost half of these same 16-year-olds have experimented with at least one street drug is seen as extremely disturbing and gives rise to urgent calls for 'something to be done'. The fact that this appetite for 'recreational' drugs occurs at a time of unprecedented reliance upon prescribed medicines and 'over-the-counter' pharmaceutical and herbal remedies is often overlooked. Pills are seen by many as a quick and easy solution to difficulties which have nothing whatsoever to do with medical disorders. General practitioners are besieged by distressed people who would much rather walk out of the

---

* Throughout this book, prevalence figures are based upon published surveys, seizure rates by police and customs, databases, and official audits. All of these sources have their shortcomings, and readers should take them as approximations rather than hard facts. Source documents are to be found in the bibliography.

surgery clutching a prescription than set about the more demanding task of finding practical solutions to their economic, social, and interpersonal difficulties.

Recreational drug use is a worldwide phenomenon, but there are considerable national and regional variations. Sixteen-year-olds from the United Kingdom and United States topped the league in lifetime experience of any illicit drug use in a comparison of 23 countries carried out in 1995 (Australia was not included in the study, but is also right up there at the top of the range). Forty-one-per cent of UK school students admitted cannabis use in comparison with 34% of North Americans, 19% of Italians, 15% of Spanish, 12% of French, and 2% of Greeks. Seventy per cent of British students admitted to a bout of drunkenness in the previous year compared to the average of 48% of the other countries. Perhaps they were just more honest!

Before trying to explain this universal attraction to both legal and illegal recreational drugs, let us first examine in more detail their profile in the UK.

Prevalence of recreational drug use

In 1995, 28% of British men and 26% of women said they were regular smokers, averaging 16 and 14 cigarettes per day respectively. Smoking among younger children has been increasing steadily, especially among girls, so that between the ages of 11 and 15 10% of boys and 13% of girls smoke regularly and by the age of 16 63% of boys and 72% of girls will have tried a cigarette. The most powerful predictor for taking up smoking is having a sibling or parents who smoke. The habit is more common among children with only one parent, living in a poor neighbourhood, or with lower educational attainments. The prevalence of regular smoking among British 16-year-olds (36%) is comparable to the average across other European nations (32%). Most people who are destined to be daily smokers as adults are already smoking at age 18. The decline in smoking among British adults has not been mirrored among children: over the past two decades, the number of boys under 16 starting to smoke has remained constant whilst the number of girls starting has doubled. Among 16-year-old regular smokers, the average consumption is 40 per week for girls and 48 per week for boys. About a quarter of university students smoke regularly with an equal sex distribution, but there is considerable variation between faculties: prevalence is at least 30% among art students and social scientists but only 5% among female student vets. Seventeen per cent of medical students still puff away in defiance of the mute testimony of the specimen jars and pathology slides that surround them.

The consumption of alcohol in the UK per head of population has doubled since 1950. By the age of 16, 94% of young people have tried alcohol and 78% of them will have been drunk on at least one occasion. In the comparison of European nations, the UK tops the league in the proportion of 16-year-olds who first became drunk at the age of 13 or less, and who report being drunk at least three times within the previous month. Consumption levels in Britain peak between the ages of 18 and 20, although the profile of consumption differs between the sexes: boys steadily increase their intake between the ages of 16 and 20, whilst that of girls declines over the same period. Among university students there are again large variations between faculties, with the highest consumption among male students of biological sciences who average 40 units per week. Overall, 40% of male and 24% of female students drink more than the levels of 'safe drinking' recommended by the Royal College of Physicians. Only 6% of white students are non-drinkers, in comparison with 50% of non-white students.

Despite prohibitive laws and the vigorous activities of police and customs, illicit drugs remain easily accessible to anyone who desires them. Not just the 'softer' drugs, but heroin and cocaine too are available on the streets or in the pubs and clubs of every town in England. About one in four of the UK population have tried an illegal drug at some time, amounting to some 10 million people between the ages of 16 and 69. Of these, around two million are regular, current users. Cannabis accounts for about 85% of this drug use with well over three million people having smoked it within the last year, and most cannabis smokers will never use any other illegal drug. Ethnic variations are considerable: among respondents to the 1996 British Crime Survey, 46% of whites admitted illegal drug use compared with 31% of Afro-Caribbeans, 22% of Indians, and 16% of Pakistanis or Bangladeshis.

Until the early 1990s illegal drug use among young people seemed to be increasing inexorably, but appears to have levelled out over the past five years although averages can mask regional variations: levels have decreased between 1994 and 1996 in London but gone up in the Midlands and the North of England. Drug use in children under 14 is more common in girls than boys. Thereafter, experimentation becomes more common in boys, but the gender ratio is equal for those who progress to repeated drug use. Less than 10% of 12-year-olds have tried any drug but exposure increases sharply in the early teens, so that two-thirds of 15-year-olds will have been offered drugs and around 40% will have accepted. One in two young people studying for A levels will have tried cannabis, a fifth to a quarter LSD or amphetamine, around 10% solvents or Ecstasy, 5% or so tranquillizers, and a tiny minority cocaine or heroin. Any 19-year-old who has not experimented with at least one illegal drug will find themselves in a minority these days, and university students are no exception: around 56% have smoked cannabis in the past and a fifth do so currently, though again there are wide faculty variations. Students of the arts and social sciences are way out ahead with more than 70% having tried the drug and 28% toking regularly, and they also consume a wider range of drugs than average. Two-thirds of first-time drug use occurs before the student reaches university.

Three-quarters of those who ever try an illegal drug will have done so by the age of 18, with peak use occurring in the late teens and early twenties and a steady decline thereafter. This decline correlates with progressive involvement in the structures of society as work, marriage, and parenthood take their toll. Married people use less drugs than those who are single or divorced, but the highest rates of all occur in men living with women to whom they are not married. It is well known that in later life women are much higher consumers of prescribed psychoactive drugs, while men seem to rely more on alcohol to soothe, or inflame, their nerves.

Most of the three and a half million young people under the age of 25 years who said they had taken an illegal drug in 1996 had used only cannabis, and more than half of all first-time users will only try a drug once or use it very occasionally. Ten per cent of 16–29 year-olds in the UK took two or more illegal drugs during 1996. The starting point is experimentation with cigarettes, wine, beer, or solvents. Frequency of drunken episodes correlates with future intake of cigarettes and illegal drugs, the first of which is almost always cannabis. The greater the consumption of cannabis, the more the chance that other drugs will be tried. Stimulants, 'party drugs', and hallucinogens might follow, and heroin or crack cocaine are the end-points for that tiny minority who have tried everything but are still searching. It must be emphasized that there is no evidence that this is a causative sequence. The argument that cannabis inexorably leads on to harder drug use is confounded by the observation that a large majority of users never touch any other illegal drug. Besides, any escalation theory would have to conclude that the horror of heroin or crack addiction must find its roots in the earliest experiences of intoxication – in other words, that first cup of sugar-laced tea or coffee!

Only 3% of the drug-using population ever injects a drug. Heroin and crack cocaine remain distinctly minority interests, with only 1% of those under 30 years admitting ever having tried either, but people who try heroin certainly find it hard to use it sparingly. In one large survey, the number of adolescents who had tried heroin was only 1.7% of the total sample. But of those who had used it once, 65% used it again, and of these two-thirds were using it weekly and 15% daily. Crack and heroin really do represent a different ball game.

It is clear from all these figures that the appetite for mind-altering drugs, both legal and illegal, remains as awesome now as it has ever been. Not content with just alcohol and cigarettes, millions of ordinary people are prepared to flout the law and face considerable risk and inconvenience in order to consume forbidden substances. Why do they do it?

This question can be approached on two levels: first, by contemplating the attraction or function of intoxication, and secondly by a more utilitarian search for those human or environmental characteristics which can be shown to make initial experimentation or persistence with drugs more likely.

The search for 'altered consciousness'

A number of writers interested in psychoactive drugs have come to the conclusion that a desire or need for the experience of 'altered consciousness' has always represented more to mankind than mere hedonistic self-indulgence. Andrew Weil (*The Natural Mind*, 1973) has argued that it is a basic human appetite, recognizable throughout history from the most primitive beginnings. Of interest here is the observation that some animals in their natural habitat seem interested in intoxication, seeking to experience it repeatedly. Dogs have been observed snuffling the fumes from rotting vegetation to the point of incoordination, and an acquaintance of the writer had a cat which confounded its carnivorous nature by gobbling up any marijuana she inadvertently left lying around.

Weil argues that drug-induced mental changes are part of a whole range of natural 'altered states' which fulfill an important revitalizing or insight-producing function. Other examples of these would include twilight states between sleep and waking, daydreams, trances, meditation, hypnosis, and delirium. He sees evidence of the in-built attraction and need for these states in the antics of children making themselves dizzy, faint, or even unconscious by whirling or breath-holding. He quotes a more famous writer, Aldous Huxley: '… the urge to escape, the longing to transcend themselves if only for a few minutes, is and always has been one of the principal appetites of the soul. Art and religion, carnivals and saturnalia, dancing and listening to oratory – all these have served, in H. G. Wells's phrase, as Doors in the Wall.'

The writings of Weil and others challenge the assumption that consciousness alteration is undesirable, dangerous, or 'wrong'. Does 'reality', he asks, really equate to ordinary waking consciousness? Huxley certainly did not think so, and modern brain research has given support to his conception of the brain as a sort of filter or reducing-valve, diverting from conscious awareness all information that has no immediate survival value. He felt that the inhabitants of a modern, materialistic society progressively stripped of the spiritual dimension had more need than ever to transport themselves beyond such sterile boundaries. Street graffiti in the late 1960s called on people to 'stamp out reality'.

This is a controversial line to pursue because it suggests that those who use mind-altering drugs, who take the chance of freeing themselves from a perceptual strait-jacket, may reap significant benefits from the experience. At the very least, they may gain insight into the robotic, stereotyped nature of much human behaviour. This can be a profoundly unsettling realization, and none of these writers suggest that it is an undertaking without risk. Weil concedes that drugs can '… hurt your body, hurt your mind, impede your development'. But the possibility does arise that these might be risks worth taking.

Reasons for experimenting with drugs

If you ask teenagers why they use drugs, most will simply tell you that they are pleasurable or exciting. Other reasons include getting rid of unpleasant feelings of shyness, anxiety, or lack of confidence, fitting in with their friends, or because it makes them feel sophisticated or pleasantly rebellious and independent. Scientists have tried to refine these simple explanations or attach numbers to them. One investigator found that fun and curiosity accounted for half, peer pressure a third, and self-medication only a fifth of the stated motivation. This pattern held true for all drug types except the stimulants; here, fun and curiosity was the prime mover for 40%, with the other two categories 30% each. Among Oxford undergraduates the main reason for using both alcohol and drugs was pleasure, with stress relief the principal benefit for around a fifth of the students in both categories. Social pressure was slightly more influential in encouraging alcohol use than it was for drugs. Several factors make drug or alcohol use at university more likely: emergence from the controls of family and school life, the excitement of a new environment and circle of friends, social and academic pressure, and enhanced availability of legal and illegal substances. Expectations of positive consequences vastly outweigh the anticipation of problems, but most drinkers, for example, can think of many reasons for *not* drinking. The most commonly expressed in one study were 'awful effects' (89%), cost (76%), health reasons (74%), risk of accidents (66%), and fear of losing control (51%). Another survey showed that the main dislikes for drug use were health risk (13%), cost (7%), breaking the law (7%), hangovers (6%), and fear of addiction (6%). However, the main reason for stopping was insufficient pleasure rather than a fear of adverse consequences. Young people say they get their information about drugs from the following sources in descending order: media, friends, school teachers, and the police.

What it all boils down to is that most adolescents and students try a drug for one of three main reasons: fun and curiosity, to fit in with their friends, or to medicate themselves for some unpleasant emotion and forget their troubles. But the interesting question remains: what makes one teenager say 'yes please' and another 'no thanks'? To answer this we have to examine some individual and environmental characteristics.

Biological explanations

The most obvious biological attribute to start with is gender. Males are much less likely to be total abstainers, and tend to consume larger average quantities of drugs and alcohol than females of similar age and social circumstances. The most frequent drug of abuse for men is alcohol and for women prescribed sedative/hypnotics – currently benzodiazepines, in previous decades barbiturates. Much of this intergender variation is no doubt culturally induced.

Our understanding of how genetic make-up may influence the response to drugs and susceptibility to pleasant or unpleasant effects remains rather rudimentary. Temperament is to some extent genetically determined, and in turn predisposes to particular lifestyles (see below). Adoption studies suggest that certain types of alcoholism can be transmitted genetically in males, and in animals a predisposition to the abuse of morphine or barbiturates can be inbred. Genetic inheritance can influence routes and rates of drug metabolism, and relevant physiological systems; for example, brain wave response (as measured by an electroencephalogram) to drug administration is in part genetically mediated. It is quite easy to breed animals which are more or less sensitive to specific drug effects, vulnerable to tolerance, dependence, or withdrawal symptoms, or likely to develop drug-seeking behaviour. There is no obvious reason why these genetic traits should not evolve naturally in humans.

The balance of the brain's chemical messengers (neurotransmitters) seems to vary between individuals. If a person happens to be a bit short of, say, serotonin in a particular brain system they may still function normally in most circumstances because other chemical messengers can compensate. If they happen to take a drug which particularly boosts serotonin activity, however, they may well experience more positive effects than someone who has a natural sufficiency of serotonin. People differ in the way they metabolize drugs and this can greatly alter the balance of pleasant and unpleasant effects. For example, some Asian people are genetically programmed to experience a large build-up of the toxic metabolite acetaldehyde in response to a modest intake of alcohol. The cracking headache which results is most unrewarding, so these individuals are much less likely to drink regularly if at all. We shall return to these pharmacological factors in more detail in examining the mechanisms of addiction in Chapter 13.

Psychological explanations

A considerable amount of attention has been focused on the personal attributes and early influences which might increase the likelihood of a child or young person experimenting with drugs and going on to develop problems as a result. Unfortunately, much of this work has targeted young people who are already problem drug users and in whom it is impossible to separate cause from effect. For example, problem drug users are often found to have low self-esteem and some investigators have been tempted to conclude that low self-esteem is likely to have been a causative factor in the development of harmful drug use. In reality, unless the study can show that the low self-esteem was present before any exposure to drugs occurred, an equally likely explanation is that the problem drug use caused the low self-esteem.

Unsuspecting adolescents in university cities throughout the world have been exposed over the years to bundles of bulky questionnaires and hordes of earnest interviewers in an attempt to give rather woolly personal characteristics a more scientific gloss. The gargantuan Minnesota Multiphasic Personality Inventory alone has formed the centrepiece for well over a hundred papers. Not surprisingly, this effort has generated a host of apparent associations and predictors of future drug use. For what it is worth, the typical drug-user-to-be is likely to possess at least some of the following characteristics: alienation, rebelliousness, nonconformity to conventional values, and a tolerant attitude towards unusual or deviant behaviour; a relative lack of ambition and commit-ment to school work or career building; independent mindedness, self-reliance, and a reluctance to abide by rules; impulsivity; a preoccupation with pleasure seeking and minimal concern for risk; poor problem-solving, coping, and 'refusal' skills; a history of physical or psychological illness; and impaired emotional well-being or consistently low self-esteem. It is calculated that up to 40% of children and adolescents experience at least minor mental health problems at some time, and up to 10% have moderate to severe problems. Such emotional difficulties are reportedly twice as common in urban as opposed to rural areas. The prevalence of depression increases steadily in the teenage years, and eating disorders peak at age 17.

Certain personal attributes, attitudes, and behaviours in early adolescence can be shown to predict, albeit weakly, experimentation with street drugs at some point in the future. On the behavioural side, these include a demonstrated fondness for beer, cigarettes, and wine; minor delinquency; early sexual experience; active participation in political or other 'protest activity' (American studies only!); and a general willingness to get involved in exciting but risky activities. Temperamental characteristics such as feeling persistently fed up or irritable, and regular tantrums in very young children, are associated with 'problem behaviours' in adolescence and delinquency in adults. Traits such as high novelty seeking and low harm avoidance in six-year-olds have been shown to predict early onset of substance use. Children who generally have internal rather than external explanations for things that happen (e.g. explaining failure in an exam because 'I didn't work hard enough' as opposed to 'the paper was too hard') are much less susceptible to peer pressure.

A measure which reliably predicts drug experimentation is called the Sensation Seeking Scale. 'Sensation seeking' has been defined as 'the need for varied, novel, and complex sensations and experiences and the willingness to take physical and social risks for the sake of such experience' (Zuckerman, 1979). The Sensation Seeking Scale is a questionnaire which provides a global score and ratings on four sub-scales labelled 'thrill and adventure seeking', 'experience seeking', 'disinhibition', and 'boredom susceptibility'. People who like cigarettes, alcohol, and stimulating foods also score high on this scale, which its author believes provides a measure of 'sensitivity to reinforcement'. He predicted that high scorers would prefer stimulants and hallucinogens to other classes of drugs, but this has not proved to be the case. It seems that high scorers value altered consciousness in whatever form it may take.

The Sensation Seeking Scale does not have much value as an explanatory tool. It is like trying to account for the consumption of cakes by a measure of liking for sweet things. A person who enjoys excitement and doesn't dwell too much on the risks is more likely to race motor-bikes or smoke cannabis than someone who lacks these attributes. So what? The majority of people with these same attributes will not do either of these things, but will select any one of a thousand other pursuits which fulfill their requirements but do not happen to be on the investigator's list. The real question to be answered is one step back: what are the biological or existential precursors of a craving for excitement and disdain for risk?

As mentioned above, the importance of low self-esteem in the development of drug-related problems remains uncertain but it is certainly true that many of the personal characteristics which have been linked with vulnerability to compulsive drug use are also associated with poor self-esteem: submissiveness, a tendency to depend upon others and constantly crave approval, lack of confidence, a sense of helplessness, anxiety, low expectations for the future, and a readiness to give up if the going gets tough. As one might expect, having high self-esteem is enormously valuable quite apart from the obvious feel-good factor. People who have it are likely to be more confident and self-determining, better able to handle stress and criticism from others, more willing to express a controversial opinion and resist pressure to conform, enjoy better relationships, and be less likely to suffer from anxiety and depression. Development of self-esteem is a multifaceted business, but the role of the family is very important. The ideal upbringing is to be on the receiving end of unconditional love and acceptance from a pair of cheerful and reliable adults whose own relationship is warm and supportive, and who evolve clearly defined rules and boundaries for the child's behaviour with plenty of latitude for individual decisions and actions within those boundaries.

Family and cultural explanations

It is hardly surprising that the personal relationships which envelop every individual are tremendously important in shaping attitudes and behaviour, and it makes sense to look first at the influence of the family. Inconsistent family practices (mealtimes, bedtimes, television allowance, homework rules, parental reliability, discipline, rewards for good behaviour), poor maternal interaction at an early age, and low expectations by the parents of future success for their offspring are all associated with regular smoking, drinking, and drug use. The children of an alcoholic father or a mother receiving prescribed psychoactive drugs are more likely to use an illicit drug other than cannabis, and the theory put forward to explain this is that they have learnt from their parents that psychological stress requires a chemical solution. The presence of one smoking adult in the family doubles the risk that the children will take up regular smoking. This influence is more powerful in girls who are also more successful in keeping their smoking secret from their parents. The risk of becoming a smoker increases fourfold if an older brother or sister smokes. Consumption of illicit drugs is higher in teenagers who lack one or both of their natural parents, who come from families with high levels of stress and conflict, whose parents themselves use illegal drugs, or who have a close relative who is 'antisocial' or 'alcoholic'. It is lower in families with pronounced religious beliefs, or warm, trusting, and conflict-free parent-adolescent relationship – a state which may exist more frequently in the pages of psychology textbooks than in the real world. Influences in families cut both ways: a difficult baby may result in weary and exasperated parents who unleash their frustrations in later childhood and heighten teenage alienation. One good parent–child relationship can provide an effective buttress against quite disturbed behaviour in siblings or the other parent.

The more time children kick their heels after school unsupervised by an adult, especially outside the family home, the more likely they are to drink alcohol excessively and smoke cigarettes or cannabis, feel depressed, indulge in more generally risky activities, and do less well in school.

Drug taking by young people may simply reflect rejection of mainstream ideas or values by the adult members of the family. Conventional, conservative families operating along more authoritarian lines are likely to produce children with an inbuilt resistance to deviating from the norm, and less inclination to buck the system. Each style has its advantages and disadvantages. Although they sometimes come a cropper we can all think of eccentrics and risk-takers who have hit life's jackpot in one way or another, and these people often have a life-enhancing effect on those who come into contact with them. The family also seems to play a vital role in determining an individual's self-esteem as described above.

Not surprisingly, members of friendship groups share attitudes and beliefs, but it is uncertain whether this is mainly due to like selecting like ('assortative pairing') or one person influencing another. In other words, do similar people simply cluster together, or do certain individuals produce conformity by inducing changes in others? Whichever explanation is true, people certainly do hang out with people of similar habits and pastimes. Three-quarters of regular smokers say that most or all of their friends smoke, while nine out of 10 non-smokers say that none or very few of theirs do. One study looked at the source of drugs on the occasion of first-time sampling. Most commonly (40%) this happens within a group of friends sharing the supply. Other sources were as follows: given by an older friend (26%) or other aquaintance (12%), bought from a friend (10%), given by an older sibling (5%), bought from a stranger (5%), given by a stranger (2%).

The effect of this immediate circle of friends and acquaintances easily outweighs any conflicting pressure emanating from society at large and, albeit temporarily, from the family. Becoming warmly acquainted with established aficionados of any particular drug, be they beery medical students or pot-smoking jazz musicians, is by far the strongest predictor that you will try that particular substance yourself.

Influence can be direct through persuasion or role-modelling, or indirect by a subtler inculcation of beliefs and values, and that of friends and associates interacts in a complicated way with that of the family. It seems that the influence of siblings fades with age, presumably as that of peers increases, but the power of one peer group declines rapidly as the person moves to a fresh milieu or social circle. Indirect influence is much longer lasting, and is the characteristic effect which the family exerts. Parental influence, although it may be swamped by succeeding peer groups from time to time, constantly re-emerges. Whilst immediate and overtly-stated parental rules may seem totally ineffective in curbing adolescent excesses, the subtler modelling of attitudes and behaviour results in psychological structures or mind-sets which remain active for a lifetime. Unfortunately, they may not result in the outcome anticipated or intended by the parents. A father preoccupied with the virtue of hard work and long hours might expect his progeny to be impressed by the money and prestige this is producing; instead, the child may be taking note of the loneliness and lack of support experienced by the mother, and planning his own life accordingly.

Interrupted schooling, academic failure, and truancy are each associated with a greater prevalence of drug use. Truants aged 14–16 are twice as likely to smoke regularly, three times more likely to abuse solvents or smoke cannabis, and four times more likely to try 'hard' drugs than non-truants. They are more likely to come from large or broken families, to have smoking parents and unemployed fathers, and to engage in heavy drinking, fighting, and vandalism.

Observation of adult behaviour outside family and peer groups also influences young people. For example, in schools which permit teachers to smoke on the premises, twice as many 16-year-olds will take up the habit. Children tend to smoke the more heavily advertised brands of cigarettes. Active promotion, availability, and cost have a significant influence on most forms of drug use, but the law does not seem to be a major deterrent. In a survey of university students, users said that the law had not been a significant factor in weighing up the decision to try a drug. Very few non-users said they would try a currently illegal drug if it was legalized.

There are regional variations in the pattern of drug use within the UK. For example, alcohol consumption is heavy in Scotland and Wales, and particularly so in Northern England where a third of men drink more than official safety recommendations.

Risk taking

Risk taking is generally accepted to be part of the normal process of developing independence and individual identity during the progression from childhood through adolescence into adulthood. Society deems some risks acceptable and some not, often with little justification to teenage eyes. There are many hidden variables which can subtly alter risk profiles. Putting a small child into a safety restraint when you drive to the supermarket is obviously sensible, but research suggests that mothers who do this drive faster than those whose children are just rolling around in the back, and are therefore at increased risk of having an accident.

Adolescents approach risk assessment differently to adults. It is rather unlikely that they will sit down and consider fully the pros and cons of any particular adventure. They may lack knowledge or tune out the possibility of danger. Powers of introspection tend to be undeveloped, they may well be impulsive and impatient, and most young people have a sense of invulnerability if thoughts of mortality or serious damage even cross their minds. External influences also impinge on risk awareness and judgement; for example, adolescents from intact families take less risks than those with divorced or separated parents. Risks cluster together: the young person overtaking you at 120 m.p.h. on his motor-bike probably smokes, drinks, and fornicates far more than the family doctor would think advisable. Smokers are much more likely to drink heavily than non-smokers.

Most people confronted with a possible course of action which seems attractive but also risky carry out some sort of rapid mental cost–benefit analysis which is subject to all sorts of idiosyncratic biases. The key calculation is the likely balance of positive and negative outcomes, and the expected intensity of those outcomes. Rewards are often immediate while possible harms are deferred, leading to an underestimate of both the likelihood and severity of the latter. The majority of young smokers remember risks being discussed within the family and can repeat the message from health awareness sessions at school. There is no doubt that awareness of the dangers of smoking among children has increased greatly over the last 10 years, but this has not been mirrored by reductions in the numbers taking up the habit.

Even if a decision to avoid risk is taken, this may be thwarted at the last moment as other factors intrude. For example, there is a large discrepancy between initial intention to wear a condom and actually using one. Spiralling lust, too much alcohol, or embarrassment may overwhelm earlier decisions. Having indulged in risky behaviour and apparently got away with it unscathed is in itself extremely rewarding and encourages further exposure.

Is experimenting with drugs 'abnormal'?

Many of the normal psychological changes associated with adolescence present challenges both to the young people experiencing them and to concerned adults looking on. This is a time of learning to exert control over emotion in the face of stress, becoming an individual separate from the family and clarifying a sense of self, developing the ability to consider alternative outcomes and make rational decisions about competing choices, and beginning to plan beyond the immediate. Experimentation in many aspects of living is an essential part of the developmental process. In an era when legal and illegal drugs are part of the environment in every school in the land, can we automatically assume that trying out illicit drugs (which include cigarettes and alcohol for certain age groups) is automatically pathological or even abnormal? One American study, controversial but scientifically impressive, would suggest not.

The investigators selected 100 three-year-old children and followed them up regularly until they were 18. At regular intervals they were interviewed and subjected to psychological testing. Quality of parenting was assessed when they were five, and feedback from teachers was obtained from time to time. At the end of the study, the subjects mostly fell into three categories with regard to their use of recreational drugs: 29 total abstainers, 36 experimenters (cannabis once a month or less and no more than one other drug), and 19 regular users (cannabis at least once weekly plus at least one other drug). Sixteen subjects could not be classified. There were significant psychological differences between the three groups and those with the healthiest psychological profile turned out to be the experimenters. These differences were discernible in the children's earliest assessments, and those who were destined to become regular users showed 'inter-personal difficulties, poor impulse control, and emotional distress from an early age'. Quality of parenting was significantly better in the families of those who turned out to be experimenters than in either of the other groups.

So it is clear that experimenting with illicit drugs is certainly not an automatic sign of an alienated or unhappy young person. On the contrary, it may be the product of psychological traits which are associated with many positive outcomes in life. Unfortunately, as we shall see in the next chapter, all recreational drug use, legal and illegal, is inevitably associated with some level of risk.

chapter 2

the consequences of drug use

An individual's reaction to a drug is shaped by many factors: the pharmacology of the drug, its purity and the presence or absence of contaminants, the route by which it is taken, the way it is metabolized and stored, and possibly by the person's unique pre-existing biological make-up; the individual's personality and experience, mood, and expectations when the drug is taken; and the physical and social environment in which the experience happens. The existence of so many variables explains the unpredictability of drug effects, and why a particular drug may affect a person differently from one occasion to another. This will be discussed further in Chapter 13.

Short-term consequences

All legal and illegal drug use, no matter how fleeting, carries some immediate risk. We cannot escape from the harsh reality that poisoning and accidental injuries are the commonest causes of death in teenagers. Intoxication can result in accidents on the road or elsewhere, and is a frequent accompaniment to crime. Alcohol is a factor in up to half of all head injuries and a third of accidental deaths, and a third of pedestrians killed on the roads are over the legal limit for driving. Half the violent crime reported in the 1996 British Crime Survey was perpetrated by intoxicated offenders. Most of the assailants responsible for the million assaults by strangers which occur each year in England and Wales are drunk at the time, and a third of these attacks happen in the immediate vicinity of licensed premises. Alcohol is a factor on nearly half the occasions when the attacker is known to the victim, and other drugs on a further 22%. A third of all adolescent suicides are intoxicated at the time.

Illegal drugs have additional immediate risks because they are manufactured, distributed, and sold by criminals who do not put quality control high on their list of priorities. Purity varies hugely, making accidental overdose an ever-present possibility. For example, analysis of street heroin shows that the diamorphine content can vary between 5% and 80%. A report in 1997 showed that the death rate among 15–19 year-olds generally has been increasing at a rate of 8% annually over the past 10 years. Among teenage opiate users the increase has averaged 27% per annum. Between 1985 and 1995, 436 young people in this age group killed themselves accidentally with drugs, with opioids the prime cause in 21% of these. These figures are likely to underestimate the true picture. Mortality rates associated with acute adverse reactions to opioids or cocaine are five times greater in men than women, and are at their highest in people in their mid to late twenties.

Street drugs can also contain toxic solvents, accidental by-product of manufacture, adulterants, or bulking agents. They may be contaminated with pesticides, fungi, or bacteria. The intensity of the psychological effects of stimulants, hallucinogens, or unusually potent forms of cannabis may prove overwhelming. Young people are particularly at risk from the lifestyle consequences of the street drug scene, such as violence and sexual exploitation.

Legal and illegal recreational drugs, both 'hard' and 'soft', can interfere with many aspects of ordinary living. Effects on energy, concentration, mood, or physical health can cause tension and disruption within families, and confrontations or disappointments at school or in the workplace. Some employers operate drug (and alcohol) policies which involve regular urine screens for illicit drugs. Positive tests can result in dismissal even if there has been no discernible effect on performance.

In Britain, the Road Traffic Act requires applicants or licence holders to inform the Driver and Vehicle Licensing Agency (DVLA) of any 'prescribed or prospective disability' which could pose 'a source of danger to the public'. Such disability includes 'addiction/use or dependency on illicit drugs' or 'chronic solvent misuse or dependency'. If the DVLA receives evidence of 'cannabis misuse' six months off driving will be required, and 12 months if abuse of other drugs is confirmed, including 'any psychoactive drug currently fashionable'. A professional driver faces revocation of his licence for at least three years, with strict criteria to be satisfied before it can be restored. It is an offence to be in charge of a vehicle whilst 'unfit to drive through drink or drugs'. Consultant-supervised maintenance on oral methadone (see Chapter 14) is no bar to retaining one's licence, but if injectable prescriptions of controlled drugs are provided it must be surrendered. Covert drug use revealed in testing following an accident may invalidate insurance cover.

Approximately a third of all North American drug users are women of child-bearing age, and more than half a million unborn babies are exposed to illicit drugs each year. Damage to the fetus, though theoretically possible with most drug types, is extremely rare when the mother is an occasional or social user, though some adulterants commonly found in street drugs are potentially very toxic. Drug users overall fall into the 'high normal' range for congenital abnormalities with an incidence of around 3% of live births. Common sense (but not much in the way of hard data) suggests that risks will be greater for addicted mothers who are likely to be consuming more drugs, and may also be suffering from the effects of poor nutrition, chronic infections, lack of family support and antenatal care, and a chaotic lifestyle. It is important to note that *all* drugs taken during pregnancy – legal, illegal, or prescribed – especially during the first three months, represent a potential risk to the fetus and should be avoided if possible. Tobacco is identified as a cause of low birth-weight and premature delivery, whilst a heavy consumption of alcohol has been associated with malformations, growth retardation, and impaired mental capacity.

Most people who use illicit drugs socially, and many who are dependent upon drugs, make as good a job of caring for their children as any other parents, in the writer's experience. In the UK, however, the Children Act (1989) requires that in cases where a child appears to be at risk in terms of health or development, it is incumbent upon social workers and other professionals to ensure that the interests and welfare of that child take precedence over all other considerations.

Interventions will almost always be aimed at helping the parent or parents to provide the emotional and physical environment that the child requires.

'Visible' and 'invisible' drug users

The great majority of people who use drugs never come to the attention of doctors, lawyers, or policemen. They are invisible to research unless briefly flushed out of cover by population surveys, and so do not feature in the statistics of the outcome literature. The problem that this presents to those with an interest in understanding the consequences of drug use beyond the boundaries of the addiction clinics can be illustrated by reference to the recent cocaine epidemic in North America. Population surveys indicated that over 25 million American citizens had tried the drug in one particular year in the 1980s. Animal experiments, emergency room surveys, and the pronouncements of 'experts' suggest that cocaine is one of the most toxic and addictive of street drugs, yet only a tiny proportion of these people presented for treatment or help of any kind, or were ever prosecuted. The rest remained completely invisible, and we have no idea how things turned out for them. Did they just snort the stuff a few times, enjoy it or not as the case may be, then simply drop it as new priorities took shape? Similarly in the case of heroin, of the 1% or even 2% of the general adult population who tell researchers that they have tried it at least once, relatively few go on to contribute to the casualty statistics.

The discrepancy between the numbers who admit to having at some time smoked cannabis, or swallowed LSD, Ecstasy, or amphetamine, and those who ever present for help with drug-related problems is even more enormous. One can only assume that the vast majority use these drugs only briefly or in small amounts, or that they prove pretty well harmless to most people.

Since next to nothing is known about the natural history of this invisible population of relatively problem-free users, one naturally looks with interest at the few studies that have been carried out. Every heroin or cocaine user in treatment can tell you about friends or aquaintances who seem able to limit their use of these drugs to weekends or special occasions, but it is all so subjective and anecdotal. Besides, who can be sure that these apparently controlled users are not simply in transit to addiction or abstinence?

A handful of American studies do give limited support to the idea that relatively stable, controlled use of opiates is possible. Such people often develop rituals and routines which ensure that the drug remains just a part of their lives, rather than its epicentre. We shall see in Chapter 13 that environmental and social context is all-important to the formation and maintenance of addictive behaviour. It seems that if the drug taking can be ritualized and compartmentalized, then it can be more easily contained. The social drinker limits her consumption of alcohol to particular times and places, sanctioned and reinforced by society's rules. Studies among opiate 'chippers' (see p. 189) suggest that many are successful in creating a similar structure around their heroin use. Such people inevitably have other strong interests and competing activities, clear plans for the future, and a sense of being in control of their lives. They are wary of tolerance, that ever-decreasing pay-off from the drug consequent upon too-regular consumption, recognizing that this is the 'hook' which can draw them into dependency.

Many chippers do give a history of episodes of addiction, but usually seem to have been able to overcome these without professional help. Some oscillate between drug and 'straight' cultures, while others lead completely conventional lives apart from this one peccadillo. Intermittent users are more likely to prefer snorting or smoking heroin to injecting it.

In one large sample of young men selected because they admitted trying heroin at least once, only a third had ever reached the point of using it almost every day. Two-thirds of those who had progressed to monthly indulgence also reported periods of daily use. This suggests that it is difficult to avoid getting hooked unless you rigorously restrict yourself to very infrequent indulgence, and is mirrored by observations on American soldiers who used heroin in Vietnam. Although the majority of these did not become addicted, three-quarters of those who tried it more than five times did become dependent. This group also demonstrated that a period of addiction does not inevitably mean that any future dabbling is bound to give rise to re-addiction; a third of the once-addicted sample did use heroin again in an infrequent, controlled manner on their return to the US.

Invisible cocaine use has been examined on a number of occasions using the 'snowballing' technique. Cocaine users identified through advertisements, personal contacts, or fieldworkers are invited to introduce the investigator to similarly inclined friends and acquaintances, who in turn are asked to do the same thing. This uncovers a sample which does not have as its common denominator a connection with treatment services, and which should therefore be more representative of drug users in general. In groups of people discovered in this way dependence upon cocaine is the exception rather than the rule, though one cannot be certain that these apparent copers are not merely in transition between control and addiction.

Six patterns of cocaine use have been described: an initial high intake slowly diminishing to zero; a slow and steady increase; stable consumption from beginning to end; escalation to high doses followed by a decline of similar rapidity; regular intermittent use; irregular intermittent use. Progression to heavy use followed by spontaneously regained control or abstinence seems to happen more often than not, but a sizeable minority are able to cope with regular or irregular intake without losing control over lengthy periods. Long-term prospective studies are very rare and involve only small numbers but, for what they are worth, also suggest that dependency upon cocaine requiring professional help is quite unusual. Most individuals who are able to take cocaine in a controlled manner over many years do so rather sparingly, no more than once or twice a month. If a period of heavy use does supervene, most people can respond to the writing on the wall: in one sample, only 20% of those who had escalated to daily use were still taking cocaine one year later. On the other hand, many years of controlled use can sometimes lead to an unwarranted sense of invulnerability, since loss of control after a decade or more of problem-free experience is also well recognized. All of this research focuses upon snorted or, much more occasionally, injected cocaine and less is known about the consequences of flirting with crack, except that certain populations seem particularly vulnerable to compulsive patterns of use (see Chapter 13).

One study showed strikingly different population characteristics between visible and invisible users of cocaine, amphetamine, and heroin. In sharp contrast to the visible group, most invisible users expressed little or no concern about their drug use and no wish for help or advice. They were much more likely to use stimulants only, less likely to inject anything or if they did so to share equipment, and less likely to use drugs on a daily basis. The invisible group showed a much lower propensity to compulsive or dependent use of any of the three drugs. The similarity in age, gender ratio, and duration of drug history argues against the alternative explanation that the two groups are simply at different stages of their drug 'careers'.

The conclusion from these various observations seems to be that addiction to heroin and cocaine occurs in only a minority of those who try them. Since addiction usually has devastating consequences for those who do fall within its grip, it is particularly unfortunate that it remains so difficult to predict with any confidence who will be so afflicted.

Longer-term consequences

In assessing the long-term impact of various drugs, it is essential to keep one stark fact in perspective: ordinary cigarettes are implicated in the deaths of more people in Britain than heroin, cocaine, alcohol, road accidents, HIV, murder, and suicide all put together.

Research of sufficient quality to tell us much about the long-term consequences of regular smoking, drinking, or drug taking in the teenage years is in very short supply, but some broad conclusions can be reached. Modest, controlled consumption of illegal drugs is much more common than regular, heavy, or compulsive use, and many young people seem able to use these substances in the same socially appropriate way as most adults are able to use alcohol. Such transient or experimental use does not seem to be associated with measurable long-term harm.

On the other hand, about 10% of those who experiment with alcohol or illegal drugs will go on to develop problems with them at a later stage. Starting with these drugs at an unusually early age or significant escalation during the teenage years are bad prognostic signs. Regular or heavy use during adolescence has a strong association with emotional and physical problems then and later, difficult family, social, and sexual relationships, and disruption of education and employment. Problem drug use overlaps with many other undesirable behaviours such as delinquency, teenage pregnancy, and school drop-out, and probably shares many causative factors. Drug effects join with these to disrupt the developmental processes involved in progressing from adolescence to adult roles and responsibilities. Such teenagers almost always have poor relations with those outside their peer group, are less good at practical problem-solving, and become cut off from those groups and organizations which most young people find reasonably helpful, such as families and schools. This alienation can eat further into an already precarious sense of purpose and ambition, and fuel anxiety, hostility, boredom, and emptiness. It is unwarranted to conclude that drug use has necessarily *caused* these effects, when it may itself be just another symptom of, say, a dysfunctional family. It is important too not to confuse the effects of a drug with the social conditions which surround it. One researcher, noting that strained parent–child relationships are more likely if the young person smokes cannabis, concluded that this was the result of the psychological effects of cannabis. Equally likely explanations are that the parents were angry about their offspring's involvement with illegal activities, or that natural rebelliousness in the child accounted for both the estrangement and drug experimentation independently. There are gender differences in the expression of distress by young people: males tend to manifest this by antisocial behaviour, girls by the development of emotional symptoms. Women tend to be more stigmatized by alcohol or drug problems in most societies.

School students who drink regularly will admit to a range of alcohol-related problems. Most commonly reported in a UK sample are problems with relationships (22% – quarrels with parents, teachers, or friends), personal difficulties (21% – impaired school work, damage to objects or clothing, loss of money or valuables, accident or injury), sexual regrets (15% – engaged in unwanted or unprotected sex), and acts of delinquency (12% – fights, victim of theft, driving while drunk, trouble with the police). Long-term follow-up of adults diagnosed as alcoholic show increased mortality rates in comparison with non-alcoholics of similar age and social circumstances.

Virtually nothing is known about the natural history of people who continue quietly consuming cannabis, amphetamine, Ecstasy, and hallucinogens intermittently or regularly during their twenties and thirties, or the impact, if any, this may have on their physical or mental health. As far as one can judge, this sort of drug use gradually peters out as middle age approaches, though no doubt many people quietly persist into their dotage.

Outcome of long-term 'hard' drug use

Most available statistics relate to heroin use. Even these must be taken with a pinch of salt because they can only focus upon *visible* drug users. Invisible users are presumably running their lives more efficiently, otherwise they would have become visible. There are variables which make it difficult to generalize beyond any particular sample, such as the availability of barbiturates on the black market. These were commonplace in the 1960s and 1970s but are now rarely encountered, and were peculiarly lethal, accounting for at least 60% of overdose deaths. Most long-term follow-up studies quoted today began in the early 1970s, so mortality figures may be misleadingly high. Again, injecting habits have demonstrably changed since the threat of HIV infection was first recognized in the mid-1980s.

A number of attempts have been made to follow the progress of opiate users over years rather than months. Addiction is seen in these studies to be a chronic relapsing and remitting process which carries a significant mortality from accidents, illness, suicide and, in the US, murder. Despite this, the outcome is not as gloomy as generally thought since up to half the subjects are found to be consistently abstinent after 10 years. Indeed, in those addicts that survive, the natural history of the condition with its unpredictable ups and downs seems slanted towards slow but steady recovery, which may lead to the beneficial effect of treatment being overestimated.

Most addicts become heroin-free by middle age, with a typical addiction 'career' lasting about 10 years. The fluctuating course is marked by longer and longer intermissions of controlled use or abstinence. Notwithstanding this trend, between 5% and 10% of addicts are more than 45 years old. Some may become dependent upon alcohol or other drugs as heroin loses its appeal.

Physical problems are mainly related to lifestyle, poor injecting technique, and adulterants in street drugs. Pharmaceutical opiates are remarkably non-toxic and there are many documented examples of doctors and others with access to pure drugs who have injected opiates over decades and still managed to lead stable and productive lives.

If this is the broad pattern of opiate addiction, the details vary considerably from study to study. There are regional variations, and conditions fluctuate even within regions. For example, a recent publication highlighted the situation in Glasgow. Drug-related deaths in the city have increased from five-yearly in the early 1980s to the current average of 100 out of the total 350 deaths of people in this age group. The average annual mortality among both male and female injectors is nearly 2%, and the average age at death is 26. This represents an excess mortality ratio of 22, in comparison with a ratio of 18 for Stockholm, 11.9 for London, and 10 for Rome. By far the commonest cause of death was overdose, accidental or intentional. It is possible that rates are so high in Glasgow because of the high prevalence of multiple drug use, especially the combination of heroin and the benzodiazepine temazepam.

American follow-up studies usually make for grimmer reading. A quarter of the sample is likely to have died over a 20-year period, and between a quarter and a half remain addicted for the whole time. Nevertheless, a benign natural history is still discernible for survivors. One respected investigator published figures on a sample of male addicts which he followed for 20 years (Table 1).

Injecting drug use (IDU) represents a massive, worldwide public health risk because of its role in the spread of several diseases. Over the past 15 years, 24 million adults have been infected with the human immunodeficiency virus (HIV) which causes acquired immunodeficiency syndrome (AIDS). Sexual contact with an injecting user who has acquired HIV through sharing injecting equipment is the most important bridge by which the virus reaches the

Table 1 Twenty-year follow-up of male addicts

	Time after first hospitalization (years)		
	5	10	18
stable abstinence	10%	23%	35%
dead	6%	11%	23%
active narcotic addiction	53%	41%	25%
uncertain status	31%	25%	17%

From: Vaillant, G. V. (1988) *British Journal of Addiction* **83**, 1147–57.

heterosexual population: a study in New York showed that 80% of cases of heterosexual spread involved an injector at some point of the chain. The spread of the virus through an injecting population can be terrifyingly rapid: in 1984, the proportion of infected users in Edinburgh leapt by 40% within a single year. There are very large national variations: in the UK, injectors make up only 6% of the total HIV/AIDS population, while in Spain and Italy the proportion approaches 70%.

Other diseases spread by IDU include hepatitis B, which is 10 times more infectious than HIV, and the even more aggressive hepatitis C which chronically affects more than 100 million people worldwide and gives rise to much morbidity and mortality. Other sexually transmitted diseases are commoner in this population, as is that ancient and currently re-emerging scourge tuberculosis.

Influences upon the outcome of dependent drug use

Treatment is but one of a number of factors which may impact upon the profile or duration of addiction careers. The common denominator of those treatments which do have some demonstrable impact seems to be their ability to introduce or enhance structure in people's lives. Natural events which achieve the same result, such as a new relationship or job, can be just as beneficial. Factors which most commonly lead people to seek treatment include health or legal problems, pressure from the family, and boredom with the whole rigmarole and risk of obtaining black market supplies.

Short-term treatment measures, though they may be a necessary preliminary or stepping-stone, have not been shown to exert any effect at all upon long-term outcome. Detoxification is a case in point, with some people undergoing hundreds of these procedures in the course of their addiction career. In one series, 100 addicts clocked up 770 detoxifications between them, and on only 3% of occasions was this followed by a period of abstinence of a year or more.

When detoxification is linked with some continuing therapy, results are often better than they appear at first glance. Although 71% of addicts in one study had sampled heroin again within six weeks of completing detoxification, many of these did not revert to dependent use and there was a steady increase in the abstinence rate over time. At six months, 45% were off drugs and living in the community, whilst a further 14% were using only on an occasional basis. Almost all lapses had occurred in the afternoon or evening, mostly in the presence of other heroin users. Doses tended to be lower than was customary before the detoxification, with less injecting. Only a minority of the abstinent group reported any problems with alcohol, though this has been more prominent in other series. A quarter regularly smoked cannabis.

The greatest number of lapses happened in the first week after detoxification, and the results from other studies show that 80–90% of full-scale relapses will have occurred within the first few weeks or months. Reasons given for relapse include re-exposure to the drug culture and drug-using friends, recurrent craving, interpersonal conflicts, unpleasant mood states or environmental conditions, and reduction of staff support.

Long-term outcome relates quite consistently to the length of time spent in treatment, and if that duration is less than three months it is unlikely to be more effective than detoxification alone or no treatment at all. Of relevance to this observation is the finding that methadone maintenance programmes, in America at least, retain clients better than drug-free outpatient programmes or therapeutic communities. Nearly half of methadone maintenance clients remain in treatment for a year, compared to a quarter of those who enter therapeutic communities and 13% of drug-free outpatients.

Predicting outcome for the individual addict is very difficult indeed. Having a serious pre-existing psychiatric illness is a definite disadvantage, and there are some other relatively weak indicators of an unfavourable prognosis: poor pre-addiction social stability, employment history, or educational attainment; heavy involvement in the drug culture, or having a drug-using partner; history of serious criminal activity; heavy alcohol use before or during treatment; an inability to maintain long-term relationships; and, with relevance mainly to the US, raised in a culture different to that of the parents. Interestingly, the severity of the addiction in terms of frequency of use or quantity consumed has little or no bearing on outcome.

Two factors stand out above all the others in determining a successful outcome. These are achieving a structured and rewarding lifestyle, and changing location after becoming abstinent.

Addicts who are successful in beating their habit are usually those who are able to find alternative sources of interest and gratification which lead to new routines and preoccupations. These may be achieved in a variety of ways such as a new relationship, a job, or even an alternative, less damaging dependence. The latter could take the form of religious involvement, or regular attendance at a self-help group. There is no doubt that membership of Alcoholics Anonymous (AA) is associated with prevention of relapse into alcoholism, and there is no reason to suppose that this would not also be the case with Narcotics Anonymous (NA). It remains uncertain whether this is cause or effect as it is entirely possible that the same factors which maintain remission also cause attendance at the meetings rather than the other way round. At the very least, AA and NA are very effective at breaking the unhealthy self-focus through their emphasis on helping others, and provide an inspiring model of attainable abstinence to those who have begun to abandon hope.

An occupation or career fulfills many functions beyond the obvious one of generating a supply of money. It provides a sense of belonging and purpose, contributes to self-esteem and confidence, permits an escape from the humdrum tasks of day-to-day living even though it may itself be quite routine and dull, introduces the worker to another circle of acquaintance, and perhaps most important, adds shape and structure to life. Unfortunately, at times of high unemployment even the most adaptive and able people can find it impossible to find work, but it seems that this is particularly true of addicts. A study of a group of New York addicts showed that by the time they were 40, they had spent only 20% of their adult lives addicted but 80% of it unemployed. It is tempting to ascribe their vulnerability to addiction at least in part to this evident inability to find any productive niche in life.

The other quite striking predictor of a good outcome is a change of domicile after coming off drugs. According to the published opinions of ex-addicts themselves, this seems to have played the decisive role in maintaining abstinence in at least a quarter of cases. One investigation followed a group of 171 heroin addicts over a period of two decades. Abstinence occurred for 54% of the time spent away from the home city and for only 12% of the time spent living in it. Abstinence lasting a year or more was three times more likely to be achieved away from home. However, 81% of abstinent addicts relapsed within one month of returning to their home city. Presumably, this can be explained by re-exposure to a familiar and welcoming drug scene, alongside a resurgence of family pressures and conflicts.

part two

alcohol

Historical background

Nobody knows just how long ago it was that humans first learnt to ferment sugars into alcohol, but the founders of the Babylonian Empire were brewing beer 4000 years before the birth of Christ. An Egyptian papyrus dating from around 3500 BC describes wine-making techniques, and knowledge of the process had reached the Atlantic coast of Europe by 2500 BC. Alcohol partially displaced the ritual and medical roles of cannabis and opium which were being cultivated by Stone Age farmers. From that time onwards alcohol has been produced wherever humans have settled.

In polytheistic Ancient Greece, Dionysus, son of Zeus and Semele, may have been a minor god but as patron of wine and dance he was certainly a popular one. Drunken revelries were held by his acolytes every spring and winter. The symposium evolved as a ritual-laden gathering at which men could indulge in bibulous conversation and riotous entertainment, with vast amounts of food and drink being consumed. Very few delegates would still be ambulant by the end of the proceedings, but public drunkenness outside of these special occasions was unusual. A love of alcohol was certainly not confined to the ruling classes. The Greeks invented the tavern and were the first to organize the mass production and systematic export of wine, and mead (derived from fermented honey) was also very popular among ordinary people. Plato and Socrates drew attention to the darker side of boozing, including its association with public disorder and violence, failure to fulfill a useful role within the family, difficulties in work and productivity, and accidents. And for high-profile casualties one need look no further than Alexander III ('the Great'), dead at 32 after one too many alcoholic binges.

Dionysus evolved into Bacchus, and Pliny the Elder reviled wine as 'a thing that perverts the mind and produces madness'. The small Roman vineyards that sprang up around 700 BC were insufficient for home consumption, so trade routes for importation developed rapidly. As the empire expanded both importation and home production soared and prices plummeted. By AD 20 heavy daily drinking had become the norm and was associated with much violence and general debauchery. Alcohol was free to the plebs on public holidays, which eventually amounted to around 160 days each year under Nero and helped to fuel the growing atmosphere of savagery and decay.

The Hebrews took enthusiastically to wine during the Egyptian captivity. The Bible veers from condemnation to endorsement, but generally there has been a tendency down the ages for Christian theologians to be indulgent towards over-imbibers and not averse to the bottle themselves. After the decline of the Roman empire it fell to the Christian monasteries in many countries (including England) to safeguard the traditions of brewing and viticulture, and it was an ingenious monk who invented the cork and opened the way to bottle ageing and secondary fermentation. Around the same period, approximately AD 616, the adherents of Islam were forbidden alcohol by the law laid down in the sacred Koran (or Qur'an) by the prophet Mohammed.

In the British Isles, ale had been the endemic tipple of the native population since pre-Roman times, and taverns appeared around the beginning of the 12th century. In medieval Britain, beer was often safer to drink than water from the local river or well, and was also seen as an important source of energy and nutrition. Ales were relatively low in alcohol content (around 3% by volume), contained useful amounts of B vitamins, calcium, and magnesium, and supplied up to 10% of dietary energy. The addition of hops to prolong storage time and enhance taste probably caught on about 200 years later. This process also permitted extended fermentation time so the resulting beer was much higher in alcohol content.

With the increasing dominance of the 'patriarchal nuclear family' a drunken husband or father increasingly came to be seen as falling down in his role as an ally of the government in maintaining social order. The drunkard became socially unacceptable because his incapacity obliged his neighbours to care for his dependants, and no excuse was accepted for what was seen as a manifestation of selfish gluttony or simple greed. English rural communities were notably charitable towards the needy in the 15th century, but parishioners came increasingly to see themselves as the true victims of the irresponsible drunkard rather than the abandoned wife and children, who were often left to fend for themselves as best they could. Alcohol-induced violence within the family was deplored by respectable people, but induced little in the way of a practical response because of the low status of women and the expendability of young children. There are documents surviving from this period which demonstrate contemporary concern about the role of alcohol in fermenting violence, causing accidents, and undermining moral behaviour.

From the 15th century onwards, alcohol consumption became increasingly located outside the family home, and the alehouse or tavern evolved as the convivial centre of the working man's social life. It also served as a labour exchange, a staging post for journeys, and a setting for such entertainments as bear-baiting, cock fights, and prizefights. This shift considerably reduced women's access to alcohol, and raised concern among the ruling classes about possible disruption of the availability and reliability of labourers.

The popular belief that alcohol was generally beneficial was endorsed by 17th-century doctors who recommended it for a wide range of conditions as disparate as depression, venereal disease, and gout. It was a staple ingredient of tonics and dietary supplements. Consumption increased steadily through the century, and the government took financial advantage of this by imposing the first ever beer duty in 1643. Beer consumption reached an all-time high in 1689 with an average intake for the year of 832 pints for every man, woman, and child in the land. Infants and younger children are not usually particularly fond of beer and women were largely excluded by social custom, so we can assume that the male population was shifting enormous quantities by modern standards (average consumption in 1976 stood at around 200 pints per person).

Considerable amounts of home-produced wine were drunk in Britain in the middle ages, but the dissolution of the monasteries by Henry VIII resulted in the destruction of virtually all British vineyards. Subsequent patterns of wine consumption were determined almost entirely by shifting treaties and taxes. When relations with the French became less than genial at the very beginning of the 18th century the Methuen Treaty was signed with Portugal, turning the wealthier English citizens from claret to port drinkers almost overnight. For the next 80 years only 3.6% of all the wine drunk in England came from France. Smuggling of French wine became vastly profitable until commercial channels were reopened by a new treaty in 1783. Around this time, the vineyards which formed the starting point for the future New World wine tradition were being planted by Franciscan monks newly embarked in California. There were notable peaks of consumption in the middle of the 18th century and the late 1900s, but the industry in Britain went into a steady decline to an all-time low in the 1940s and 1950s. Since then, however, the taste for wine has caught on again in a big way and consumption per capita is far greater now than at any time in the past.

The process of distillation had been developed in the Middle East around the 12th century AD with medicinal applications in mind, but the consumption of 'acqua vitae' was quite widespread in Europe by the beginning of the 16th century. Until around 1700, various restrictive practices ensured that distilled drinks were consumed in Britain almost entirely by a tiny group of wealthy topers. Then the decision was taken to cancel the monopoly hitherto enjoyed by the Worshipful Company of Distillers, leading to the infamous 'gin craze' among the poor which peaked between 1720 and 1750. Gin was first created in 17th-century Holland by the addition of juniper berries to grain alcohol. When King William III severely restricted importation of French wine and brandy, the deregulated home gin industry went into overdrive, and in London alone 8000 'dram shops' sprang up in which one could become 'drunk for a penny, dead drunk for tuppence'. The craze was brought to an abrupt end by the imposition of swingeing taxes and a clamp-down on the gin houses.

The debauchery and squalor associated with this crisis was a shock to the respectable citizenry, but alcohol in all its forms was still absolutely central to the everyday life of polite society. Drinking among men tended to be heavy and competitive and public figures such as William Pitt and Richard Sheridan were certainly not ashamed of their reputations as 'six-bottle men'. Gin may have plummeted downmarket but the respectable image of brandy ('bernenwijn' evolving to 'branntwein' or 'burnt wine') remained untarnished. Whisky ('usque-baugh') was hugely popular in Scotland and Ireland. In the US, despite the prominence and influence of the Puritans, the early colonists adopted similar habits to their countries of origin. The local cider industry developed rapidly along with production of mead and fruit wines, and distillation became widespread early in the 18th century. Alcohol consumption per capita in 1790 was at least twice that of 1990 levels.

The 18th century saw the zenith of both British and American drinking, but it was also the period when organized opposition to the habit began to emerge. Doctors began to refer to drunkenness as a disease in the first half of the century, and as early as 1724 George Cheyne wrote about the eroding power of 'craving' and the physical risks inherent in sudden abstinence after regular, heavy boozing. This 'medicalization' of alcohol abuse was accelerated greatly by the writings of such physicians as Benjamin Rush (1790) in the US and Thomas Trotter in Britain, who declared in 1804 that the 'habit of drunkenness is a disease of the mind'. The acute withdrawal syndrome was named 'delirium tremens' in 1813, and the term 'alcoholism' coined in 1849 by the Swedish physician Magnus Huss who defined it as follows: 'Those disease manifestations which without any direct connection with organic disease of the nervous system take on a chronic form in persons who, over long periods, have partaken of large quantities of brandy'. The appropriation of the new syndrome by doctors was just part of a wider professional expansionism. This included the birth of the new specialism of 'psychiatry' which sought to redefine abnormal behaviour according to moral and medical principles. Then, as now, there were outspoken critics of these attempts to explain interpersonal or social problems in medical terms, and notable in modern times are the writings of Thomas Szasz.

The earliest pioneers of the Temperance Movement were not so much preoccupied with the need for abstinence but rather sought to promote the concept of moderation. They were much less concerned about beer, wine, and cider than punch, rum, and whisky. But as the alcoholic increasingly came to be seen as ill and needy rather than immoral or degenerate, so the argument for complete abstinence began to take centre stage. The fervour of the adherents escalated frighteningly alongside the growing power of psychiatrists and the increasing use of asylums. Restrictions on alehouse opening hours were introduced in 1828 and tightened further in 1848 and 1854, and by then American temperance associations could boast more than a million signed-up members. Paradoxically, at around the same time the number of public houses shot up as a result of the Beer House Act which made it much easier to obtain a liquor licence. Wine, too, enjoyed an impressive peak of consumption in the last quarter of the century.

In the American West, the first saloons appeared in the aftermath of the Civil War and soon cropped up in every one-horse town. The combination of cheap whisky, heavily-armed customers brutalized by war and deprivation, and the complete absence of any manifestation of law and order ensured an environment that fully justified the concerns of the temperance campaigners back East. An 'Antisaloon League' emerged, and was influential in persuading some states to tackle the problem by going 'dry'. In 1913 the League joined the political movement calling for national prohibition, which was duly enacted in 1919. Initially this had quite wide support, but demand for bootleg liquor shot up in the 1920s, and a host of private drinking clubs ('speakeasies') sprang up in every city. Organized criminals took full advantage of this window of opportunity. Then, as now, quality control was not a major consideration and there were many casualties from impurities in the 'moonshine'. A combination of pressure from the voters and a desperate need by the Federal government for taxation income lead to the repeal of the prohibition in 1933 during the Roosevelt era. From that moment onwards all control over alcohol retail and distribution was turned over to administration by individual states.

With many short-lived oscillations along the way, consumption of beers, wines, and spirits fell steadily in Britain from the beginning of the 20th century to the start of the 1950s. Popularity of wine and spirits has rocketed since then, particularly the former whose consumption per capita now easily eclipses the previous all-time high in the 1740s. Beer showed a much more modest recovery until the mid-seventies, but has declined again more recently. In the England of 1750, 94% of all alcohol was consumed in the form of beer but in 1980 the proportion had slumped to less than 50%.

Levels of alcohol consumption are determined by a complex interaction of price, availability, and promotion, national prosperity, social upheavals and periods of recovery, cultural pressures, and educational or moral campaigns. Price seems to be the most influential factor, and taking account of inflation the real cost of a pint of beer in 1980 was less than half that of 1950. A bottle of whisky would have been one third of the cost. In the case of wine, a determined commercial onslaught on the UK market and the startling impact of New World energy and enterprise within the wine-making industry have changed the drinking habits of a nation.

Attempts to ban juvenile drinking are really a modern phenomenon. In the Middle Ages, infants received ale as part of their normal diet and a page in the Court of Edward IV could expect to receive an allowance of two quarts a day. Prepubertal children were advised to be moderate, restricting intake to two or three glasses with meals, but there was no question of abstention. This acceptance of modest consumption alongside stern condemnation of excess along with the associated indulgences of whoring, gambling, lying, and cheating continued without any legal enforcement until the 20th century. In 1908 it became illegal for children under 14 to enter bars, and in 1923 sale of alcohol to under-18s was forbidden.

Preparation and distribution

The alcohols are a group of organic compounds characterized by the presence of one or more hydroxy (OH) groups and having a wide range of industrial applications. Ethyl alcohol (ethanol) forms the basis of intoxicating drinks, and the basic method of its production is the fermentation of glucose by yeast.

Yeast consists of a collection of oval vegetable cells, each of which is capable of existing independently as a tiny plant. If yeast cells are placed in a solution containing sugar in conditions of low oxygen concentration to encourage anaerobic metabolism, they will split each molecule of glucose into two molecules of ethanol plus carbon dioxide. The chemical equation is as follows:

$$C_6H_{12}O_6 = 2C_2H_5OH + 2CO_2$$

The pay-off for the yeast cells is energy generation but the ethanol is a toxic by-product so they excrete it back into the solution. Once the concentration of ethanol in solution approaches 13 or 14% the yeast cell finds it overwhelming and becomes dormant. This is, therefore, the maximum strength which can be achieved for alcoholic drinks which rely on fermentation alone. Different species of yeasts have been found to lend themselves more efficiently to production of particular types of beer or wine.

Drinks such as wine and cider are manufactured in this single-stage operation by direct fermentation of the sugars in grapes and apples. Allowing secondary fermentation after bottling results in champagne. In the case of beer, fermentation is preceded by the malting process in which grain of one sort or another (usually barley) is allowed to germinate in water, roast-dried, and crushed. The malted barley is then mixed with hops and yeast in hot water for fermentation. The strength of beer and wine ranges between 3–9% and 8–14% alcohol by volume respectively. Fortified wines such as sherry or port are boosted with extra alcohol (brandy, in the case of the latter).

Distillation relies upon the fact that ethanol evaporates at a lower temperature than water. If a fermented solution is heated but kept well below the boiling point of water, collecting the resulting vapour by condensation will generate an ethanol concentration up to a maximum of around 96% by volume. The strength of an alcoholic drink is usually defined by this measure. The British 'proof' system, which dates from the 17th century, is centred around the concentration of alcohol required for a solution containing gunpowder to explode – this threshold is taken as 100° proof. Spirits are generally around 40% alcohol by volume, which equates to 70° proof. The American proof value is obtained by simply doubling the percentage of alcohol by volume. All very confusing.

The taste and character of alcoholic drinks do not depend primarily upon the alcohol content. For example, the flavour of wine is greatly affected not only by the type of grape but also soil, climate, additives, and production techniques. The character of spirits will be shaped by both the material from which it is derived, which may be grapes (brandy), grain (whisky), molasses (rum), or juniper berries (gin), and the maturing conditions (e.g. malt whisky stored in sherry barrels). All alcoholic drinks contain widely varying amounts of organic materials, minerals, and other chemicals collectively known as congeners. These greatly influence the colour, aroma, flavour, and hangover potential of each particular drink, and include phenols, sugars, tannins, sulphur, esters, and amino acids. Vodka has the lowest level of congeners, whilst port, brandy, and rum absolutely bristle with them.

On the subject of taste and presentation, a phenomenon of the 1990s has been the appearance of a wide range of 'alcopops' ('spiked sodas' in the US), which are sweet and fizzy drinks containing 5% alcohol or more. In the opinion of the editor of the scientific journal *Addiction*, 'If there were a gold medal for cynical marketing it would surely be awarded to sections of the alcohol industry for the marketing of alcohol products targeted at young people'. His own research suggested that by the age of 14 more than half of all teenagers have been drunk at least once, and that white ciders, fruit wines, and alcopops are most closely associated with intoxication in this age group. Among children aged 11–16, 27% of girls and 21% of boys had consumed alcopops within the previous month.

Methanol (CH_3OH), known as wood alcohol, is widely used as a solvent but sometimes crops up as a constituent of illicitly manufactured alcohol ('moonshine'). Methanol is highly toxic because it is broken down in the body to formaldehyde. Unfortunately, there is a high concentration of the enzyme responsible for this process in the retina of the eye where the resulting formaldehyde destroys the light receptors and causes blindness.

Scientific information

Ethanol is soluble in both water and fat, so absorption from the stomach and intestine and entry into cells is fast and efficient. Absorption is slowed by fatty or carbohydrate-rich food in the stomach and speeded up by carbon dioxide in champagne or mixers. Drinks with an alcohol concentration greater than around 20% may be absorbed slower because the movement (peristalsis) of the stomach is inhibited and the valve ('pylorus') between the stomach and small intestine goes into partial spasm. The timing and height of peak alcohol blood levels will be determined by the size of the dose and rapidity of consumption, the alcohol concentration of the drink, the consumer's gender, the presence of food, and the time of day (because of the influence of diurnal rhythms on hormone levels). Peak levels normally occur about an hour after consumption.

Well over 90% of the absorbed ethanol is oxidized to acetaldehyde which in turn is broken down to acetic acid, carbon dioxide, and water. The remainder is excreted unchanged in the breath, urine, and sweat. The enzyme which brings about the first step, alcohol dehydrogenase (ADH), exists in nature to break down the ethanol and other alcohols produced by bacteria in the guts. The quantity of ADH contained in the liver and other body tissues varies tremendously between individuals, depending upon liver size, genetic make-up, and the regularity and quantity of alcohol intake. Heavy drinking boosts ADH production and results in tolerance – the need to consume more alcohol to achieve the same level of intoxication. Not only is ADH less efficient in females but women also possess less of it, for example in the walls of the stomach. Unlike men, however, they do not face decreasing ADH activity as the years roll on. There are a number of other reasons why women are more susceptible to alcohol: absorption occurs more rapidly; smaller bodies and a lower proportion of body weight made up of fluid lead to higher tissue concentrations of alcohol per unit dose; hormonal changes influence peak blood levels; certain tissues are more sensitive to the damaging effects of ethanol. Drugs such as aspirin interfere with the efficiency of ADH.

Quite apart from this effect on ADH, genetic make-up influences the response to alcohol by regulating other metabolic mechanisms and altering the tone of relevant brain chemicals and systems, including the dopamine-powered 'pleasure pathway'. Almost half of all Asian people produce a relatively inactive form of acetaldehyde dehydrogenase, the enzyme responsible for driving the second stage of ethanol metabolism. The resulting build-up of acetaldehyde in the blood produces headache, flushing, dizziness, nausea, and a pounding heart.

There is enormous individual variation, but the average person is able to metabolize approximately 8 g of alcohol (roughly equivalent to a 'standard drink' such as a half pint of ordinary bitter, a glass of wine, or a single shot of spirits) each hour, causing the blood alcohol level to fall in that period by 15 mg per

100 ml of blood (%). The legal limit for driving in the UK is 80 mg% (equivalent to 35 micrograms per 100 ml of expired air), but considerably lower in many other countries (e.g. 50 mg% in the US and France). With larger amounts or more rapid consumption, the metabolic and elimination processes become overwhelmed, so blood and tissue levels increase much more rapidly. The liver begins to be overwhelmed if it is presented with more than about 80 g of alcohol in 24 hours. The risk of liver disease is increased sixfold by levels of consumption averaging more than 40 g daily in men and 20 g in women.

Ethanol produces both stimulant and depressant effects within the brain and interacts with various chemical messengers ('neurotransmitters') such as dopamine, serotonin, GABA, and the endorphins. Its main direct effect is probably upon the channels which permit charged chemicals to pass in and out of nerve cells, blocking or generating impulses. Ethanol powerfully inhibits glutamate receptors and this is probably an important source of the impaired coordination and cognitive function.

Finer judgements, prudence, and self-concern are among the earliest casualties of even mild intoxication. Visual and auditory acuity, recovery from glare, colour discrimination, muscle coordination and balance, concentration, decisiveness, and reaction time are all measurably impaired after a single drink. The accident rate for drivers is doubled at the British legal limit of 80 mg%.

Alcohol produces a wide range of physical effects. Blood vessels in the skin dilate, increasing heat loss, while blood pressure and pulse rate increase. Blood sugar first goes up then drops below normal (hypoglycaemia). A direct effect on hormones controlling fluid balance results in the production of larger amounts of dilute urine and net fluid loss (diuresis leading to dehydration). Alcohol has both painkilling and sleep-inducing effects, though it upsets the balance between REM and slow-wave sleep and often produces rebound insomnia half way through the night. Sexual function is impaired in men, though desire may be enhanced in both sexes. Labour is delayed. Alcohol is directly toxic to the liver and the lining of the stomach. Nausea and vomiting can be induced by a direct effect within the central nervous system. Small doses of alcohol probably give a slight boost to the immune system. A gram of alcohol delivers seven calories.

Possible beneficial effects

Over the centuries, the positive image of alcohol in the public mind has never been remotely dislodged by the dreadful toll it has exacted on individual and public health, or the pronouncements of temperance campaigners of various ilks. The folklore of medicinal attributes has survived in one form or another with little or no evidence to support it, and alcohol is often portrayed in the context of rude good health, virility, courage, and friendship.

Most doctors now accept that a modest intake is unlikely to be harmful and indeed may be beneficial in offering some protection against diseases of the heart and circulation. Red wine is said to be particularly useful in this regard, possibly due to the presence of certain phenols such as quercetin and rutin which reduce the clotting activity of blood components, boost the right sort of fats (high-density lipoproteins) in the plasma, and also have highly desirable antioxidant activity. Whether or not red wine is particularly special in this way, very few people would doubt that where alcohol is concerned, a little bit of what you fancy does you good.

Recreational use

Based on recent league tables, alcohol consumption in the UK, US, Canada, Australia, and New Zealand is broadly comparable at around 8 litres of absolute alcohol per head per year. France tops the table with 13 litres, but this still represents a considerable reduction from the 1960 level of 16 litres per head. In contrast, the consumption of alcohol in the UK went up by two-thirds over the same time period. The proportion of alcohol sold as beer fell from 74% to 56%, while that of wine increased from 8% to 19%.

Recent household surveys indicate that 93% of British men and 87% of women drink at least some alcohol. As with most non-Muslim countries, alcohol remains central to most social rituals but is much less politically correct in the workplace than it was a decade ago. The teetotaller is still regarded by many as a social deviant. Some trades and professions carry an awesome reputation for heavy consumption and a high prevalence of alcohol-related problems. Factors which are likely to contribute to this are ease of access (bar staff, caterers, restaurateurs, business men with generous expense accounts), hedonistic or sociable working environment (showbusiness, advertising industry, journalism), prolonged separation from family and home environment (seamen, oil-rig workers, servicemen) and stress (doctors, farmers).

In 1987 the Royal College of Physicians recommended 'sensible limits' for safe drinking of 21 and 14 units weekly for men and women respectively (where a unit, containing 8 g alcohol, is equal to a half pint of ordinary strength beer, a glass of wine, or a single measure of spirits). There has been consensus between several Royal Colleges in supporting the Health Education Authority's three categories of drinking: 'low risk' (0–21 units per week for men, 0–14 for women); 'increasing risk' (22–50 units for men, 15–35 for women); 'harmful' (>50 units for men, >35 for women). In 1996 the average daily consumption in the UK fell within these limits at three units for men and one unit for women. However, more than a quarter of all men were drinking more than 21 units weekly, and 6% were downing more than 50. This proportion has been remarkably constant between 1984 and 1996 but the average conceals a steady rise in intake by 18–24 year-olds, always the age of heaviest consumption. In 1996, 41% of these young men were drinking more than 21 units weekly. Half of all male drinkers admit to having been drunk within the previous three months, and 7% say they get drunk at least once a week. Fourteen per cent of women drink more than 14 units weekly, 15% were drunk in the last three months, and 2.5% get sozzled every week.

It is an offence to be drunk (and not necessarily disorderly) in a public place. Wherever young men gather together in large numbers, there is a serious risk of alcohol-fuelled mayhem. For this reason, the Public Order Act 1986 forbids alcohol on trains or coaches travelling to and from designated sporting events.

In Britain it is illegal for those under 18 to buy drinks at a bar. Over-16s can buy beer or cider in a restaurant for consumption with a meal. Despite these restrictions a quarter of 15-year-olds admit to having been drunk at least 10 times in the last year, a figure which puts Britain third from top in a league comparing 25 countries. The figures for France, Italy, and the US were 3%, 4%, and 8% respectively. Forty per cent of British children aged 13 or under have been drunk at least once, and the UK tops the league for the prevalence of alcohol-related problems in young people under 17.

Even in countries where alcohol is central to social life there are large variations in what is acceptable. For example, public order problems related to alcohol are much more common in France than in Italy, where drunkenness is regarded by most people as a disgrace to the individual and his family.

Unwanted effects

Alcohol is thought to be responsible for 40 000 deaths each year in the UK, and 70 000 yearly in France. The cost to the US economy of 'alcohol abuse' in 1990 amounted to over $100 000 million. Almost a quarter of American men and 5% of women can be expected to experience problems related to alcohol at some time in their lives, and the US is nowhere near the top of the league in this regard. The relationship of dose to mortality is J-shaped because total abstainers have a higher overall mortality than light drinkers. Mortality begins to climb at levels of intake over three units daily for men and two units for women. In a 20-year follow-up of problem drinkers, mortality rate was raised by 364% over that expected for people in this age group. The negative consequences of alcohol can be considered under two headings: acute effects including the potential consequences of intoxication, and risks which result from long-term heavy consumption.

Acute effects

Anyone who has ever been drunk is familiar with the price to be paid the morning after. The hangover is made up of some or all of the following: nausea, dry mouth, thumping headache, lethargy, light-headedness, irascibility, reduced tolerance to noise, and general all-round misery. All this is due to a combination of dehydration, build-up of acidic metabolites of alcohol, and the direct effects of toxic congeners in certain drinks. Memories of the night before are mercifully blurred.

Levels of intoxication can be related fairly accurately to blood levels of alcohol. Levels between 50 and 150 mg% will produce emotional instability, reduced visual acuity, and impaired coordination and reaction time in most people. At between 150 and 300 mg% these handicaps become more pronounced, other perceptions may be affected, and slurring of speech becomes apparent. Levels between 300 and 500 mg% usher in severe mental and physical impairment, potentially life-threatening falls in blood sugar, body temperature, and depression of the heart, and the risk of fits. Above 500 mg% coma is likely, with depression of breathing and other vital functions including the cough reflex. There is a risk of asphyxiation by inhaling vomit, so an unconscious drunkard should always be placed in the recovery position rather than left snoring on his back. After a huge binge the plummeting blood sugar can be enough to cause brain damage, and the build-up of acidic metabolites (lactic acid, ketones) can bring on kidney failure.

The danger of drunken driving has been recognized since the earliest days of the motor car, and scientific tests in the 1930s clearly quantified the risk. This knowledge did not prevent drunken American drivers killing 60 000 people each year in the 1960s, and more recent studies show that alcohol is involved in more than half of all fatal crashes. In an average year in the UK, 1000 people will be killed and more than 20 000 hospitalized as a result of accidents caused by drivers over the limit. The introduction of the breathalyser in 1967 reduced road deaths by 15%, but this proved a transient effect. Recently there has been discussion about lowering the limit from 80 mg% to 50 mg% or even to zero in recognition of the fact that even the most modest alcohol intake measurably impairs performance. Alcohol is a major risk factor for pedestrians and cyclists, and also plays an important part in accidents in the home and elsewhere. Drunkenness is closely associated with violence. The 1996 British Crime Survey revealed that 53% of people who attack strangers are drunk at the time, a third of such attacks occur within the immediate vicinity of pubs or other licensed premises, and a further third at or near bus or railway stations. Alcohol plays a significant part in nearly half the fights between acquaintances and a third of domestic incidents. The risk of becoming a victim of violence is increased by drinking, since those with robbery or sexual attack in mind often target people made more vulnerable by befuddlement. A study among young Swedish soldiers showed a clear association between alcohol intake and the risk of dying as a result of a violent attack.

Alcohol freely crosses the placenta and is toxic to the developing fetus. The greater the dose, the greater the likelihood of damage, but many paediatricians believe there is no completely safe dose and that abstention during pregnancy is the wisest course. It is possible that ordinary social drinking can result in subtle impairments of the infant's mental functioning. A woman quaffing two units daily has twice the chance of suffering a miscarriage than a teetotaller. Heavier maternal drinking may cause the 'fetal alcohol syndrome' (FAS) which now occurs once in every 600 births in the UK. It is possibly related to peak acetaldehyde levels, so a binge-drinking pattern would be the most harmful. Affected infants are small and floppy with a characteristic facial appearance including a flattened nose and small eyeballs, and variable amounts of brain damage. The fetus is at its most vulnerable during the second and third months of pregnancy, a period of important brain development and limb growth. Three-quarters of children with FAS turn out to be hyperactive, and the average IQ is around 70. Drinking alcohol during pregnancy is the only preventable cause of mental retardation.

Chronic effects

Ethanol is toxic to most tissue, so heavy alcohol consumption over a lengthy period can result in damage to almost any body system.

In the brain, there is loss of nervous tissue in the higher centres which can lead to confusion, memory loss, and deterioration of personality. Associated deficits in Vitamin B_1 (thiamine) can produce Wernicke's encephalopathy with its characteristic combination of confusion, abnormal eye movements, and staggering gait. Untreated, many patients will go on to develop severe and permanent loss of memory and ability to learn new information ('Korsakoff's psychosis'). The cerebellum can be injured, leading to problems with balance and coordination. Damage to nerves outside the brain ('peripheral neuropathy') will cause numbness and muscle weakness. The muscles themselves can be affected, especially those in the upper arm and thigh.

Susceptibility to liver damage seems to be affected by gender (higher in women), genetically determined tissue types, and general quality of nutrition as well as the quantity of alcohol imbibed. Enlargement of the liver due to fatty infiltration is quite common in heavy drinkers but is usually fully reversible following abstinence. Alcoholic hepatitis (inflammation of the liver) is much more serious and may even prove fatal. Cirrhosis is a progressive disease which occurs when damaged liver cells are replaced with scar tissue and the whole organ contracts to a fraction of its normal size. Eventually, not enough remains to meet the body's metabolic needs and the signs of liver failure appear. Other bodily signs of alcoholism usually evident at this stage include skin blemishes ('spider naevi'), red palms, swelling of the parotid salivary gland, excessive bruising, and clawing of the hands due to tightening of tendons in the palms ('Dupuytren's contracture'). Liver cancer develops in up to 11% of people with cirrhosis.

Alcohol irritates and inflames the digestive tract all the way from the mouth and pharynx down the oesophagus to the stomach and beyond, and is associated with increased risk of cancer in many sites. Malnutrition results from a combination of this direct effect with the narrowing of dietary intake which is so common among dependent drinkers. The B vitamins are particularly affected, especially thiamine, with potentially dire results as outlined above. Interference with disposal of urates can lead to gout. The pancreas is particularly vulnerable to alcohol, and both acute and chronic pancreatitis are heralded by severe abdominal pain. Long-term damage to pancreatic cells can produce diabetes mellitus because of the loss of insulin production, and further impairment of nutrition because key digestive enzymes are no longer secreted. Chronic pancreatitis is associated with an increased risk of cancer of the pancreas. The strong association between alcoholism and tobacco smoking is presumably the cause of the much increased prevalence of lung cancer.

A large binge can produce an irregular heartbeat, and heavy long-term consumption is associated with a raised blood pressure and risk of strokes. Direct toxicity to the heart can result in an enlarged or flabby organ ('cardiomyopathy') which often proves fatal. Production of blood cells in the bone marrow is suppressed, leading to various anaemias and further increasing the strain on the heart.

Because of its effects upon sex hormones and other related mechanisms, alcoholism is associated with impaired libido and sexual function, and infertility in both sexes. Women sometimes stop having periods. Overproduction of the hormone cortisol can lead to obesity and raised blood pressure among other problems.

Dependence upon alcohol runs in families, with the close relations of alcoholics having a fivefold increase in prevalence in comparison with the general population. No doubt this is due to both genetic and environmental factors ('nature and nurture'). Various typologies have been invented in an attempt to delineate

different categories of alcoholism, and the best known of these originated with
E. M. Jellineck in the early 1950s. Jellineck described five distinct patterns of
abnormal drinking: alpha alcoholics drink far too much but with no evidence of
physical dependence (i.e. withdrawal symptoms, tolerance); betas are as above
but with some physical damage becoming evident; gammas show physical
dependence with a fluctuating intake and intermittent 'loss of control' (seen as
the typical British drunkard); deltas are physically dependent with a steady intake
and inability to abstain (i.e. the French); epsilons indulge in huge destructive
binges interspersed with periods of guilty abstinence.

Typologies have been superceded by the concept of the 'alcohol dependence
syndrome' which has seven characteristics: 'narrowing of repertoire' as the
drinker relies less on social cues and more on the need to maintain a steady intake
by an increasingly inflexible routine; making the regular supply of alcohol the
main priority in the organization of day-to-day activities; increasing tolerance to
the effects of alcohol; repeated withdrawal effects (see below), especially first
thing each morning; relief of such symptoms by more drinking; awareness of a
growing compulsion to drink; and rapid reinstatement of all these symptoms
after a period of abstinence.

When someone who is physically dependent upon alcohol stops drinking
abruptly, withdrawal effects appear after a few hours and reach a peak within a day
or two. Initially these consist of tremulousness, nausea, sweating, anxiety, and
insomnia. In severe cases this may progress to a full-blown toxic confusional state
known as delirium tremens (the 'DTs'). The victim becomes agitated and dis-
orientated, suffers from fleeting delusions and hallucinations, and may develop
epileptiform fits which can prove fatal. This syndrome is usually accompanied by
other physical disorders, including dehydration, increasing blood pressure, and
plummeting blood sugar.

Alcohol dependence is associated with a number of psychiatric problems, including intermittent auditory hallucinations, pathological jealousy which can be
extremely disruptive to relationships and not infrequently results in physical attacks
or even murder, and serious depression. There is an association with eating disorders, especially the bingeing/starving condition known as bulimia nervosa. The
risk of suicide is greatly increased among alcoholics.

Finally, the dependent drinker is likely to run into a raft of problems socially and at work. Families are often wrecked by drunkards with violence directed against the partner or children, neglect of duties of caring or material provision, and diversion of resources to maintain the flow of booze. The impact upon children is potentially devastating with an increased likelihood of physical and emotional abuse, and a greater prevalence of 'hyperactivity', truanting, and delinquency.

Jobs are lost through poor performance or absenteeism, education and training are disrupted. Social life narrows to the dimensions of the pub, relations with non-drinking friends or neighbours degenerate. Loss of work and family support sometimes ends in complete financial disaster and homelessness. Alcohol is a lubricant for violence and crime.

Such is the savage impact of our favourite drug on personal and public health. The Royal College of Physicians calls it 'a great and growing evil' but mostly the rest of us seem remarkably complacent in the face of this vast array of carnage and suffering. This response is in marked contrast to the usual reaction to disasters associated with less familiar drugs, for example the national outcry that recently followed the sensational reporting of a single death associated with an idiosyncratic response to Ecstasy. A huge police operation aimed at catching the teenage peddler of the fatal tablet and a national publicity campaign followed rapidly. On the same night this tragic death occurred, hundreds of young people of similar age would have been maimed and some of them killed as a direct result of alcohol intoxication, yet this outrageous daily carnage is almost entirely ignored. Strange.

chapter 4

tobacco

Historical background

We have no idea when North American Indians (and Aztecs in central Mexico) first incorporated tobacco into religious rituals and social interactions, but Christopher Columbus certainly found the custom well established by the time of his arrival towards the end of the 15th century. The dried plant was smoked in pipes or roll-ups made from leaves. The addictive quality of the habit was soon appreciated by the missionaries who were quite successful in converting the Indians to Catholicism but found it more difficult to persuade the new recruits to desist from smoking in church. There was much bemusement in Spain when the travellers returned with what was, for a short while at least, the original duty-free supply of tobacco. Its reputation as a medicinal plant spread quickly through mainland Europe. At various times it was used to treat intractable headaches, asthma, gout, tumours, and labour pain.

Tobacco probably reached England around 1550 when some Indians arrived in the custody of Sir John Hawkins, carrying with them generous supplies for their own consumption. Many of the sailors sampled it during the voyage and liked it so much that it became the custom to plant seeds at various stopping points around world trade routes to ensure a ready supply wherever the call of commerce or military necessity might lead. Sir Walter Ralegh is credited with introducing it to the fashionable world in London towards the end of the 16th century.

The popularity of tobacco soared during the 17th century with demand always exceeding supply, and the first commercial plantation was established in Jamestown, Virginia in 1612. Chewing tobacco and inhaling it as snuff also caught on, and at one point tobacco was literally worth its weight in silver. However, the possibility of harmful effects and the difficulty of consuming it in moderation were appreciated right from the start, and it had some influential opponents. King James I published his 'counterblaste to tobacco' in 1604 to emphasize his view that the 'manifold abuses of this vile custom' were 'loathsome to the eye, hateful to the nose, harmful to the brain, dangerous to the lungs'. The realization that truly massive tax revenues could easily be exacted from habitués soon overcame such considerations, and James' government became the first beneficiary of a massive bonanza which continues to the present day.

Measures aimed at restricting supplies or introducing punitive taxation merely increased the value of tobacco and made smuggling profitable enough to run any risk. No country has ever been successful in suppressing it once use has become endemic, notwithstanding the proclamations of tyrants, the formal decrees of popes, and the direst of penalties: hand and foot crushing in Turkey; nostril slitting in Russia; total confiscation of all assets in Japan; molten lead poured into the throat in Persia. Sooner or later, most governments just settle back and enjoy the immense profits to be made by sale of monopolies or taxation, and formal tobacco duties were introduced in England in 1660.

The first machine-made cigarettes appeared in Havana in 1853, and factories were established in London in 1856 and the US in 1872. The demand for these was small at first but grew rapidly towards the end of the century, and by the end of the First World War it had become the most popular formulation. The filter cigarette was introduced in the 1930s but didn't catch on for another 30 years.

UK cigarette sales increased steadily from 11 000 million in 1905 to 74 000 million in 1939, of which less than 1% were filtered. Up to this point, smoking was a more or less exclusively male habit but it became much more popular among women during the Second World War. Consumption soared in the immediate postwar period to more than 113 000 million annually (of which 20% were filtered) and thereafter increased more slowly to an all-time peak of 137 000 million in 1973 (83% filtered). The actual weight of tobacco sold peaked earlier in 1961 at which point 60% of men and 50% of women were smokers, but then fell off because of the rapid increase in popularity of filter tips. However, the average smoker's daily intake of cigarettes went up steadily from 14 in 1949 to 22 in 1973.

During the course of the 1960s cigarettes killed more Americans each year than the total combined casualty list of the First World War, Korea, and Vietnam. Health campaigns and adverse publicity in the UK, notable among which were the reports published by the Royal College of Physicians in 1962, 1977, and 1983, were associated with a 25% fall in the number of smokers between the mid-seventies and mid-eighties, by which time women were smoking around 45% of all cigarettes manufactured. By 1987, smokers made up around a third of the adult population as compared to well over half 10 years earlier. Male smokers have a consistently higher average daily consumption than women. More recently, the extent of further reductions in smoking has been quite disappointing.

There have been some striking shifts in the pattern of smoking over the years. Before 1958, smoking was much more prevalent among the higher income groups but more recently the opposite is true: a survey in 1987 showed that in social class 1 (SC1) only 13% smoked compared to 46% in SC5. Among smoking women in SC1 half will quit when they become pregnant, whereas in SC5 only 13% can be expected to do so. The reduction of smokers has been more rapid among men than women. The proportion of boys starting smoking under the age of 16 each year between 1965 and 1987 remained constant at around 30% but the rate among girls of the same age increased from 6% to 14% over the same period. More recently, it is apparent that girls are more likely to smoke regularly in their earlier teens than boys.

Despite the fact that UK custom duties went up by 900% between 1939 and 1977, and the proportion of the retail price made up by tax went up by 75% between 1956 and 1989, the real cost of 20 cigarettes actually decreased from 1.1% of the average weekly wage packet in 1960 to 0.6% in 1989. In 1990, duty was calculated on the basis of 21% of the retail price plus £34.91 per 1000 cigarettes, and the government received more than £5000 million revenue from tobacco taxes in that year.

Although there was a trend in many developed countries for a reduction in the prevalence of smoking between 1970 and 1985, overall world consumption increased by 7% over this period. This disappointing situation has come about because of very large increases in the Third World; up 22% in Asia, 42% in Africa.

Preparation and distribution

The solanaceous plant *Nicotinia tabacum* was so called in honour of a French ambassador to Portugal, Jean Nicot, who was a strong believer in its medicinal properties. The modern production and global distribution of cigarettes and other tobacco products is overwhelmingly dominated by a handful of vast, multi-national companies: Imperial Tobacco, Rothmans International, Philip Morris, R. J. Reynolds, British American Tobacco (BAT), and American Brands. Profit margins are impressive – BAT made £2495 million pre-tax profits in 1996. Astonishingly, tobacco enjoys higher EU subsidies per hectare than any other crop even though much of the product is unsellable and has to be dumped on the undeveloped countries at knock-down prices.

According to the organization Action on Smoking and Health (ASH), more than 81 000 million cigarettes were sold in the UK in 1996–97, and 90% of these were supplied as brands marketed by Imperial, Rothmans, Philip Morris, and Gallaghers, which was demerged from American Brands in 1997. Gallaghers owns Britain's leading brand, Benson & Hedges, which corners nearly 17% of the total market. Tobacco is the fourth largest consumer product behind clothing, beer, and meat. The business currently employs more than 13 000 British people and generates around £9000 million yearly for the British Exchequer in the form of Tobacco Excise Duty and VAT. On the other hand, ASH estimates that the total health costs directly attributable to smoking add up to well over a billion pounds. Taking the effects of inflation and wage rises into account, the real price of cigarettes has fallen consistently over many decades. This is unfortunate because smoking is quite responsive to price: an increase of 1% in retail cost can be expected to result in a 0.5% fall in consumption. The UK tobacco industry spends more than £100 million yearly on advertising and promotion, while the government forks out less than a tenth of this in health campaigns. It is now clear that advertising does have a significant effect in boosting consumption, and that in countries where it has been banned the subsequent fall in smoking cannot reasonably be attributed to any other influence or intervention.

Under the terms of the Children and Young Persons (Protection from Tobacco) Act (1991), it is illegal to sell tobacco products to children under 16, yet 450 children start smoking every day in the UK and this age group consumes over 1000 million cigarettes yearly. Prosecution of shopkeepers is a rare event. The Health and Safety at Work Act (1974) prohibits smoking in certain places such as commercial kitchens and petrol filling stations.

Ready-made cigarettes contain a number of additives, including humectants (glycerol, diethylene glycol), casing agents, and flavourings. Traces of pesticides and fertilizers sometimes turn up. Ventilated filters were introduced in the 1970s and by the beginning of the 1990s had come to dominate the market.

Routine surveys of cigarette tar and nicotine content by the Laboratory of the Government Chemist (LGC) were initiated in 1972, and carbon monoxide estimates from 1978. The average tar yield of cigarettes halved between 1960 and 1990 from 30 mg down to 15 mg. Current LGC classification bands are as follows:

low tar = 0–9.99 mg
low to medium = 10–14.99 mg
medium = 15–17.99 mg
high = 18 mg +

Over the same period, carbon monoxide generation reduced less impressively from 19 mg to 14 mg. Nicotine content in plain cigarettes has come down steadily, but the average filter cigarette still delivers around 1.3 mg, hardly different at all to the levels in the 1970s. The problem is that there is little evidence that 'safer' cigarettes are actually any safer: people who switch to low tar brands may just increase the frequency and depth of inhalation.

Health warnings on packets appeared as part of a voluntary agreement between the UK government and manufacturers until they were made compulsory by EC directive in 1992.

Scientific information

The tip of a cigarette achieves temperatures of more than 1000°C during a puff and this tiny furnace releases more than 4000 chemical substances, one of which is nicotine. This drug, which reaches the brain within 10 seconds of inhalation, resembles in structure the naturally occurring neurotransmitter (chemical messenger) acetylcholine and has a very complicated network of effects. Individual reactions to it vary, and sensitivity to the pleasurable effects may be genetically linked.

Absorption of nicotine through mucous membranes in the mouth will only occur to any significant extent if the smoke is alkaline, as is the case with pipe and cigar tobacco. In these circumstances, the drug remains un-ionized and therefore highly fat soluble. Most cigarettes produce acidic smoke which must be inhaled into the lungs for the nicotine to be absorbed. Absorption from the lungs is a highly efficient process which hoovers up 90% of the nicotine in the smoke, giving an average dose per cigarette of 1 mg. Nicotine is broken down quickly in the liver and elsewhere to inert substances, so that blood levels halve every two hours or so. Cotinine is a metabolite which is itself broken down quite slowly, and is a useful marker in research which requires an accurate measure of tobacco intake.

Nicotine can either stimulate or depress various parts of the brain and nervous system depending on the dose, environmental conditions, and the mood and personality of the user. The complexity of its effects relates to this variability, and to its ability to cause the release of many other hormones and neurotransmitters, including noradrenaline, dopamine, serotonin, growth hormone, corticotrophin, and antidiuretic hormone. The result is that the reward experienced by smokers will range from calm relaxation to stimulation and euphoria, depending upon circumstances. Larger doses have a purer stimulant effect leading to agitation, hyperactivity, vomiting, trembling and shaking, and convulsions.

Nicotine has a wide range of consequences outside the nervous system, including an increase in heart rate and blood pressure; irregularities of the heart beat; constriction of some blood vessels and dilation of others; increased concentration of potentially damaging fats (triglycerides, cholesterol) in the blood and a reduction of protective fats (HDL cholesterol); stimulation of certain components of the blood-clotting process; and increased general metabolic rate. Tolerance (reduced sensitivity) to many of the effects of nicotine comes on quickly but is also lost within a few hours. Thus the regular smoker notices dizziness or skin tingling from the first cigarette of each day because tolerance has been lost overnight.

Regular smokers become physically dependent upon nicotine, and withdrawal is associated with changes in electroencephalogram readings (which map the electrical activity of the brain), tests of physical and mental functioning, mood (e.g. irritability, depression, poor concentration), appetite, and sleep pattern. The psychological component of the addiction is represented by craving for, and preoccupation with, cigarettes.

The 4000 or so chemical components of tobacco smoke are classified as solids ('particulate phase') or gases. Tars are combustion products of organic materials and are therefore absent from unburnt tobacco, snuff, and chewing tobacco. They are responsible both for the pleasurable taste of cigarettes and much of the damage which ensues. Reducing the tar production of cigarettes causes many smokers to increase the rate and depth of inhalation in an attempt to compensate. Sidestream smoke, which enters the environment without first passing through the smoker, contains more tar than mainstream smoke. Many tars are polycyclic hydrocarbons or N-nitroso compounds which are known to be capable of producing cancerous changes in cell preparations and whole animals. Apart from such long-term effects, irritation produced by particulates causes an immediate reduction in the efficiency of the lungs. The tiny hair-like structures (cilia), which swirl rhythmically about on the surface of the larger airways to clear foreign matter out of the lungs, at first work harder to try and counter the sudden surge of incoming toxins but gradually become overwhelmed and give up.

Tobacco smoke contains up to 5% of carbon monoxide (CO) which combines with the haemoglobin to form carboxyhaemoglobin (COHb). This reduces the oxygen-carrying capacity of the blood and makes the heart work harder because it has to deliver more blood to the vital organs to maintain a constant supply of oxygen. COHb is very stable and, once formed, hangs around for a long time. So we have a situation where the heart of the smoker is facing an increasing workload and direct stimulation by nicotine. At the same time its oxygen supply is being reduced by the presence of COHb and a nicotine-induced constriction of the arteries which supply it. As a final insult, the blood-clotting mechanism is also being stimulated by nicotine. The result, as detailed below, is a huge increase in mortality from heart attacks among smokers.

Possible beneficial effects

Dementia of the Alzheimer type is said to be less common in smokers, and tobacco has been shown to improve performance in tests of memory function.

Smoking reduces quite markedly the chances of developing Parkinson's disease and improves some of the symptoms of the neurological condition Tourette's syndrome. This might be due to an influence of nicotine on brain mechanisms powered by acetylcholine, which it resembles, or to its effect on reducing levels of the enzyme monoamine oxidase (B).

Recreational use

The 1996 General Household Survey showed that 29% of men in Great Britain and 28% of women admit to being regular smokers. Until 1994, the trend in both men and women was for a slow but steady decline, but 1996 showed a small increase (which was statistically significant for women). Prevalence of smoking has decreased in the last 10 years among men and women of 35 and older and boys between 16 and 19, remained unchanged in both sexes between the ages of 20 and 34, and increased in girls aged 16–19.

Smokers give various explanations for persisting with a habit which they know to be risky. Some say it improves their mood or helps them relax, 'calm down', or generally cope better. Smoking can reduce aggression or anxiety, improve tolerance of other people's annoying behaviour, or improve vigilance and task performance. Women and young girls often say it helps keep their weight down.

Most new recruits are under 18, and uptake of smoking among teenagers has remained constant over the past decade despite numerous public health campaigns. Year after year, presumably to the delight of the tobacco companies, 450 children in Great Britain start smoking every day. Girls tend to start at an earlier age but smoke fewer cigarettes each week than boys (an average of 40 for girls, 48 for boys). Children say that the strongest influences are parental and sibling habits, advertisements, and smoking in films and on TV.

Reasons why young people might choose to take up tobacco or any other drug are discussed in Chapter 1. Knowledge of health risk has not been found to be a strong deterrant because the process of risk assessment by adolescents, insomuch as it happens at all, is different to that of adults. Teenagers exhibit a strong bias towards optimism in the consideration of personal risk. Unpleasant outcomes such as illness are delayed long into the future whereas the rewards in terms of status, peer solidarity, affront to adults, and illusions of maturity are immediate.

Environmental factors have a huge influence on the uptake of smoking quite apart from the obvious impact of parents, siblings, and peers. Religious belief (even when no direct restrictions on smoking are made explicit) has an inverse relationship with prevalence. Comparisons between schools in similar neighbourhoods demonstrate that the presence of a smoking teacher can double the prevalence of smoking among older pupils. The average prevalence of smoking among 16-year-olds in a group of schools with no restrictive policy on staff smoking was 32% compared to 20% in those that did have a policy. Banning smoking in public places also has an impact on uptake rates.

A third of women becoming pregnant are regular smokers, and only a quarter of these will stop during the course of the pregnancy. Of these, two out of three resume smoking within a few weeks of the birth. Ninety per cent of women who continue to smoke throughout pregnancy are still smoking five years later.

Unwanted effects

Smoking tobacco causes more deaths worldwide than all other avoidable causes put together. It is directly responsible for approximately 300 000 deaths each year in the United States and 150 000 in the UK. In these countries, 15% of 35-year-old non-smoking men can expect to die before their 65th birthday: for smokers of up to 14 cigarettes daily the figure is 22%, 15–24 cigarettes 25%, and 25 or more cigarettes 40%.

Tobacco is the primary cause of at least a third of all cancers, and the most familiar association is with lung cancer. Between 1920 and 1950 the prevalence of this disease in men went up 20-fold, and it currently kills 30 000 people each year in the UK. Smokers are more likely to contract it by a factor of 1000%, and passive smoking is thought to be a contributory factor in a proportion of the 15% of cases which occur in non-smokers. The earlier in life the individual starts smoking, the greater the risk. The prevalence is now decreasing in men but increasing in women. Tumours of the mouth, throat, and oesophagus are up to 10 times more common in smokers, and there is also a proven association with cancers of the stomach, pancreas, kidney, and bladder, and certain types of leukaemia.

Coronary heart disease is the leading cause of death in the developed countries, killing 180 000 annually in the UK and 750 000 in the US, and smoking is one of the three major risk factors (along with high blood pressure and raised blood cholesterol). The damage is done by reducing the oxygen-carrying power of the blood through the formation of carboxyhaemoglobin and so starving the heart of oxygen; narrowing of the coronary arteries which supply the heart muscle as a result of the building up of a rim of fat (atherosclerosis); and increasing the clotting tendency of the blood by effects on several of its constituents (e.g. red blood cells and platelets). The good news is that the greatly increased risk falls off rapidly if the smoker quits, and after four years of abstinence is no different from that of a person who has never smoked.

Smoking damages other parts of the circulatory system too. Ninety per cent of people with diseased leg arteries are smokers, who also have an increased risk of high blood pressure, strokes (double the risk in smokers), and ballooning (aneurysm) of the aorta (the biggest artery in the body).

The risk of fatal chronic bronchitis and emphysema (chronic obstructive airways disease) is six times greater in smokers and kills 20 000 people yearly in the UK. Smoking is associated with a long list of other dreadful illnesses which include ulcers in the stomach and small intestine, eye damage, pulmonary tuberculosis, tooth and gum disease, and impairment of the immune system. Nicotine interacts unhelpfully with a number of prescribed drugs, and increases the cardiovascular risks associated with the contraceptive pill 10-fold.

Fertility in women is reduced, and there is a higher prevalence of spontaneous abortion (25% up), toxaemia of pregnancy, congenital malformations, labour complications, and stillbirth (perinatal mortality up by 33%). Smoking mothers produce babies which are on average seven ounces lighter than those born to non-smokers. This finding is more striking in older mothers and the magnitude of effect correlates with the number of cigarettes smoked, especially in the second and third trimesters. The effect has remained constant over the last two decades, despite reductions in tar and nicotine levels over that period. Paternal smoking seems also to have some negative impact on birthweight, either through a chromosomal mechanism or by passive smoking by the mother.

The spotlight on the damaging effects of passive smoking (inhalation of someone else's fumes) has intensified in recent years, and in particular the impact upon children of smoking parents. Such a child inhales the equivalent of between 60 and 150 cigarettes each year. The smoke inhaled passively is largely sidestream, and this contains much greater quantities of nicotine, carbon monoxide, ammonia, and certain carcinogens than mainstream smoke.

Maternal smoking is associated with a fivefold increase in atopic (allergic) symptoms in the child, a greater chance of admission to hospital with a chest infection in the first year of life, and an increased prevalence of the sudden infant death syndrome (SIDS – 'cot death'). This link with SIDS is dose related: in comparison with a non-smoker, the risk for a mother who smokes less than 10 cigarettes daily is increased by a factor of 1.8, and more than 10 by 2.7.

If one parent smokes the annual incidence of pneumonia or bronchitis in the child increases from 7.8% to 11.4%, and if both parents smoke this rises to 17.6%. The risk of the child developing asthma increases by at least a third. Glue ear is much more common, and the child's growth is likely to be stunted if the parents smoke more than 10 a day each. It seems probable that the prevalence of many cancers, including leukaemia, is higher among children in smoking households.

The impact upon adults of exposure to smokers in public places is of growing concern: half of all non-smokers living in cities are found to have significant levels of nicotine in their blood and urine. Living with a heavy smoker increases the risk of lung cancer by between 10 and 30%, and may also increase the chances of developing bronchitis or heart disease.

There has been a reluctance to accept that regular cigarette smokers are in the grip of a genuine addiction, but there can be no doubt that this is the case. The American National Institute on Drug Abuse has laid out the case: patterns of tobacco use, withdrawal, and relapse are very similar to those of other addictive drugs such as heroin and alcohol; tolerance and physiological changes appear in response to nicotine; nicotine is 'reinforcing' in a range of animal species in a dose-related manner by all routes of administration. Regular smokers who quit usually experience a predictable pattern of physical and psychological withdrawal effects. Over 90% of cigarette smokers fulfill the criteria for dependence arrived at by the American Psychiatric Association. According to documents revealed through recent court cases in the US, the tobacco industry have for at least two decades been 'aware of the addictive or habit-forming nature of nicotine, experimented with 'dosages' of nicotine, and did not reveal to consumers the extent of their knowledge'. Litigation against the tobacco companies by victims of smoking-related illnesses or the health care industry seems to be gathering momentum.

The reality is that the likelihood of progression from occasional to regular, daily use is greater for tobacco than any other addictive drug, including heroin and crack cocaine, and the long-term damage associated with this particular drug and its delivery system is in a class of its own. Of all the risky temptations facing young teenagers that responsible parents may lose sleep about, cigarette smoking should head the list.

cannabis

Historical background

A robust but otherwise undistinguished weed has provided the world with one of its most remarkable drugs. For centuries the psychoactive properties of cannabis have been put to use in religious and social rituals, and it has an intriguing history as a nostrum for many of life's most ubiquitous and irksome discomforts. The use of cannabis as a medicine is described in the Egyptian Ebers papyrus of the 16th century BC, at which time it was prized as a powerful painkiller. It went on to become a valued remedy in all succeeding civilizations up to and including our own.

In the modern world, no other prohibited drug has provoked such polarization between its defenders and detractors, with reason frequently swamped by rhetoric on both sides of the divide.

The hardy annual now labelled *Cannabis sativa* was probably the first crop to be grown for reasons other than food production. The first systematic account of the painkilling, fever-reducing, anti-inflammatory, and anti-emetic properties of cannabis appeared in China nearly 5000 years ago. It was particularly prized for its ability to relieve labour pain, speed up delivery, and reduce post-delivery bleeding. The Assyrians made use of it in the eighth century BC, the Chinese were certainly cultivating it by the fourth century, and it is described in Indian religious writings in the second century. It also found an important place in ancient Chinese and Greek pharmacopoeias. Ceremonial, recreational, and therapeutic use has continued uninterrupted throughout Asia, Africa, Arabia, and South and Central America down the centuries. Traces of cannabis were identified in the remains of a young girl who died near Jerusalem in the fourth century AD. Scientists have deduced that she was in all probability given the drug to ease the pains of childbirth. This has been one of the most ubiquitous historical applications, extending across many civilizations and persisting to the present day in some cultures.

The other great asset of the plant, its fibrous stem so useful for rope-making and weaving, was utilized by the Romans who initiated cultivation of the plant in Britain. By Tudor times, this had been expanded on a very large scale but still the demand for the fibre could not be satisfied. The early settlers in North America were encouraged to grow the plant early in the 17th century, and this soon developed into a considerable rural industry. Apart from the fibre, the seeds were a source of oil for fuel and other commercial applications, and found to be most nutritious for birds.

This tenacious relative of the nettle grows wild throughout the world. Its psychoactive product is available in the East in many forms varying in potency, refinement, and expense, and goes under many names, including bhang, charas, ganga, kif, dagga, kabak, and hashish. In these endemic areas it is used ceremonially, but also quite casually by ordinary folk to alleviate fatigue and boredom. It was introduced into the Caribbean from Bengal, and the population took to it most readily. The psychoactive and herbal properties of cannabis were probably first introduced to Europeans in any quantity about 1000 years ago by the Moorish marauders who were then ravaging Spain and Portugal.

The weed was known in the West as Indian hemp until Linnaeus christened it *C. sativa* in 1753, and it only began to emerge here as a herbal remedy on any scale in the 18th century. It soon gained a popular reputation as a rival panacea to opium in Britain, Europe, and North America but it was not until the 19th century that Western doctors became fully aware of its potential as a mainstream medicine. The person who is credited with making cannabis respectable was the Irish scientist and physician, W. B. O'Shaughnessy. He observed its use in India as a painkiller, anti-epileptic, antispasmodic, anti-emetic, and cure for insomnia. After carrying out experiments on goats and dogs to convince himself of its safety, O'Shaughnessy began giving it to patients suffering from a variety of conditions, including rheumatism, epilepsy, and tetanus, and was impressed with the results. Dissolved in alcohol solution it proved a most effective painkiller. He was also struck by its particular usefulness as an anti-vomiting agent, a finding that has been fully replicated in 19th- and 20th-century research.

When O'Shaughnessy returned to England in 1842 bringing a substantial supply with him, he published an account of his findings and the medical use of cannabis expanded rapidly. Other clinicians emphasized '… the remarkable power of increasing the force of uterine contractions, concomitant with a significant reduction of labour pain', mirroring French reports of its effectiveness in reducing uterine haemorrhage, and its usefulness in the treatment of chloral and opium addiction. By 1854 it had found its way into the United States Dispensatory. Cannabis was soon available 'over the counter' in pharmacies throughout England and Scotland. Queen Victoria apparently found it useful in relieving menstrual cramps.

J. Russell Reynolds, 'Physician in Ordinary to Her Majesty's Household', wrote in the *Lancet* of his more than 30 years' clinical experience with cannabis. In his opinion, '… Indian hemp, when pure and administered carefully, is one of the most valuable medicines we possess'. He found it incomparable for 'senile insomnia', 'night restlessness', and 'temper disease' in both children and adults, but not helpful in melancholia, 'very uncertain' in alcoholic delirium, and 'worse than useless' in mania. It was very effective in a range of painful conditions including neuralgia, period pains, migraine, 'lightning pain of the ataxic patient', and gout, but useless in sciatica and 'hysteric pains'. He had found it impressive in certain epileptiform convulsions related to brain damage from tumour or trauma, but no good at all in petit mal or 'chronic epilepsy', tetanus, chorea, or paralysis agitans. It effectively relieved nocturnal cramps, asthma, and dysmenorrhoea. Reynolds warned of inconsistency of effect consequent upon 'great variations in strength' of the different preparations since the 'active principle has not been separated', and held that toxic effects only occurred with excessive doses.

Reynolds was writing at a time when the zenith of cannabis as a prescribed medicine and home remedy was already past. Although Sir William Osler was still recommending it for migraine sufferers in 1913, by the First World War it was in steep decline. Reasons for this include variable potency of herbal cannabis preparations, unreliable sources of supply, poor storage stability, unpredictable response to oral administration, uncertainty as to optimal dosing regimes, increasing enthusiasm for parenteral routes of administration, the growing availability of potent synthetic alternatives, commercial pressures, and, progressively, concern about recreational use, particularly in the United States.

Recreational use does not seem to have been widespread in 19th-century Europe and North America, but it became a firm favourite among artists and intellectuals in the bigger cities. Dr Jaques Moreau de Tours was introduced to hashish whilst touring North Africa, and on his return to Paris in the 1840s founded the *Club des Haschishchiens* at the Hotel Pimodan with like-minded cronies such as Dumas, Balzac, Flaubert, and Baudelaire. The doses consumed by the members of this club were heroic by modern Western standards, and the effect upon their already fevered imaginations was florid indeed.

Awareness of a growing popularity of cannabis among the poor and labouring classes in the British colonies, alongside pressure exerted by a distilling industry increasingly alarmed by the popularity of this competitive product, led the British government to instigate a massive scientific enquiry into cannabis use and its possible dangers in Asia. The Indian Hemp Commission produced its seven volume report in 1894. This very comprehensive survey revealed no convincing evidence of 'mental or moral injury' from moderate use of cannabis. Excessive use was no more likely to occur than was the case with alcohol, and seemed to be more or less confined to those with an established tendency to be idle or dissipated. These findings have been broadly confirmed by the various detailed reviews that have appeared at regular intervals up to the present day. These will be referred to in more detail below.

Cannabis was outlawed in Britain in 1928 when the government ratified the 1925 Geneva Convention on the manufacture, sale, and movement of dangerous drugs. It did, however, remain available in pharmacies for use in psychiatric indications until its absolute prohibition under the terms of the Misuse of Drugs Act (1971).

In North America, the drug was associated in the earliest years of the 20th century with the poorest sections of the community, and the reefer (marijuana cigarette) was introduced into the country by wandering Mexican labourers. However, it soon began to catch on more widely, initially among the mainly black jazz musicians and their followers, and started to develop an extremely negative image in the newspapers of the deep South. Lurid stories linking it with horrific violence and sexual debauchery became commonplace, and induced a truly hysterical reaction to the drug in some quarters. This seems to have been driven, at least in part, by the hate and fear inspired by the minority groups which were particularly associated with it – immigrants and blacks.

A rich folklore and grammatical idiom developed around the use of cannabis, which became known by such names as weed, tea, gage, loco-weed, and Mary-Jane. The reefer or 'joint' was sometimes referred to as a 'mezz' after the white jazz musician Milton Mezzrow who seems to have enjoyed access to material of particularly fine quality. After a highly eventful life, Mezzrow died in 1972 at the age of 73.

By 1930 the steady flow of scare stories, most of which appear to have been entirely fanciful, had led 16 states to ban cannabis and in the same year the Bureau of Narcotics was formed within the Treasury Department. The first Commissioner was Harry Anslinger, and he was to spend the next 30 years doing everything in his power to blacken the image of cannabis and all who used it or spoke up in its defence with truly fanatical zeal. In 1937, the Marijuana Tax Act effectively outlawed the drug nationwide despite the opposition of a number of doctors and psychiatrists, as well as people concerned with civil liberty.

All the contemporary scientific investigations contradicted Anslinger's propaganda campaign, but were studiously ignored or their authors pilloried by the Bureau and the media. The scholarly La Guardia Report (1944), for example, was based upon a detailed review of the medical, psychological, and social aspects of marijuana use in New York City. The report concluded that there was no evidence to suggest that cannabis induces aggressive or antisocial behaviour, increases sexual crime, or significantly alters the personality of the user. The scientists could find no evidence of addiction or mental or physical deterioration in their subjects. Then, as now, sensational anecdote was preferred to painstaking enquiry.

Contrary to the Bureau's statistics, cannabis use had a low prevalence in the general population right up to 1960, even though the weed was growing wild and unrecognized in millions of gardens throughout the nation. To most English people it was almost unknown as a fun drug until the 1950s when immigration from the Caribbean increased greatly, and the incomers brought their cannabis with them (ganja in some form was said to be used by up to 70% of the population of Jamaica at that time). Marijuana began to turn up in London folk and jazz clubs, and the first white teenager to be busted found himself in the dock in 1952.

In the 1960s, as everybody knows, cannabis exploded out of these narrow confines. It became integral to the developing hippy and psychedelic movements, but also found its way into student life and the homes of otherwise quite unre-bellious and non-deviant people. By 1970, upwards of 25 million Americans had puffed on the weed, and there were 10 million regular smokers. In England four million had tried it, including a third of all university students. That tell-tale aroma even became familiar in and around the conservative corridors of the London medical schools in those heady years.

Prevalence expanded steadily through the 1970s, perhaps reaching its peak toward the end of the decade. By this time, the figures from contemporary surveys are rather remarkable (but see footnote, p. 3): 50% of people aged 18–25 questioned in the US said they had tried it at some time; 43 million Americans had sampled it, and 16 million were regular smokers. Ten per cent of American high-school students were puffing on it daily. In Britain, 20% of employed people between the ages of 20 and 40 had smoked it within the previous month. These were not criminals or deviants. Millions of ordinary people liked dope and used it regularly, but seemed to be able to combine this with an ordinary lifestyle. The level of demand had, and still has, enormous economic implications for the countries where cannabis has always been an important cash crop. In the early 1980s the annual export from the Lebanon alone far exceeded 2000 tonnes, a significant contribution to the national economy.

So concerned was the British government that it commissioned Baroness Wootton to head an investigation. Her report (1968) concluded: 'Having reviewed all the material available to us we find ourselves in agreement with the conclusions reached by the Indian Hemp Drugs Commission appointed by the Government of India (1893–1894) and the New York Mayor's Committee on Marijuana (1944) that the long-term consumption of cannabis in moderation has no harmful effects.' She also found no evidence to support the escalation theory which suggests that cannabis is dangerous because it leads on inexorably to experimentation with more dangerous drugs. She proposed that cannabis should be separated from heroin in the eyes of the law, and that the drug should be available for research and for use within medicine.

Despite its carefully argued, unsensational style, the report received the sort of histrionically hostile press reaction that Anslinger would have delighted in, and was ignored by the Callaghan government. Other investigations have concurred with the findings of Wootton. The Canadian Le Dain Commission (1972) came to a similar conclusion. The British Royal College of Psychiatrists (1987) stated that '… on any objective reckoning, cannabis must at present get a cleaner bill of health than our legalized "recreational drugs"'. In February 1998, *New Scientist* magazine revealed that the World Health Organization had suppressed a report on the harmful effects of cannabis which concluded that on balance cannabis is safer than alcohol or tobacco.

Strong calls for decriminalization have arisen from time to time. In 1972, the American Presidential Commission on Marijuana and Drug Abuse recommended that the possession of a small amount of cannabis for personal use should no longer be a criminal offence, and in 1977 the Carter administration formally advocated legalizing the possession of up to one ounce of cannabis. Public opinion oscillates according to the image the drug has in the media at the time: a Gallop poll in 1983 revealed 53% of Americans to be in favour of decriminalization, but this figure had decline to 27% in 1986. Generally, politicians seem to have concluded that espousing the decriminalization of cannabis has no value as a vote winner.

Preparation and distribution

Whilst there are a number of varieties of *C. sativa* named after their geographical location (e.g. *C. indica*, *C. americana*), they are all essentially the same plant.

Resin content and shape depend upon ambient conditions. If grown in peaty or heavy soil in a warm, wet climate, tall solid plants ideal for fibre extraction result. Plants grown in sandy soil in hot, dry surroundings are rich in resin, most of which is exuded from the flowering tops of female plants, coating nearby leaves and stalks. The plants are harvested between July and September. A particularly potent form known as *sinsemilla* (literally, without seeds) is obtained by culling out the male plants before pollination can occur. This results in larger flowering heads in the female plants, and a particularly abundant yield of the resin which contains the mind-altering ingredients.

Cannabis is usually less adulterated than most other street drugs, but may contain other inactive or active (e.g. datura-containing) plant material, bacteria, and fungi. Hashish may be contaminated with solvents or other chemicals. Poor quality cannabis has sometimes been impregnated with the dangerous hallucinogen phencyclidine (see Chapter 7) to increase its impact. Cannabis grown in the US or imported from Mexico or Central America may be contaminated with paraquat or other highly toxic herbicides sprayed from aeroplanes as part of eradication programmes.

Scientific information

More than 400 chemicals have been identified in the resin, including at least 60 psychoactive compounds (cannabinoids). The most important active ingredient is called delta-9-tetrahydrocannabinol (THC) which was isolated in 1964. Cannabis is available on the street in many different forms which vary considerably in their THC content. These include herbal material (often called marijuana or grass), resin compressed into blocks (hash), or less commonly a thick oil or tincture. As a rough guide, dried herbal material contains anything from 1–10% THC by weight, resin around 10–15%, and oil 15–30%. Highly potent preparations much richer in THC, such as sinsemilla and skunk weed, are becoming much more widely available.

In recent years important advances have been made in clarifying how cannabis actually produces its effects. Specific receptors have been discovered both inside and outside the brain, and in 1992 a naturally occuring chemical ('anandamide') which activates this receptor was identified. Others have subsequently been discovered. So it turns out that the body manufactures its own cannabinoids, analogous to the brain's own opiates, the endorphins. The natural role of the anandamide system remains to be clarified, but it may be concerned with mood, memory and awareness, sensory perception, movement, coordination, posture and balance, sleep, hormonal regulation, temperature control, appetite, and the regulation of the immune response. Cannabis is known to impair short-term memory, and this is consistent with the high density of receptors found in the hippocampus, a brain structure particularly associated with learning and the coding of sensory information.

The drug is metabolized within the body to both active and inactive metabolites, some of which are absorbed into fat stores and take a very long time to get rid of, so that urine tests for cannabinoids can remain positive for weeks after a single exposure. Levels of THC in plasma or urine can be measured accurately by a number of methods but there is no consistent relationship between blood levels and the intensity of drug effects. It is theoretically possible for passive inhalers of other peoples' cannabis fumes to test positive if sensitive immunoassay techniques are used. THC is capable of crossing the placenta into the unborn child, and is detectable in breast milk.

Many findings from animal experiments are inconsistent and of dubious relevance to humans. Cannabis is a powerful painkiller in animals by an unknown mechanism. Although this effect is definitely not mediated through opiate receptors, cannabis greatly reduces opiate withdrawal symptoms in animals. The release of reproductive and thyroid hormones is suppressed, as are certain aspects of the immune response. In monkeys, aggression is reduced but so is the motivation to perform complex tasks. The drug reduces susceptibility to fits. Animals given huge doses show long-lasting learning deficits and what are described as 'subtle changes in brain cell connections'. Cannabis tar is definitely carcinogenic.

Hormonal changes in the brain are similar to those produced by addictive drugs, and it is possible to produce withdrawal effects in animals given a cannabinoid antagonist after long periods of heavy dosing. However, animals given access to the drug show no inclination to self-administer it, in sharp contrast to cocaine, alcohol, or tobacco.

Medical uses

As a drug classified under Schedule 1 of the Misuse of Drugs Regulations, cannabis has no currently recognized therapeutic indications despite its world history as a medicine extending back over the centuries. The synthetic cannabinoid nabilone is currently available in the UK under a licence which restricts its use to the treatment of severe nausea and vomiting in cancer patients resistant to other treatments. THC capsules ('dronabinol') are not licensed here, but can be imported on a 'named patient' basis provided the doctor is not averse to a mountain of paperwork.

Notwithstanding this virtual ban, there is a wealth of anecdotal evidence and some scientific evidence that cannabis and cannabinoids have potential benefits in a wide range of medical conditions for which conventional medicines are far from satisfactory. Apart from a wider application in conditions associated with nausea and vomiting, these include multiple sclerosis and other neurological disorders which produce spasticity, glaucoma, chronic pain, certain types of epilepsy, anxiety, insomnia, detoxification from opiates, and conditions associated with loss of appetite and weight such as cancer or AIDS. The discovery of cannabinoid receptors and the anandamide system is important because it opens the way to the development of new drugs with improved side-effect profiles.

Surveys have shown that most doctors believe that cannabis and its derivatives should once again be available on prescription. In defiance of the present restrictions, a large number of otherwise law-abiding people have though it worthwhile to expose themselves to the risk, inconvenience, and unnecessary expense of the black market to obtain a drug which they believe can alleviate symptoms inadequately controlled by conventional medicines. A 1997 British Medical Association report concluded that '… individual cannabinoids have a therapeutic potential in a number of medical conditions in which present drugs or other treatments are not fully adequate' and '… present evidence indicates that they are remarkably safe drugs with a side-effect profile superior to many drugs used for the same indications'. The report went on to call for a change in the law which would open the way to both therapeutic use and clinical research. In 1998, a

Select Committee on Science and Technology of the House of Lords, after an extensive inquiry, recommended that the law should be changed to allow doctors to prescribe an appropriate preparation of cannabis if they saw fit. The Government rejected this recommendation on the day of publication. So it seems that politicians will continue to allow a potentially useful medicine to be tangled up in the complicated agendas which surround the 'War on Drugs'.

Recreational use

There are said to be at least 300 million recreational cannabis users in the world today. Approximately 60 million North Americans (a third of those aged 12 years and above) and somewhere between 5 and 10 million British people are thought to have smoked it at some time.

Following a period of steady decline between 1979 and 1992, rates of consumption in the US are rising again, and the number of current users among 12–17 year-olds doubled between 1992 and 1994. Somewhere in the region of 20 million American citizens are current users, of whom as many as 5 million smoke it daily. Americans spent in excess of $40 million on the drug in 1994. According to the 1996 British Crime Survey, 42% of young people under the age of 24 had tried cannabis, of whom 16% were regular consumers. School surveys suggest these are conservative estimates.

Cannabis is the target of more than 80% of all drug seizures by the British police and customs authorities, and the number of seizures continues to rise steadily year by year. The figure was 91 000 in 1995, weighing in 58 tonnes. The number of people found guilty of cannabis-related offences has increased from 42 000 in 1991 to 77 000 in 1995, representing 82% of all drug-related offences.

Current sources of cannabis for the British black market include Nigeria, Jamaica, Ghana, Morocco, Pakistan, and Afghanistan. Lebanese and Nepalese hashish is now rare but highly prized, as are the famed 'Thai sticks' (high-quality herbal material tied into tight reefers). Average street prices for the small-scale customer have remained remarkably constant over the years (though reducing in real terms); around £25 for a quarter-ounce of hash, more for good quality, imported herbal cannabis. It is usually bought as chunks of resin or bundles of herbal material, but occasionally appears as powder, sticks, tablets, or hash oil. Rough and ready home-produced 'grass' generally consists of a *mélange* of shredded leaves, seeds, and stalks and is rather low in THC, but is usually a good deal cheaper. Current street names include blow, puff, spliff, draw, grass, pot, shit, and weed.

An average marijuana roll-up or 'spliff' contains around 300–400 mg of herbal material. The quality of the street supply and the consumer's smoking technique will have a profound effect on the amount of drug absorbed, but even the most expert smoker cannot achieve more than 50% absorption; 25% would be a more likely figure. The dose of THC delivered by a single spliff could be as little as 1 mg or as much as 30 mg depending on the quality and type of material. Since the threshold dose for intoxication is around 2 mg, the impact of a single cigarette will be rapidly apparent. The placebo effect is not unimportant in cannabis smoking, and is more prominent in naïve smokers or those with suggestible personalities. However, most effects of cannabis can be shown to be dose related.

Intoxication will be discernible within a few minutes, peak around 30 minutes, and last for three to four hours. If you eat it, onset is delayed for one or two hours depending on whether the stomach is empty or not, but the effects last much longer. The main effects are upon mood, attention and memory, perception, and patterns of thinking. These psychological effects are quite variable, and are described below. Heart rate is increased, clumsiness and slurring of speech may be noted, and the eyes become reddened, but the physical effects of the drug are generally very mild. Body temperature may be slightly reduced. Fatal overdose due to cannabis alone has never been reliably reported.

Most users in the West smoke the drug in handmade cigarettes ('joints', 'spliffs' or, for those of Churchillian dimensions, 'blunts') with or without tobacco, or more ostentatiously in clay 'chillums' or water-pipes. It is also sometimes brewed up as a tea, or used in cooking. When consumed by mouth, it is more difficult to get the dose right and people may get much more 'stoned' than they had intended. The onset of activity by this route may seem particularly sudden and overwhelming.

There are hundreds of descriptions in print of what it is like to take cannabis. Although these accounts are rather variable, the discernible common theme is the essential lightheartedness of the experience. This is not, for most people, a serious or heavy drug. Its effect has been described as whimsical in nature, and the high it produces labelled, presumably by a non-enthusiast, as 'fatuous euphoria'.

The effect of any drug is greatly influenced by a range of factors quite apart from its pharmacology, and this is particularly true of cannabis. The personality, mood, and expectations of the user; the quality of the drug and the amount actually absorbed into the body; the nature of the environment, and the attitude and behaviour of other people who are around at the time will all shape the experience quite fundamentally. Some have argued that cannabis intoxication is a 'learned behaviour', that one has somehow to discover how to recognize and welcome the effects, and label them in one's mind as enjoyable. Others are unconvinced by this thesis, feeling it may be based upon a lack of firsthand experience or hash of inadequate quality!

Smoking dope is usually a sociable activity. A spliff, usually containing a mixture of cannabis and tobacco, is rolled from one or more cigarette papers to achieve the desired dimensions, and then handed round until it is nothing more than a tiny glowing stub (roach), highly prized for its heavy potency. This may get so hot and wizened that it requires a special holder (roach-clip). The experienced cannabis smoker inhales deeply and retains the smoke in the lungs for as long as possible to maximize absorption. This sometimes induces a peculiarly strangulated conversational style which may enrage the non-smoking listener whose patience is already sorely tried by the antics of the group.

After a few minutes of smoking, a sense of calm, contentment, and well-being is noted, often accompanied by a peculiar expanding or tight sensation in the head that users find hard to describe. A growing feeling of hilarity and sense of the absurd transforms the most mundane or banal observation or witticism into the funniest thing in the world. There is usually good will towards all of humanity and a sense of optimism and well-being. Inhibitions are reduced or dispelled entirely. The party may be seized with paroxysms of laughter or helpless giggling which can be most unappealing to the non-intoxicated observer.

In moderate doses, the effect is to enhance perception rather than distort it. Music, food, and sex, for example, seem more pleasurable and intense than usual but the user remains firmly in touch with reality. Time seems to crawl by very slowly, but the consumer feels active and talkative. With slightly larger doses, there may be a more pronounced sedative effect.

As time passes, enhanced appetite may become evident, and many people feel a particular desire for sweet things ('the munchies'). A rather dry mouth generally requires a steady intake of fluids. Sudden feelings of depersonalization or unreality sometimes come on in waves, and the degree of intoxication often seems to ebb and flow.

Novices who have misjudged the dose may occasionally find themselves physically transfixed. Their thoughts are racing and they may desperately wish to say something or get up and move about, but are effectively frozen to the spot. On the other hand, more experienced users claim to be able to master their intoxication if circumstances demand it. One chap remembered an occasion on which he was very high indeed, when suddenly the doorbell rang. Giggling inanely to himself, he went to answer it and there stood a policeman in uniform. The constable had been passing and had noticed a car parked with its headlights on in the drive. Being public-spirited, he had decided to alert the householder and prevent the inconvenience of a flat battery in the morning. This fellow claims he was able immediately to master his hysteria, find the keys to the car and nonchalantly stroll over to it with the officer, engaging him in small talk and not arousing in any way the suspicion that this might be a drug fiend in the grip of his habit. He was uncomfortably aware of the sounds of jollity that continued unabated from within the house. When he rejoined his friends, he relapsed instantly into the prevailing merriment which was no doubt enhanced by a shared sense of relief that the party had not been 'busted'.

To the aficionado, this sort of intoxication seems valuable and life-enhancing. Musicians may be convinced that their playing is more free-flowing and inspired, talkers that they are more witty and interesting, lovers that their sexual energy and enjoyment are augmented, writers that their imagination is broadened. Sceptics or 'straights' would say that any idea of improved creativity is pure illusion, literally a pipedream. Users, they say, are banal, clumsy, infantile, irritating, illogical, and almost entirely lacking in judgement.

Unwanted effects

The acute toxicity of cannabis is extremely low, and no deaths from overdose have ever been recorded in humans. A quantitative measure of acute toxicity in animals can be arrived at by working out the ratio of the therapeutic dose of a drug to its lethal dose. The ratio for alcohol is about 10, while that for cannabis is 40 000. However, as with all intoxicants, people under the influence of cannabis are more prone to accidents or miscalculations. Impaired reaction time, depth estimation, time sense, recovery from glare, coordination, ability to track a moving object, and lack of judgement may prove to be a lethal combination for drivers, pilots, or others performing tasks requiring skill and prudence.

Most of the unwanted effects caused by cannabis are minor in nature and brief in duration. Anxiety, occasionally building up to full-blown panic attacks, may result from misinterpreting the rapid heartbeat which usually accompanies use of the drug as evidence of an impending heart attack, or the psychological effects as a precursor to complete loss of control or madness. Dizziness or depersonalization may similarly be assumed to herald impending catastrophe. These symptoms are more common in less experienced smokers who may also be more vulnerable to transient mood disturbances. Cannabis tends to heighten whatever mood was dominant before exposure; depressed or anxious people often feel worse. Some users may feel 'paranoid' from time to time, imagining they are being watched or followed, or that everyone is against them. Awareness that these suspicions are the product of the drug rather than anything real is usually retained, and abstention generally results in a rapid recovery. There may be interactions with other drugs, especially brain depressants.

Hangover from moderate use of cannabis is usually mild, but it is easy to oversleep the following morning, possibly by several hours. Larger doses may accentuate the sedative potential of the drug, or result in sensory distortion or frank hallucinations. Members of the *Club des Haschischchiens* referred to earlier in the chapter took huge doses by today's standards, and Gautier has left an interesting description of the phenomenon known as *synaesthesia*, where the senses become interchanged. Describing a vase of flowers, he wrote: 'My hearing became prodigiously acute.

I actually listened to the sounds of the colours. From their blues, greens, and yellows there reached me sound waves of perfect distinctness.'

There are hundreds of published reports of more serious adverse effects of cannabis, but the scientific validity of many of them is questionable. This is because of the many difficulties inherent in this sort of research, which include the need to rely on uncorroborated, retrospective accounts of illegal activities by the subjects under study; lack of information on physical, psychological, or personality problems that may have existed before the subject began to use drugs; covert continuation of cannabis use or undisclosed use of other drugs currently or in the past; variations in the quality of illicit drugs, and the amounts absorbed; lifestyle factors such as poverty and deprivation, or unrecognized physical or mental illness. The design of the studies is usually unsatisfactory, with inappropriate tests, inadequate statistics, or overinterpretation of the results. The prior assumptions of the experimenter may shape the design of the study or the interpretation of the findings.

The heart speeds up and therefore has to work harder and blood volume may be increased through salt and water retention. The absorption of carbon monoxide by cannabis smokers reduces the oxygen content of the blood, and thus the oxygen supply to heart muscle. These effects seem of little relevance for the healthy individual, but may add up to trouble for someone with pre-existing disease of the heart or circulatory system, including those with high blood pressure.

A cannabis cigarette delivers a significantly greater burden of insoluble particulates (tar) per unit weight than a tobacco cigarette, assuming a similar smoking profile. In practice, the larger puff volume, increased depth of inhalation, and longer smoke retention by the cannabis smoker can deliver four times as much tar to the lung as would result from a tobacco cigarette. Particle size has a similar profile to that of tobacco. Tar from a marijuana cigarette contains as much as 50% more unpleasant chemicals of known carcinogenicity than tobacco smoke, and produces precancerous cell changes in a variety of animal experiments. Heavy cannabis consumption (3 to 4 spliffs daily for five years or more) is associated with sinusitis, pharyngitis, shortness of breath, chronic cough, and bronchitis.

The impact of four joints daily on the lungs is said to equate to 20 tobacco cigarettes. Inflammatory and precancerous changes have been identified in the airways of chronic smokers, and these changes are most marked in those who smoke both tobacco and cannabis. There are anecdotal reports of an increased incidence of tumours of the mouth, larynx, and airways in cannabis smokers. On the other hand there doesn't seem to be any firm epidemiological evidence of an increased prevalence of these cancers or chronic lung disease in countries where large amounts of cannabis are consumed. This may simply be due to lack of systematic investigation, or a predominance of eating the drug rather than smoking it. The delay between exposure and development of disease, allied to the relatively short time-scale of mass use, might explain why nothing has yet shown up in the West. Doctors rarely inquire into, and document, their patients' use of cannabis, and may not get an honest answer if they did. The consensus among the experts is that daily cannabis smoking probably poses all the potential long-term risk to the airways that cigarette smoking does, and that smoking both cannabis and tobacco will maximize this risk.

The effect of cannabis on memory, in particular the ability to learn new information, is another genuine cause for concern. There is no doubt that impaired concentration, learning, and short-term memory can be confidently anticipated when a person is high on cannabis. What is far from certain is whether this impairment can persist after a person has stopped taking the drug, and if so, for how long. One study showed that in subjects abstinent for 12 hours, residual effects were entirely restricted to recent memory; long-term memory, immediate and delayed recall, attention, and concentration were all unaffected. A more important question is whether memory might remain impaired for weeks, months, or even years after a person has stopped using the drug. This dilemma remains unresolved. One study does suggest that memory may remain abnormal in humans after several weeks of abstinence, but it has scientific limitations and requires confirmation. This is an area which cries out for high quality research.

In North American samples, at least 10% of women have smoked cannabis during pregnancy, and presumably a similar picture pertains in the UK and elsewhere. Does this matter? Cannabis freely crosses the placenta and, given to animals in large doses, it is damaging to the fetus (teratogenic) and increases lost pregnancies. The picture in humans is much less clear, but the main effects which have been suggested are an association with prematurity and babies of low birth-weight. However, there are many complications in interpreting findings since continued cannabis use during pregnancy is often associated with low income, social deprivation, poorer education, younger age of conception outside a stable relationship, heavier alcohol and tobacco use, use of other illicit drugs, and poorer maternal nutrition and general health. All of these factors are themselves associated with an increased risk to the fetus. Medications given to the mother, natural birth complications, maternal bonding, feeding practices, and sibling interactions can also confuse the issue. Animal studies show an interaction between exposure to cannabis and a low-protein diet in the induction of stillbirths, postnatal deaths, and delayed developmental milestones.

The possibility of delayed effects upon the offspring is another font of contro-versy. An American study suggested that babies born to cannabis-smoking mothers showed increased startle reactions, fine trembling, disrupted sleep patterns, and signs of immaturity of the visual system lasting up to 30 days. When the children were followed up at one year, no abnormalities attributable to cannabis were found. Four years later, children of regular marijuana users performed relatively poorly on tests of verbal ability and memory, but were indistinguishable from other children at the five-year point.

So, experts continue to differ in their views on whether smoking cannabis during pregnancy puts the unborn child at risk. The most sensible conclusion is that pregnant and breast-feeding women would be prudent to avoid this and all other unnecessary drugs.

A highly controversial question is whether cannabis is capable of producing a full-blown mental illness in someone who was previously perfectly healthy. It is certainly possible to take such large doses that a state of toxic psychosis may be induced with confusion, hallucinations, and delusions. Relatively unusual in the West, such reactions are reported more frequently in Asia and the Caribbean. Occasionally, weird frozen postures may be taken up in such cases: a student who, fearing detection at an airport, swallowed a large chunk of hash was found some hours later by his flatmates half-reclining on the floor with his limbs held rigidly in an extraordinarily uncomfortable-looking and contorted way. He was fully conscious and seemingly undistressed, though bemused, but remained unmoving in this position for many hours. Within a day, he was completely back to normal, albeit somewhat sheepish.

Although it is undoubtedly possible to develop a short-lived psychotic illness as a toxic reaction to high doses, there is no conclusive evidence as yet that it can cause long-term psychiatric illness in a previously normal person. People consuming large doses over long periods may continue to suffer psychotic symptoms as a form of prolonged toxic reaction, and this phenomenon may explain at least in part the many anecdotal reports of 'cannabis psychosis' which emanate from the East. Such formal surveys as exist in the Western world suggest that the prevalence of serious mental illness is no more common in regular, moderate smokers than in the general population. However, though it seems reasonable to accept, on present evidence, that 'cannabis psychosis' persisting for weeks, months, or longer after complete cessation of all illicit drug use is in reality schizophrenia, it remains an open question as to whether heavy use of cannabis may be one of the risk factors for the development of this condition. The drug is certainly capable of provoking relapse or a worsening of symptoms in psychologically vulnerable people or those already in the grip of a mental illness. On the other hand, some people with chronic mental illness have claimed that the drug calms them, or reduces the intensity or intrusivess of distressing experiences such as hearing voices when there is nobody there, or imagining that the TV is broadcasting messages to them personally. On balance, most doctors would recommend that people with a serious mental disorder or marked emotional instability would be wise to avoid cannabis.

Another high-profile problem that has been laid at the weed's door is that it induces a state of chronic apathy, passivity, and indolence which amounts to a change in personality. This reputation goes back a long way, and certainly finds its way into the pages of the Hemp Commission report as a cause of concern in 19th-century India. One must bear in mind that the subjects described tended to be marginalized, unhealthy people perhaps suffering from malnutrition and almost entirely lacking in prospects, who were using potent cannabis in very large doses over long periods. There was some indication that people who were 'mentally unstable' to start with were more likely to use cannabis excessively; in other words, that mental abnormality was possibly a cause of drug use rather than a consequence.

'Amotivational syndrome' was a term coined in the 1960s to describe a cluster of symptoms said to occur frequently in regular cannabis users, including apathy, loss of ambition and determination, impaired concentration, and deterioration in school or work performance. There are many possible explanations for this group of symptoms in young people, including physical illness of various sorts, psychiatric disorder, sleep disturbance, 'chronic fatigue syndrome', or enforced proximity to uninspiring teachers. Where cannabis was a major factor, chronic intoxication was probably the key. The case to support the concept of amotivational syndrome was built upon the sand of case reports and is not at all convincing. Separate from the effects of chronic intoxication, there is no evidence to suggest that use of cannabis leads to a deterioration in personality.

Psychological dependency upon cannabis does occur, but seems relatively uncommon. Heavy or compulsive users of cannabis may well have a history of emotional or mental disorders, and are statistically much more likely to be using other illicit drugs such as amphetamines, cocaine, or hallucinogens. Smoking cannabis sometimes induces flashbacks in LSD users. There seems to be growing acceptance of the existence of mild physical dependency in heavy users, with abrupt withdrawal sometimes resulting in irritability, anxiety, gastrointestinal upsets, and disturbed sleep for a few days.

Part of cannabis's folklore is that it provides a great stimulus to crime, violent and otherwise. Although cannabis use is highly prevalent in prison communities and among the criminal classes, there is absolutely no evidence to suggest that it has a causal role. Cannabis-smoking school students do not commit more crime than non-smokers, for example. Some prison officers express the belief off the record that prison society would be considerably more violent and disrupted if it ceased to be freely available.

A long list of other terrifying consequences of cannabis use have been fielded, including shrinkage of the brain, chromosome damage, deleterious effects on reproduction and the immune system, and so forth. The evidence to support them is not convincing from the scientific point of view, but one cannot totally discount the possibility that real dangers lurk as yet undiscovered.

Certain groups of people are probably more vulnerable to adverse effects. These would include those already anxious, depressed, or psychotic; heavy users of other drugs; pregnant women; some epileptics; diabetics; patients with existing heart or lung disease; and younger adolescents.

A recent review of the evidence concluded that the implications of heavy cannabis use over many years remain uncertain, but that there are *probable* and *possible* adverse effects. The former are respiratory diseases associated with smoking, persistent impairment of memory and concentration, and cannabis dependence. Possible risks are cancers of the respiratory system, an increased risk of leukaemia among offspring exposed *in utero*, a decline in occupational or educational performance, and birth defects among women using cannabis during pregnancy.

These risks must be taken seriously. But as things stand at present, the simple truth is that none of the exhaustive reviews of the available scientific data carried out repeatedly at the instigation of various governments have revealed any convincing evidence that light to moderate use of cannabis does any harm whatsoever.

chapter 6

cocaine, amphetamines, and other stimulants

Cocaine

Historical background

Chewing coca leaves has been part of everyday life in many South American cultures for several thousand years. For millions of people the habit continues to fulfil a comparable role to that of coffee or tobacco elsewhere in the world. A wad of leaves tucked into the cheek for several hours, with perhaps a little woodash mixed in to increase salivation and enhance absorption of the active ingredients, will produce a sense of well-being, reduced hunger, and increased endurance; highly adaptive for a peasant in the mountains of Peru.

Stories about this interesting plant first reached Europe in the 16th century, but it was not until the middle of the 19th century that its attributes became widely publicized through the writings of an Italian physician who had witnessed its use amongst the Indians of Peru. The main active constituent, christened cocaine, was isolated in 1859 and soon appeared in an ever-widening array of patent medicines and tonics. A famous example was Vin Mariani, containing the relatively modest dose of 8 mg per glass, which was available in France from the 1860s. This became extremely popular at all levels of European society, and reached the US in 1885. The medical response had at first been muted but interest grew rapidly, with articles by some famous physicians extolling the properties of the drug as little short of miraculous for a variety of ailments. Sigmund Freud was one of the many professionals swept along in the rush. In 1884, his great friend, the scientist Ernst von Fleischl, received morphine for the relief of severe postoperative pain and became addicted. This seemed an excellent opportunity to try out the wonder-drug. Freud got hold of some to treat his friend, and was so encouraged by the initial results that he was inspired to write a review article which was, in his own words, 'a song of praise to this magical substance'. A frequently quoted advertisement of 1885 described coca as 'a drug which through its stimulant properties can supply the place of food, make the coward brave, the silent eloquent, free the victims of alcohol and opium habit from their bondage, and, as an anaesthetic, render the sufferer insensitive to pain …'. Coca-Cola, containing a few milligrams of cocaine in each glassful, was introduced in 1886 and marketed as a refreshing and stimulating alternative to alcohol.

In England, a growing recognition that the miracle drug could have a dark underbelly, reinforced by an element of professional expansionism, resulted in an abrupt restriction of outlets for cocaine alongside the opiates under the Pharmacy Act (1868). In America, more and more people had begun to sniff or inject cocaine rather than imbibe it, and public awareness of the possibility of addiction began to grow in the last quarter of the century. The prominent American physician, Halsted, became a compulsive user as a result of his explorations into its local anaesthetic properties. By 1887, even such uncritical adherents as Freud had begun to experience a downturn of enthusiasm. His friend von Fleischl had become pitifully enslaved by the miracle drug, injecting well over a gram of it every day and able to think of little else. Commercial acknowledgement of this sea change in public opinion was signposted when caffeine replaced the coca in Coca-Cola in 1903.

Increasing legal restriction at state level in the US heralded the appearance of illicit sources of supply. It is interesting that the cost of cocaine on the streets of New York in 1907 was almost identical in relative terms to that in 1985. The Harrison Act (1914) limited the use of cocaine to medical prescription nation-wide. In 1919, the Supreme Court ruled that maintenance prescribing to addicts was not a part of legitimate medical practice and outlawed it.

The black market in Britain was much less developed, but there were some widely published scandals involving cocaine in the early years of the 20th century. During the First World War, concern grew over the sale of cocaine to soldiers on leave in London, and in 1916 Regulation 40 of the Defence of the Realm Act proscribed the supply of cocaine and a number of other drugs to members of the armed forces except on prescription from a doctor. With some additions, this Regulation was transferred to the Civil Law in 1920 as the Dangerous Drugs Act.

Cocaine underwent a progressive decline through the second quarter of the 20th century in both Britain and North America, use being largely restricted to marginal groups in society, reaching a nadir in the early 1950s. It began a comeback in the middle 1960s, and the public and professional perception of the drug gradually came to resemble that benign and complacent view of a century before. Rapid expansion of use followed in the US, peaking around 1979. At that time, surveys indicated that 10% of North Americans between the ages of 18 and 25 had used cocaine within the last month. By 1986, it was estimated that 40% of Americans aged 25–30 years had tried it, and some three million people were regular users. The drug's social impact was greatly aggravated by the appearance of smokeable cocaine (crack) in 1985. The epidemic subsequently spread into mainland Europe but, despite dire predictions by American experts, it has not afflicted Britain or Australia to any comparable degree at the time of writing.

Preparation and distribution

The slopes of the Andes and the vastness of the Amazon basin play host to the two major species of coca-yielding shrubs. The demand for cocaine emanating from the developed world has created a black economy of dramatic proportions. Peru, for example, produced 250 000 tonnes of coca leaf in 1987, compared to 11 000 tonnes in 1959. Peru, Bolivia, and Colombia between them produce 98% of the world's coca, and there is evidence that the amount harvested has doubled since 1985. All three retain a legal coca market at the time of writing, but the vast majority of production is destined for the black market where the price to farmers greatly outstrips the official rate. The trade in cocaine was worth US$3.5 billion to Colombia in 1991, and for Bolivia the supply of coca products makes up almost half of the total export market. The effects on society of the titanic criminal organizations which have grown up around this industry are devastating.

Coca leaf is converted in the country of origin to coca paste, containing up to 80% of the active ingredient. The paste is further purified and refined to produce cocaine hydrochloride, a water-soluble powder which is very well absorbed by mouth and through the membranes of the nose. The pattern of cocaine use in these countries has changed markedly as this industry has developed. Paste smoking, virtually unknown before 1970, is now widespread and associated with much physical and psychological harm. The snorting of cocaine salt is on the increase amongst the more sophisticated users, but has yet to catch on in a big way.

Scientific information

Cocaine is not very effective if swallowed because the liver destroys most of it before it can reach the brain. Once absorbed, rapid metabolism in the liver, blood, and elsewhere results in a halving of the blood level every 60–90 minutes. When the powder is sniffed ('snorted') absorption may be delayed because the drug narrows the blood vessels in the nose, reducing the flow of blood. It causes numbness of the tongue and mucus membranes if taken orally due to its local anaesthetic effect, and this attribute is sometimes used as a measure of purity of street supplies. The powder can also be dissolved in water and then injected into a vein. This results in much higher and more rapid peak concentrations in the blood, and cocaine hits the brain within a few seconds of the injection.

Cocaine powder must be heated to over 200°C in order to vaporize it. At this temperature, most of the active ingredient is destroyed, the result of which is a disappointed smoker. Freebase, which consists of cocaine stripped of its hydrochloride salt by a process of alkalinization and chemical extraction, vaporizes at a much lower temperature so that most of the active ingredient remains intact. Smoking freebase delivers drug to the brain at least as rapidly as would be achieved by injection, albeit at slightly lower peak concentration. A cocaine smoker can be distinguished from a snorter by the presence in the urine of a particular metabolite called methylecgonidine.

Crack is a crude and impure form of freebase, easily prepared from cocaine hydrochloride and bicarbonate of soda in an illicit laboratory or somebody's kitchen, and so called because of the popping and clicking given off by exploding impurities during smoking. Also known as 'wash', 'stone', or 'rock', it usually takes the form of soapy crystals containing up to a quarter-gram of cocaine and costing around £25. It is smoked in a pipe or some form of improvised delivery system, such as a soft-drink can with holes punched in it, or heated on a piece of foil and the fumes inhaled.

Cocaine stimulates the brain mainly by increasing the activity of the chemical messengers noradrenaline, serotonin, and dopamine. Its effectiveness as a local anaesthetic derives from its ability to block the initiation and conduction of impulses along nerves.

The effect upon one particular bundle of dopamine-containing nerves seems central to the drug's ability to produce a 'high'. It seems that this bundle of nerves may play a vital role in mediating the experience of pleasure in everyday life. Animals find electrical stimulation of the bundle very enjoyable indeed, and will perform any number of tasks to obtain this reward. Dopamine concentration in the bundle has been shown to be raised during exposure to such rewards as food or sex. Many of the drugs to which people can become addicted have now been shown to stimulate these nerves, but none more powerfully than cocaine (or amphetamine). These drugs rev the bundle up much more than any of the gratifications or delights life normally offers. This may account for the fact that animals, when given the choice of either cocaine or food (or sex, or warmth) will go for the cocaine every time. They will press a bar thousands of times to obtain a tiny dose. And given unlimited access, they will continue to dose themselves until they finally die of exhaustion.

Cocaine also stimulates the part of the nervous system nicknamed the 'fight or flight' mechanism (sympathetic nervous system). This produces an increase in heart rate and blood pressure, widening of blood vessels to muscles and narrowing of those to skin, a toning-up of the body's chemical systems generally, and an increase in the amount of oxygen entering through the lungs. The body is prepared for action.

Cocaine hydrochloride (coke, snow, charlie, Bolivian marching powder(!)) is usually sold as an off-white crystalline powder, currently priced at between £50 and £80 per gram depending upon the size of the deal and the buyer's closeness to the wholesale source. It has a bitter, tongue-numbing taste. Purity is variable, but averages between 50% and 70%. Contaminants include related substances such as procaine, active but cheaper (and often more toxic) substitutes such as amphetamine or phencyclidine, or any suitable powder that comes to hand as inert bulking agents.

Frequent use by any route quickly results in reduced sensitivity to the euphoric effects of cocaine, but not to all of the unwanted effects (see below).

Medical uses

Cocaine was used by doctors as a local anaesthetic for decades, but it has now been superceded by safer alternatives such as lignocaine and bupivacaine. Apart from very occasional use in anaesthetic eye-drops, no other medical indications remain.

Recreational use

Cocaine seizures by police and customs in Britain increased rapidly in the 1980s, from 500 in 1981 to a peak of nearly 2100 in 1989, falling back slightly in 1990, and rising steadily thereafter to 3654 in 1995. The quantity seized fluctuates widely, with the highest level recorded so far occurring in 1994 at 2260 kg. Average purity of material seized in 1995 was 53%. Crack seizures increased sharply up to 1990, but the rise since then has slowed considerably, reaching 1442 in 1995. Out of a total of 93 631 people found guilty of drug offences in 1995, only 2073 (2%) were charged primarily in relation to cocaine, a proportion which has remained constant for many years.

The limited information available suggests that prevalence has remained fairly constant in recent years. In 1985, 2–3% of young adults questioned in surveys said they had used cocaine at some time, and the 1996 British Crime Survey produced the same figure. Other studies suggest that many of these would be infrequent or once-only users (see footnote, p. 3). In many countries, regular cocaine use is the domain of two very disparate social groupings who also have very different profiles of use. On the one hand there are young professionals, typically unmarried males in their late twenties, who use cocaine by the nasal route relatively infrequently and in the context of their work or social lives. These people would also tend to be heavy consumers of alcohol. Only rarely do they present to doctors or drug services with cocaine-related problems. Surveys repeatedly show that women are much less likely to use cocaine in large amounts or over long periods.

Then there is the hard drug scene, peopled by men and women of low socio-economic status, unemployed and often homeless, who would very frequently choose to inject the drug or smoke it in the form of crack. They would very likely also be injecting heroin, be involved in criminal activities or prostitution to support their drug habits, and would experience a lot of high-profile, drug-related problems. A recent study showed that the number of heroin addicts using cocaine increased from 13% to 29% between 1987 and 1989. In the same period, those taking their cocaine in the form of crack went up from 15% to 75%. The increase in numbers of cocaine addicts notified to the Home Office (1085 new addicts in 1990) has not kept pace with the rising seizure rate, suggesting that the large majority of cocaine users are 'invisible'; either they are not experiencing problems, or they are not presenting the problems they do have to doctors or other helping agencies.

In 1990 it was estimated that at least 30 million Americans had snorted cocaine at some time in their lives, with almost 50% of adults between the ages of 25 and 30 years having tried it at least once. There were six times as many cocaine addicts presenting to medical centres for treatment as heroin addicts. The cocaine epidemic was approaching its peak in 1979, at which time 10% of those aged 18–25 randomly selected in surveys had used cocaine within the last 30 days. By 1986 it was estimated that three million Americans were using it regularly, with a total population prevalence of 3%. It appears that, in the course of 1990, 6.2 million people in the US tried cocaine at least once, half of these went on to use it regularly, and at least 200 000 ingested it daily. The proportion of cocaine consumed in the form of crack in the US and Canada increased very sharply over the same period. For example, two-thirds of the cocaine consumed by the youth of Toronto in 1989 was taken in this form. Since 1990, there seems to have been a decline in cocaine use among the general US population but a steady rise among young adolescents. Overall, this is still a very popular drug: it is thought that an average of 1.4 million North Americans used cocaine every month in 1994.

Although it can be taken by mouth or, at the other extreme, dissolved in water and injected into a vein, most users arrange the powder into a 'line' on a hard surface and snort it into the nose through a tightly rolled piece of paper such as a banknote, ideally of high denomination. Some people achieve the same result with a tiny silver spoon or other equipment specially designed for the purpose, amid the sort of ceremonial ritual that would seem excessive even to an unusually obsessional pipe smoker. An average line delivers around 25 mg cocaine.

As with all drugs, the effects are shaped to an important extent by the user's expectations, and the setting in which it is taken. In the case of street drugs, purity and the nature of contaminants are also important factors. Usually, a sense of well-being appears within a few minutes and grows rapidly. Confidence, optimism, energy, self-esteem, and sex drive are all enhanced, and there is an overall feeling of exhilaration and happiness. Most normal pleasures are augmented but not distorted. The drug often enhances social skills, and part of its reinforcing property lies in the positive feedback which may be forthcoming from the user's companions. There is a reduced need for food, rest, and sleep. The heart speeds up, the pupils dilate, and body temperature rises.

Since cocaine is rapidly broken down in the body, the duration of action will tend to be measured in minutes rather than hours. Many people will content themselves with one or two lines, but some will seek to hang on to the high by snorting repeatedly. Once this pattern is established, decreasing sensitivity to the euphoric effects will necessitate rapidly increasing doses at ever briefer intervals. This may get out of control as an all-out binge, ending only when money or drugs run out, or exhaustion supervenes.

One survey indicated that around 29% of cocaine users are content to take the drug opportunistically if it happens to be around. A further 29% buy their own supply but use it in a controlled, infrequent way. Twenty-eight per cent tend to use the drug more frequently and regularly, and find they devote a considerable amount of time to cocaine-related friends or activities. The remaining 14% are likely to be compulsive, 'addicted' users.

The lungs are a highly efficient absorption system from which the blood carries its cargo directly to the brain without having to swirl round the whole body or pass through the liver, where much of it would be broken down before it could have any effect. For this reason, crack produces sudden euphoria so powerful that words seem to fail people when they are asked to describe it. It delivers a 'rush' or 'high' comparable to that obtained by injecting the drug. Unfortunately, the physical and mental jolt associated with this is savage indeed. There is an extremely short-lived euphoria lasting 10 minutes or so, often followed quite rapidly by a very unpleasant down-swing of mood. Regular smokers feel irritable and 'wired', and an increasingly common method for dealing with this is to smoke or inject heroin. Many dealers in crack also sell opiates for this reason, and increases in crack use may therefore be signposted by an upsurge in heroin-related problems. An even more dangerous way to use cocaine is by smoking coca paste, a practice virtually unknown in the US and UK but becoming alarmingly prevalent in South America.

A number of people use cocaine in the context of multiple drug use, and they may well choose the intravenous route in order to maximize the intensity of the effect and the 'value for money'. It may be combined in the same syringe with heroin ('speed-ball') or a benzodiazepine such as temazepam to smooth off the rough edges of the stimulant high. Most people using a number of drugs intravenously, and many crack smokers, are leading the sort of generally chaotic and dangerous lifestyle which will greatly augment the risks to their physical and mental health.

Not surprisingly, injecting or smoking cocaine produces many more casualties than snorting it. When traffickers introduced freebase into the Bahamas in 1984, hospital attendances for problems associated with cocaine abuse increased seven-fold. Every year, smugglers (mules) stuff condoms or clingfilm packages with cocaine and swallow them. Should these burst or leak, a fatal outcome is by no means unusual.

Unwanted effects

In estimating the risks associated with cocaine (and amphetamine) it is import-ant to bear in mind that those who are drawn to it are also likely to be involved in other risky behaviours such as unsafe sex and driving while intoxicated. Cocaine users almost always drink a lot of alcohol and smoke both cigarettes and cannabis. Use of opiates, sedatives, and hallucinogens is far higher than in the general population.

It was estimated that 15 out of every 1000 American users of cocaine were seen in the emergency room of a hospital for drug-related problems in 1989. The yearly death rate was reckoned to be one in every 2000 users (the figure for cigarette smokers was 12.6/2000 users). In 1994, 28% of all drug-related visits to US hospital emergency departments were associated with cocaine. The highest rates of cocaine-related problems occur in men aged between 26 and 34. Since 1989, half of all deaths officially designated as drug related have implicated cocaine. This picture is in sharp contrast to findings in countries such as the UK and Australia, where morbidity and mortality associated with cocaine appears to be very low.

Excessive doses are likely to produce sweating, dizziness, high body temperature, dry mouth, trembling hands, and a ringing in the ears. Anxiety and irritability may be evident, as may repetitive skin-picking and involuntary grinding of the teeth. Blood pressure goes up, sometimes to the point of bursting a blood vessel in the brain and producing a stroke. A direct toxic effect on the heart may cause it to beat irregularly and be less efficient, or stop altogether. Fits can occur and may lead to unconsciousness. Treatment of these emergencies is symptomatic as there is no direct means of neutralizing them. Injectors expose themselves to life-threatening infections and many other hazards.

It is possible that long-term use may irreversibly damage certain nerves or small blood vessels in the brain. More prosaically, narrowing of nasal blood vessels in snorters can lead to a chronic runny nose, ulceration, or collapse of the nasal cartilage with striking effects upon facial architecture. Crack smoking is very hard on the lungs, and is associated with severe chest pain, asthma, and bronchitis.

Impulsivity, disinhibition, and impaired judgement may lead to disaster. High doses or a susceptible individual can result in anxiety, panic, irritability, aggression, or confusion. Hallucinations or delusions very similar to those seen in schizophrenia sometimes occur. If the delusional beliefs take a persecutory form, there is a risk that dangerously aggressive behaviour may result without warning. Rarely, this loss of contact with reality (psychosis) persists even if no further stimulants are consumed.

Between 10% and 15% of people who experiment with a snort of cocaine are destined to become compulsive users, usually within two to four years of the first exposure, but it is very difficult to predict who will fall victim in this way. Compulsive use is more common among crack smokers than snorters, especially when taken in the context of social deprivation or emotional disturbance, but is by no means as inevitable as the average tabloid reader might assume.

Compulsive use of both crack and powder cocaine often involves a series of binges lasting hours or days, during which huge amounts may be consumed and ending only when supplies are exhausted or the user has a physical or mental collapse. At the end of such a run three phases of withdrawal have been described. First comes the 'crash'. After a few hours of intense depression, agitation, and desire for more stimulants, the need for sleep becomes irresistable, and this may be induced with depressants such as alcohol, heroin, or benzodiazepines. Intermittent sleep may last as long as two days, possibly interrupted from time to time with avid guzzling of food. Next comes a period of low energy and motivation, depression, boredom, and a lack of any sense of pleasure or enjoyment which sometimes goes on for many weeks. This is likely to be accompanied by a powerful desire for cocaine which tends to come in waves and is brought on by contact with people, places, or things associated in the person's mind with previous drug taking. If this desire is successfully resisted, the third phase consists of a gradual improvement in mood and the ability to find pleasure in ordinary things. The intensity and frequency of the bouts of craving steadily diminish.

Individuals in the grip of compulsive cocaine use, particularly female crack smokers, may become involved in dangerous or humiliating sexual behaviour in the pursuit of supplies.

People with a history of psychiatric illness are more at risk of becoming compulsive users, and psychotic or depressive illness may be initiated or exacerbated by stimulants (and many other drugs). In the mid-1980s, one in every five people who committed suicide in New York was found to have cocaine in their bodies at post-mortem. An analysis of 300 psychiatric in-patients showed that 64% could be categorized as 'substance misusers', of whom more than half were cocaine users.

It must be emphasized that there are important differences between clinical or forensic ('visible') populations and users who remain invisible. The large majority of the latter are not at all concerned about their drug use and certainly have no desire for help or advice. In studies using well-validated measures, cocaine seems to have a low addictive potential in these people in sharp contrast to 'visible' populations. Heavy intranasal users definitely have higher levels of physical and psychological disorders than abstainers, but light and 'light–heavy' (using up to once a week for no longer than a total of 12 months) do not.

There are reports of impaired hormonal and reproductive function in some long-term users, but of more concern are the effects of cocaine in pregnancy. This is seen as a tremendous problem in some North American cities where, in certain neighbourhoods, as many as a quarter of newborn babies test positive for the drug. Cocaine can interfere with the supply of oxygen and nutrients to the fetus through its constricting action upon uterine and placental blood vessels, and this can also result in premature labour or stillbirth. The drug has been shown to cause fetal damage in animal studies, but it is unclear whether this also occurs in humans. Many pregnant women using crack are also seriously undernourished or physically ill, or leading the sort of lifestyles which pose tremendous risks to themselves and the unborn child. Even allowing for these associated factors, low birth-weight is undoubtedly related to cocaine use during pregnancy in a dose-related manner. The effect is more pronounced if the cocaine has been taken in the form of crack, or if other drugs have also been taken. Separation of the placenta during pregnancy, which can kill both mother and baby, is four times more common in cocaine users.

The phenomenon of 'crack babies' has received a lot of publicity. The offspring of crack-addicted mothers may be small for dates, irritable, trembly, poor feeders, and unresponsive to cuddling. These effects usually wear off in the course of a few days. The possibility of longer-term behavioural problems has been raised, but there are so many confounding variables, including social deprivation, poor nutrition, and general health, that this is likely to remain uncertain. What is clear is that crack-using households are potential breeding grounds for domestic violence and all forms of personal abuse.

Amphetamines

Historical background

The amphetamines lack the historical lineage and eloquent advocacy peculiar to cocaine. By and large, amphetamine sulphate is a rough and ready drug with a rough and ready clientele. Injectable or smokeable methamphetamine is a cyclical international scourge, especially in North America and parts of South East Asia. Despite being second only to cannabis in prevalence in many countries throughout the world, the amphetamines attract relatively little coverage in either the scientific literature or the lay media. In the US, they are often kept from the limelight by the glare emanating from cocaine and crack.

Amphetamine was synthesized in 1887 and methamphetamine in 1893, but they were not tested on humans until the 1920s. Amphetamine sulphate was first marketed as a nasal decongestant in 1932, and for use in asthma, obesity, pathological somnolence (narcolepsy), and depression soon afterwards. The unwanted effect of sleeplessness was recognized very quickly, but this did not inhibit the ever-widening range of suggested applications from Parkinson's disease, migraine, addictions and seasickness to mania, schizophrenia, impotence, and apathy in old age (for which it seemed quite convincingly effective). This therapeutic enthusiasm was fuelled by many papers in the medical literature reporting very favourable results. In retrospect, the poor scientific quality of most of this work is all too evident.

The first non-medical application of amphetamine was to counter fatigue among soldiers in the Spanish Civil War, and in the Second World War this became commonplace in all armies. In the British Army, it was to be used when the men '… were markedly fatigued physically or mentally and circumstances demanded a particular effort', with a recommended upper dosage limit of 10 mg every 12 hours. Hitler was said to have received regular injections of methamphetamine (also barbiturates and other drugs) on a daily basis in the closing phases of the war, and this seems entirely consistent with descriptions of his spiralling emotional turmoil and erratic behaviour.

The first recorded outbreak of widespread abuse occurred in Japan immediately after the war when large military stocks of methamphetamine were dumped on to the civilian market. A combination of abundant supplies, low price, heavy advertising, social dislocation, and lack of awareness of the risks fuelled an accelerating epidemic. In 1950 an injectable form appeared, and the epidemic reached its peak in 1954 when there were an estimated half million regular users. Fifty thousand people were treated that year for amphetamine psychosis, and there was a very clear association with crime and violence.

By the 1950s, pill misuse in the US was becoming commonplace, and the term 'speed freak' was coined. This did not inhibit the continuing expansion of the legal use of amphetamine, with weary politicians and tired housewives alike using it as a pick-me-up. It wasn't until 1956 that the first restrictions on use were introduced in Britain, but this did little to rein in demand. In the early 1960s, neurasthenia (chronic fatigue) was accounting for a quarter of all amphetamine prescriptions. In 1964, nearly four million prescriptions for amphetamine were issued in Britain, making up 2% of all prescriptions written that year, and in 1971 12 billion tablets were manufactured for medical use in the United States. In combination with short-acting barbiturates, amphetamines were found to be a useful aid to interrogation by operatives of various security services.

Pill misuse reached London early in 1960, and had captured the interest of journalists and other observers by 1962. A survey among Borstal boys at that time revealed that a third were regular users. A growing black market developed in amphetamine sulphate (Bennies), dexamphetamine (Dexies), methylphenidate (Rit), methamphetamine (Meths, crystal), and Durophet (Black Bombers). A particular favourite among the Mods (a youth cult identified by a particular taste in music and dress) was Drinamyl (Purple Hearts), a potentially lethal combination of amphetamine and barbiturate. In 1964 the law in Britain was tightened, but expansion of the black market sustained the growing epidemic. The prescribing of injectable methamphetamine by doctors in the newly formed drug dependency units enjoyed a brief vogue, but several cases of psychosis among recipients caused this to go rapidly out of fashion.

Illicit amphetamine was available in the US from 1962 onwards, but the industry only really took off when the drug was withdrawn from prescription. In the mid-1960s, motorcycle gangs became heavily involved in the manufacture and distribution of methamphetamine ('crank'), a drug whose effects matched closely the violent, high-energy, and high-risk lifestyle they represented. Methamphetamine has always been particularly popular in the West and South West of the United States, and this has been linked to the particular targeting of cannabis by the authorities in these areas leading to a gap in the market. A similar explanation has been put forward to explain the sudden and very damaging epidemic of methamphetamine smoking in Hawaii in the late 1980s when socially integrated use of cannabis was remorselessly suppressed, leaving the way open to the infinitely more damaging 'ice'. On the mainland, methamphetamine enjoyed a new resurgence in the 1980s but was eclipsed in the media by the emergence of the crack phenomenon.

The risks were well recognized by the streetwise. As one famous rock musician (Frank Zappa, quoted by Shapiro (1988)) put it: 'I would like to suggest that you don't use speed, and here is why: it will mess up your liver, your kidneys, rot out your mind. In general, this drug will make you just like your parents.' Restraints in the US during the 1970s were associated with an apparent reduction in consumption, but this period also coincided with rapidly increasing availability of cocaine, a much more compelling reason for giving up amphetamine.

In Britain as in the US the progressive withdrawal of pharmaceutical products from the market encouraged the emergence of a succession of illicit local manufacturers. The volume of this production has consistently been sufficient to maintain amphetamine as the most widely used illegal drug in the UK after cannabis, although its quality and purity are generally very poor indeed.

Preparation and distribution

Pharmaceutical products are nowadays limited to dexamphetamine and methylphenidate.

Since the mid-1980s there has been a rapid, worldwide upswing in the illegal manufacture of amphetamines and methcathinone, as indicated by the number of seizures (up 900% between 1978 and 1993) and the number of illicit laboratories discovered. Vast increases in sales of the chemical precursors (e.g. ephedrine) required for synthesis have also been noted. Easy availability of the necessary ingredients and the simplicity of the manufacturing process mean that supplies are usually produced near the point of consumption, and can accurately reflect local demand. Most European, Australian, South American, and African laboratories produce amphetamine sulphate, whereas in the US and much of Asia the emphasis is on methamphetamine (84% of US laboratories detected in 1995). Worldwide seizure rates, already high, doubled between 1993 and 1995. Methcathinone is largely restricted to the countries of the former Soviet Union, though it is said to be gaining popularity in the American Midwest.

The process of manufacture gives off a penetrating and instantly recognizable stink, so early pioneers of bathtub manufacture would hang wet blankets over doors and windows. Clandestine producers usually operate within areas of maximum of demand such as, in the US, San Francisco and San Diego, and laboratories are easily dissembled and moved about.

Scientific information

Dexamphetamine sulphate is well absorbed when swallowed or sniffed into the nose. After taking it by mouth, peak levels in the blood are reached within an hour or two, and the level then halves every 12 hours or so. Its effect therefore lasts much longer than that of cocaine, and it is also less vulnerable to immediate neutralization on its first pass through the liver. Methylphenidate (Ritalin) has a similar pattern of onset and peak activity, but is broken down in the body much more quickly.

Amphetamine bears a close structural relationship to two of the brain's essential chemical messengers, noradrenaline and dopamine. The pharmaco-logical effects are very similar to those of cocaine, the only important practical difference being the much longer duration of action. If this is disguised experi-mentally, experienced users are surprised to find that it is difficult to distinguish between the two drugs.

Animals will self-administer amphetamine enthusiastically in tests of dependency potential. This behaviour is inhibited by the dopamine-blocking drug pimozide, and long-term amphetamine use is associated with depletion of dopamine stores in the dopamine-powered 'reward pathway' referred to in the cocaine section. Amphetamine is capable of producing irreversible damage to dopamine nerves in animals, but the significance of this for humans remains unclear.

Amphetamine stimulates the 'fight and flight' mechanism in the same way as cocaine, but the effect is more pronounced and prolonged. Its ability to induce powerful contraction of various sphincters led to a brief vogue in the treatment of bed-wetting children.

Potentially dangerous interactions occur with a variety of other drugs, including anaesthetics (heart irregularities), antidepressants (heart irregularities, soaring blood pressure), blood pressure-lowering tablets (antagonizes effect), and 'beta-blockers' (soaring blood pressure).

In overdose, the elimination of amphetamine is much more rapid when the urine is acid. In hospital, this is achieved through the use of ammonium chloride, but the same result can be achieved when medical help is not at hand with large doses of vitamin C.

Medical uses

Use of dexamphetamine and methylphenidate in medicine is now limited to the treatment of severely overactive children in whom it has a paradoxical calming effect, and narcolepsy (pathological sleepiness), with maximum oral daily doses of 40 mg and 60 mg respectively.

Recreational use

There are estimated to be 30 million regular amphetamine users in the world, in comparison with 13 million cocaine and eight million heroin users. Amphetamine attracts little attention in the US media and scientific literature at the moment, though in the past it has been calculated that more than 80% of the world's illicit speed is consumed there. In Britain, amphetamine is second only to cannabis in the illicit drug market, having been firmly established as an endemic drug since the 1960s. According to the 1996 British Crime Survey, at least 16% of young people have tried it by the age of 19 and more than a quarter of males by the age of 24. School surveys suggest these might be rather conservative estimates. Use of the drug is particularly prevalent among clubbers, prisoners, prostitutes, and heroin injectors. Quite a lot of young mothers in socially deprived areas seem to buy it as a pick-me-up and aid to housework.

The number of seizures by UK police and customs rose steadily from 2787 in 1987 to 6800 in 1991, and the quantities seized also increased spectacularly from between 100–200 kg yearly in 1990, 1991, and 1992 to 550 kg in 1993. These figures have continued to rise so that in 1995 nearly 16 000 seizures generated over 800 kg of confiscated material. The number of people charged each year with amphetamine-connected offences trebled between 1991 and 1995 to 10 364, during a period when the total number of drug-related convictions only doubled. The average purity of seized amphetamine in the UK has always been remarkably low, and was around 10% in 1995. The other 90% consists of glucose, caffeine, milk powder, talc, or anything else that comes to hand of a convincing colour and texture. In sharp contrast, North American methamphetamine has been up to 90% pure in recent seizures.

Dexedrine (dexamphetamine) is marketed as a small, white 5 mg tablet, while illegally manufactured amphetamine sulphate (speed, whizz, sulphate, Billy, uppers) is usually sold in wraps or packages of whitish powder costing £10–15 per gram or less. A particularly pure batch was once dyed pink in order to identify it as a quality product, but odd colours are now much more likely to represent a marketing gimmick. The powder can be wrapped in a cigarette paper and swallowed ('bombed', 'Rizla'd'), stirred into a drink, snorted into the nose, or dissolved in water for intravenous injection. Smoking it is less rewarding because the high temperature required to vaporize it destroys most of the active material. Smokeable methamphetamine ('ice') is available in some parts of Britain, but powerful side-effects seem to have limited its appeal.

When inhaled into the nose, the powder often stings most unpleasantly, being likened on some occasions to snorting broken glass. Within a few minutes there is an onset of effects which closely resemble those of cocaine: good cheer, vivacity, and optimism; increased energy and self-confidence; sharpened perception and concentration; reduced appetite for food and sleep. The main differences lie in the much longer duration of action, and the greater relative intensity of peripheral effects such as a racing heart and dry mouth. Decreased sensitivity (tolerance) to the euphoric effects develops rapidly, so that in compulsive users the same binge profile as occurs with cocaine can be anticipated. The intensity of the effects will be limited by the purity of the material, which is likely to be very much lower than would be usual with cocaine. This difference may have given rise to the false impression that cocaine is a more powerful drug than amphetamine. When injected, a powerful 'rush' or 'flash' is noted within seconds, and both the mental and physical effects are much more powerful.

Unwanted effects

As with cocaine, frequent ingestion causes rapidly diminishing sensitivity to the euphoric effects but not to the potentially dangerous effects on the heart, yet reported deaths due to overdose are rare. High blood pressure, and damage to small blood vessels in the eye, may occur in chronic users. It seems often to cause rashes, and heavy users may find their teeth rot because of a loss of dentine.

Amphetamine taken in pregnancy may pose a risk to the healthy development of the baby's heart and bile system, has been linked with cleft palate, and is said to be associated with small-for-dates babies. Reliable information is hard to come by, however, and the true likelihood of these effects is unknown.

Irritability, suspiciousness, heightened aggression, and an unpleasant 'wired' sensation may be prominent, for the relief of which the user may turn to alcohol, sedatives, or opiates. Rapid changes in mood, flight of ideas, and evident physical tension with restlessness are warning signs to companions or bystanders that impulsive violence may occur. As the drug wears off, the user is likely to feel depressed and washed out.

The pattern of immediate and long-term unwanted effects is very similar to that described above for cocaine, except that the time between the escalating doses as the run builds momentum is longer because of the slower rate of metabolism. Binges are followed by a short period of exhaustion and sleep, from which the user emerges into a phase of lethargy and inertia, often accompanied by anxiety or depression which may become intense enough to induce thoughts of suicide or actual self-harm. The temptation to use more amphetamine is tremendous at this stage but, if successfully resisted, the mood can be expected gradually to return to normal. Occasionally, anxiety or depression persists for months or even years.

The original description of amphetamine psychosis in 1958 has become a classic paper in psychiatry. This alarming condition usually occurs in long-term, high-dose users, but has been recorded after a single ingestion. It comes on a day or two after exposure, and consists of hallucinations (false perceptions which may be visual, auditory, or skin sensation, or any combination of these), disordered thinking, and delusions of persecution. These experiences seem completely real to the sufferer. Pointless, repetitive behaviours sometimes appear, and there may be involuntary picking and scratching at the skin. These symptoms usually disappear gradually after a week or so of abstinence, but occasionally last much longer or become indistinguishable from schizophrenia.

Tolerance (diminishing sensitivity to the drug) causes many regular, long-term users to build their doses up to several grams of street material daily. See-sawing moods, poor concentration, insomnia, fluctuating suspiciousness, and paranoia are quite common. Heavy consumption of alcohol, benzodiazepines, or opiates may represent an attempt to overcome these effects. A physical withdrawal syndrome is not prominent on giving up amphetamine but depression, fatigue, lack of pleasure in life, extreme craving for drugs, and sleep disturbance are common and may last for weeks or months.

Community surveys indicate that the majority of amphetamine consumers use the drug quite infrequently in relatively modest doses by the oral route, and in these circumstances the prevalence of problems seems low. Adverse effects correlate quite closely with dose and frequency of use, and are much more common in those who inject. The likelihood of drug-related problems is unsurprisingly greater in those with pre-existing mental health problems, and inversely related to educational attainment.

Miscellaneous stimulants

Khat (or Qat)

The stems and leaves of the shrub *Catha edulis* contain a number of psychoactive chemicals, and can be chewed or made into a tea. The most powerful constituent is cathinone, an amphetamine-like stimulant, which is extremely unstable and breaks down spontaneously within days of the plant being picked. Cathinone is prohibited under the Misuse of Drugs Act (1971), but Khat itself is not a prohibited substance.

The shrub is cultivated over large areas of East Africa, where chewing the leaves has been customary for centuries. Like coca leaves, they induce a sense of energy and well-being, but are also prone to cause stomach upsets, irritability, or sleeplessness. Their use has also been associated with oral cancer and liver disease, but it is difficult to tease out a direct effect from that of detrimental environmental conditions. The risk of psychosis and compulsive use is well recognized locally. Unless the leaves are fresh, diarrhoea is likely to be the only consequence noted by the consumer.

Among a group of Somalis living in London, three-quarters of those interviewed had used khat in the past and 86% of these were current users. On average this would happen three times weekly in the evening in a social context. The leaves are sold in bundles costing £4, and the average consumption was seven bundles a month. Adults questioned would much prefer their children to use khat rather than alcohol or cigarettes (though 60% of the sample themselves smoked).

Unwanted effects were common but generally mild, and included sleep disturbance, reduced appetite, mood swings, anxiety and panic, depression, and irritability. Dependency upon khat appeared unusual, but many people admitted using more in London than they had in Somalia.

Pemoline

Pemoline (round, white, bi-convex tablets marked P9) is a milder alternative to amphetamine in the treatment of overactive children, with a similar duration of action. In addition to the usual amphetamine-like unwanted effect, it sometimes proves damaging to the liver and bone marrow and is no longer available on prescription in the UK for this reason.

Appetite suppressants

Some appetite suppressants act by exerting mild amphetamine-like effects, and thus have some modest value on the black market. They include diethylpropion, mazindol, and phentermine.

chapter 7

psychedelics and hallucinogens

The defining characteristic of this group of drugs is their ability to induce profound changes in sensory perception, patterns of thinking, and emotion without at the same time clouding the mind. Terminology is difficult, because it always seems to be judgement-laden; one person's *psychotomimetic* (psychosis mimicker) is another's *psycholytic* (literally mind loosener, and by implication, consciousness expander). *Hallucinogen* is a widely used label derived from the Latin *alucinari* ('to wander in the mind'), which somehow fails to do justice to the complexity of the human response to these substances. It is perhaps most appropriately applied to crude natural preparations, or to those drugs which disrupt mental functioning to the point of delirium (a mixture of delusions, hallucinations, confusion, disorientation, and memory disturbance). For those drugs which have the property of 'blowing the mind' without impairing orientation and consciousness, the word coined in the 1950s by the psychiatrist Humphrey Osmond in the course of his correspondence with Aldous Huxley seems very suitable. '*Psychodelic*' was derived from the Greek words *psyche* (mind) and *delos* (visible). It was rapidly modified to the etymologically unsatisfactory, but possibly less psychiatry-orientated neologism, psychedelic.

Historical background

There are hundreds of plants and fungi with hallucinogenic properties which have been used for centuries in a prodigious variety of rituals throughout the Old and New Worlds, but the serendipitous discovery of an immensely potent, synthetic psychedelic in the mid-20th century had a much wider impact upon Western society. It provided the motive force for a counter-culture which developed with great rapidity, ushering in a period of artistic creativity and carrying at its heart a philosophy of life which posed a short-lived but formidable challenge to the existing world order. But how rapidly it all turned sour.

Hallucinogenic plants, along with fermented drinks and cannabis, have been used for thousands of years in social and religious rituals, for healing, and as a means of brief escape from a life which might well have been, as in medieval Britain, 'nasty, brutish, and short'. Indeed, some people think that occasional periods of altered consciousness are a necessity for mental health (see Chapter 1), though there are of course many ways to achieve these without recourse to drugs. In modern life, such experiences have been associated with listening to music, meditating, having sex, and even jogging.

Solanaceous plants were the source of a number of these hallucinogens, often of peculiar toxicity. Datura, pituri, mandrake, and henbane, reeking as they do of the sorcerer's art, are rich in substances which interfere with the action of acetylcholine, one of the brain's important chemical messengers. Traces of black henbane have been discovered at the sites of prehistoric settlements in Britain, and medieval witches were wise in the ways of hallucinogenic potions and unguents, mirroring shamanic activities continents away in the Amazon basin. Apart from alcohol, opium, and cannabis the ingredients of ancient European concoctions might include thorn apple, sweet flag, deadly nightshade, black henbane, and mandrake, bearing their heavy load of scopolamine and atropine.

The Europeans who first settled in North America were fascinated by a local weed which had been a favourite of the native population for centuries. They christened it Jamestown Weed, and as jimsonweed it is still known today. Such substances induce a delirious state, but may also produce loss of muscular control, temporary blindness, and paralysis. Many of their less toxic derivatives still find a use in medicine today.

More than 100 psilocybin-containing mushrooms grow freely worldwide. The Aztecs were familiar with the easily recognizable, bright yellow Liberty Cap, which they called the 'flesh of the Gods', but they were also well aware that the safety margin of many other hallucinogenic mushrooms, for example *Amanita muscaria* or 'fly agaric', is dangerously small. These mushrooms produce a similar range of effects to LSD, although less intense and shorter in duration.

Harmaloid alkaloids, found in the seeds of various shrubs and vines growing in Arabia and Southern and Central America, provided the kick in a whole range of hallucinogenic snuffs and drinks still used ritually today. Ibogaine, containing similar compounds, retains an important role in ceremonials of certain African societies. The search for new sources of such material left no stone, or creature, unturned; the fact that the skin secretions of certain toads were rich in a powerful hallucinogen did not escape notice. This produces a trance state awash with intense visual effects lasting around six hours. Pleasure may be somewhat constrained by paroxysmal vomiting or vertiginous dizziness. Ibogaine, which was described by European missionaries in Africa in 1860 and extracted from root material in 1901, is yet more powerful and long-lasting, with enhanced toxicity to boot.

Highly toxic mescal beans, psilocybin mushrooms, lysergic acid diethylamide (LSD)-containing seeds of the Morning Glory plant, and the mescaline-rich tips of the peyote cactus were used ritually in the Americas thousands of years before the birth of Christ. Partially suppressed for centuries, a formidable peyote cult resurfaced amongst Native Americans towards the end of the 19th century. At that time, peyote enjoyed a brief vogue as a constituent of patent medicines and tonics. As a result of this interest, mescaline was isolated in the 1890s and quickly established a place in Bohemian circles. It also found a niche in psychiatric practice, mainly in the hands of people who were observing and trying to understand psychotic illness (loss of contact with reality). The use of peyote in the religious practices of the Native American church grew steadily during the 20th century, and is now the only legally sanctioned use of hallucinogens in the Western world. Four or five cactus tops will produce effects similar in intensity and duration to a modest dose of LSD, though possibly with a greater effect on heart rate and blood pressure.

The key event which was to unleash the phenomenon of psychedelia upon the world occurred in 1943 when Albert Hofman, a research scientist at the Sandoz pharmaceutical company, accidentally ingested a microscopic amount of a chemical he had isolated five years previously while searching for a new heart stimulant. He felt very odd indeed, and decided to explore its effect further by taking what he thought was a miniscule dose, 250 micrograms, of the new substance which he had labelled lysergic acid diethylamide-25. Bearing in mind that anything over 50 micrograms is enough to produce a hallucinatory effect, the impact of the ensuing 'trip' upon Hofman can readily be imagined. Although at times he feared for his sanity and, consistent with the thousands of first-hand accounts that have since been recorded, experienced a *mélange* of the awesome, the inspiring, and the grotesque, he was in no doubt as to the significance and potential benefits of what he later referred to as 'my problem child'.

Hofman's report of his experience unleashed a flood-tide of scientific articles, books, and conferences. The medical and psychiatric use of LSD expanded rapidly after it was first marketed in 1949 with well over 100 000 patients in the US and Europe receiving it during the 1950s. Indications included depression, alcoholism, neuroses, sociopathy, physical symptoms with no discoverable cause, tiredness, chronic pain, comfort for the dying, and, most frequently of all, as an adjunct to various forms of psychotherapy. Many positive outcomes were reported in the scientific literature.

The CIA became interested in applications of a decidedly non-therapeutic nature, since this appeared to be a substance which might facilitate interrogation or the reprogramming of those who had been 'brainwashed'. Field tests included the administration of LSD to agents and others without their knowledge or consent, and on at least one well-documented occasion this had a tragic outcome when an individual in the grip of a prolonged psychotic state a couple of weeks after receiving the drug threw himself out of a window. It is a regrettable fact that even some of the more mainstream scientific explorations of the time were rather dubious from an ethical viewpoint, using as they did such subjects as prisoners, autistic children, and psychiatric patients whose mental state made it impossible for them to understand properly the nature of the experiment.

Many hideous words were coined to describe these new drugs, including *phantastica, psycholytics, psychotogenics, psychodysleptics*, and others with even more syllables, as well as Humphrey Osmond's *psychedelics*. Osmond was an imaginative psychiatrist working in Canada at the forefront of clinical research with LSD. Visiting California, he got into correspondence with Aldous Huxley who agreed to act as an experimental subject in an investigation and analysis of the subjective effects of mescaline. The resulting experiences were published in the book *Doors of Perception* (1954), the title taken from the quotation by William Blake: 'If the doors of perception were cleansed, everything will appear to man as it is, infinite.' Huxley thought that mescaline '… lowers the efficiency of the brain as an instrument for focusing mind on the problems of life on the surface of our planet'. This interference with the brain's efficiency ' … seems to permit entry into consciousness of certain classes of mental events which are normally excluded because they possess no survival value'. Huxley believed that the relentlessly materialistic focus of modern Western society had robbed its citizens of the spiritual dimension without which they could never rest content. He came to believe that psychedelics could bring this psychic contentment within the reach of Everyman, that permanent and beneficial changes in attitudes and values would result from allowing ordinary people access to them.

The use of psychedelics soon spread beyond the little world of clinicians and lofty aesthetes into the grasp of earthier souls. Writers such as Ken Kesey and Allen Ginsburg became high-profile users and protagonists, and William Burroughs boasted his experiences with yagé. Jazz musicians such as Thelonius Monk, Dizzy Gillespie, and John Coltrane were into the scene very early, but classical musicians also experimented with the effects of psychedelics on musical creativity and interpretation. Timothy Leary, a somewhat unconventional Harvard psychologist, took psilocybin mushrooms in 1960 and was 'swept over the edge of a sensory Niagara into a maelstrom of transcendental visions and hallucinations'. Feeling that his life had been changed fundamentally and irrevocably, he began a series of psychedelic experiments with friends, colleagues, and students. His catchphrase 'turn on, tune in, drop out' became a mantra for the hip generation and an excoriant for parents, teachers, and the rest of that great army of ready-to-be-shocked-and-outraged 'straights'. He also drew attention most effectively to the importance of 'set and setting' in determining the effects of drugs; the attitudes, personality, and expectations of the taker, and the nature of the environment in which the drug is taken. He launched a personal attack on convention and ritual. Accused of being a psychopath, he riposted that 'there is no such thing as personal responsibility'. Introduced to LSD by Allen Ginsberg and Michael Hollingshead, he also gained access through them to the musicians, writers and millionaires who were spearheading the new cultural movement. The scandal generated by the Harvard connection was important in gaining the interest of the mass media and nurturing the growth of the hippy movement.

Sacked from Harvard in 1963, Leary founded with others the International Foundation for Internal Freedom (IFIF) to pursue the study and propagation of psychedelia. He foresaw a time when every student would be 'turned on' in order to spearhead a New World order. Expelled from his base in Mexico, he returned to the US to set up the Millbrook Foundation in 1964 with the backing of a stockbroker friend. Meanwhile, Michael Hollingshead had set up the World Psychedelic Centre in London, patronized by the hip rock musicians and street poets of emergent 'swinging London'. The dissolution of the amphetamine-driven Mod scene in favour of the hash and acid atmosphere of hippiedom had begun.

On the proceeds of his novel *One Flew Over The Cuckoo's Nest* (1960), Ken Kesey bought a large estate close to San Francisco which became a focus and magnet for like-minded writers, musicians, and acolytes, and a setting for the notorious 'acid tests' in which gatherings of people drank Kool-Aid spiked with LSD and talked, played music, or made love. A folk–rock band called 'The Warlocks' were inseparable from these happenings. Later they changed their name to 'The Grateful Dead' and spearheaded the West Coast acid rock scene. Kesey's riotous and creative band of 'merry pranksters' voyaged in their ancient fluorescent bus in a stoned odyssey across America, shocking and outraging the straights and recording it all on 48 hours of uneditable film. They journeyed to Millbrook for a meeting of minds with the Leary group, but found them disappointingly staid and serious! Anyone wishing to pick up the flavour of these extraordinary times should read Tom Wolfe's account of them in *The Electric Kool-Aid Acid Test* (1969).

The hippy philosophy had at its heart an unstable mixture of straightforward pleasure seeking, rejection of existing cultural values and conventional morality, snippets of Eastern religion, and repudiation of personal and institutionalized violence. Its epicentre in the early days was in the Haight-Ashbury area of San Francisco, but its cultural energy washed through England and mainland Europe. The psychedelic movement injected its unique style of music, art, and life-view into almost every level of Western culture. Scarcely a single segment of society could avoid reacting to it, even if this reaction took the form of disparagement or contempt. But even a politician's flowery, multicoloured tie proclaimed it. It generated its own journalistic voice; *Berkely Barb*, *International Times*, *Oracle*, *Oz*.

The Grateful Dead, Cream, Jefferson Airplane, Pink Floyd, Soft Machine, The Incredible String Band, Traffic, Donovan – the list of musicians reflecting the psychedelic influence is endless. The Beatles' musical style changed strikingly as they became caught up, as is clear from the album *Rubber Soul* onwards. The music industry in general was not slow to recognize the enormous bonanza on the horizon; it was the time that the long-playing record first came into sharp commercial focus. Some have even argued that the 'acid revolution' was largely funded and driven by the profit-seeking strategies of the record industry. Perhaps the peak, the heyday, of the hippy era was represented by the 1967 'summer of love' in Northern California, where flower power found its finest hour.

The consumption of LSD skyrocketed within this cultural revolution. In 1962 it was estimated that 25 000 Americans had tried LSD, and by 1965 this figure had leapt to four million. In the same year, the first federal law controlling its manufacture stopped short of outlawing individual possession, but more restrictive state laws soon followed and created the climate for the nationwide ban introduced in 1968. Britain had already proscribed it in 1966, and it was in this year that Sandoz ceased production for the licit market. These developments ushered in the era of the entrepreneurial underground chemists some of whom, such as Augustus Owsley Stanley III – 'the man who did for LSD what Henry Ford did for the motor car' – were ideologically involved and not primarily driven by the profit motive. These individuals were often skilled enough to make a high-quality product, one of Stanley's more memorable vintages being immortalized by Jimi Hendrix's chartbuster, *Purple Haze*.

After 1967, the tawdriness that was never far from the surface became more evident. The commercial exploitation of the hippy culture by both commerce and the criminal underworld grew rapidly in scale. Nowhere was this deterioration more clearly seen than in Haight-Ashbury itself, whose denizens had to cope with daily violence on the street over methamphetamine deals or poor-quality acid cut with phencyclidine (PCP), while busloads of gawping tourists patrolled the area as if it were some kind of wildlife theme park. Icons tumbled. In 1968, Timothy Leary was jailed on marijuana charges, and although his life remained no less colourful with escapes, recaptures, and eventual pardon, he never regained his former influence or prominence. Even the musical associations began to turn sour: at the Altamont Rock Festival in 1969, Hell's Angels stabbed and beat a man to death in front of the stage where the Rolling Stones were performing. This and the subsequent free-for-all were blamed on the mixture of amphetamine and bathtub-quality LSD freely available at the concert. In fact, the giga-units of alcohol consumed by all concerned was probably the real driving force for the mayhem.

Scare stories surrounding LSD gathered pace in the media. Accounts of suicides, madness, blindness from staring into the sun, sexual orgies involving prominent people, and acid-head mothers giving birth to deformed babies began to change the public perception of psychedelics. Charles Manson shocked the world with his insane violence, his compulsive hold over his 'family' apparently greatly enhanced by their shared use of LSD. Enforcement of the law became more determined, and a number of underground chemists were caught and given long prison sentences in the early 1970s. From the middle of the decade until the early 1980s, LSD was in short supply and the trade in mushrooms and mescaline (usually PCP or similar artificial substitute in reality) took over. After this, the illicit industry recovered, and reasonably pure LSD has been available in most cities in Britain and the US to the present day.

Preparation and distribution

Lysergic acid forms the nucleus of a group of chemicals called ergot alkaloids. Ergot is a fungus which, given half a chance, colonizes rye grasses, and has a fascinating history. When bread made from infected rye is eaten, two sets of symptoms may result. Most commonly, there is excruciating pain in the hands and feet due to constriction of the arteries which can cause actual death of the tissue (gangrene). The popular name for this affliction in medieval times, St Anthony's Fire, derived from the observation that sufferers who travelled to pray at the shrine of the saint often recovered. Cynics may surmise that the saint's influence must have been boosted by a lack of fungus in the region of the shrine. The other effect was to produce fits, hallucinations, coma, and not infrequently death through heart failure or depression of breathing. It was appreciated by the 17th century that ergot was the cause of these outbreaks, but epidemics have continued to occur right up to the present day, the most recent being in France in 1953. Doctors found that some of the active ingredients in ergot were useful in the treatment of migraine and for speeding up childbirth, but there are now much less toxic alternatives.

Hofman synthesized LSD whilst searching among the derivatives of lysergic acid for a compound which might act as a breathing stimulant. It was later found to occur naturally within the seeds of the Morning Glory plant. It induces peculiar behaviour in many different animal species, but is not self-administered by animals in tests of dependence or reinforcement. It does not seem to damage the brain or nerves and the lethal dose in animals is huge, death in such experiments being due to arrest of breathing.

LSD belongs to the group of substances called indolealkylamines, which are similar in structure to one of the brain's chemical messengers, 5-hydroxytryptamine (5HT, serotonin). The group also includes dimethyltryptamine (DMT), psilocin, psilocybin, the harmaloid alkaloids (such as William Burroughs' yagé), and ibogaine. The other major group of chemicals producing psychedelic effects are the phenylethylamines, which include mescaline, MDA, and MDMA. These last two have a distinct profile of activity and are discussed in Chapter 9.

LSD is a white, tasteless powder which dissolves easily in water to a colourless solution. It is immensely potent, being hallucinogenic in doses from 50 micrograms (0.05 mg) upwards. When used as an adjunct to psychotherapy, doses between 200 and 500 micrograms were usual, and current street doses range between 50 and 250 micrograms.

There are approximately 10 species of hallucinogenic mushrooms to be found in Britain, but the most easily recognized and widely used is *Psilocybe semilanceata*, popularly known as Liberty Cap. This can be found in abundance in autumn and early winter, and 20 or so will provide sufficient psilocybin for a hallucinatory experience. Picking and eating the mushrooms is not illegal, but drying, crushing or boiling, and condensing them in order to arrive at what might be called a preparation of psilocybin is forbidden. Another mushroom, *Amanita muscaria* (Fly Agaric), also makes an appearance around September and is not controlled at all by UK law. Unfortunately, its effects can be unpleasantly toxic and it can easily be confused with similar-looking fungi which are even more poisonous.

Phencyclidine (PCP) was marketed in the 1950s as an anaesthetic free of respiratory or heart depression, but was soon restricted to veterinary use as its side-effects became apparent. The most notable of these were delirium and confusion on emergence from anaesthetic. It was completely withdrawn in 1965 as awareness grew of escalating street use. PCP is a powerful painkiller, which both stimulates and depresses the brain. It is hallucinogenic but acts through different chemical pathways to LSD-like drugs and, unlike LSD, it is self-administered by animals in dependency tests. After an oral dose, it produces hallucinatory effects lasting about four hours, followed by a longer period of irritable depression, and remains detectable in the urine for several days. Ketamine (ketalar) is a derivative of PCP which was synthesized in 1962. Shorter acting and safer than its parent, it is still in use today as an anaesthetic.

Scientific information

The psychedelic drugs produce changes in sensory perception, mood, intellectual and physical performance, and the pattern of thinking, all of this in the absence of any alteration in consciousness. Memory is relatively unimpaired. It is difficult to have much confidence in the results of psychological testing carried out on those under the influence. Either the subject lacks the concentration or inclination to participate, or fluctuations in one modality will interfere with another being tested; for example, a sudden shift in mood from elation to despair would greatly influence performance in a problem-solving task. For this reason, reliable non-subjective information on the effects of the psychedelics on intellectual functioning is not available.

Psychological effects begin to appear about 20 minutes after an oral dose of LSD, and the concentration in blood halves every five hours or so. The duration of action is variable but averages around 12 hours. Sensitivity to repeated doses rapidly decreases, but returns equally rapidly after a brief abstinence.

Only a tiny fraction of an oral dose actually reaches the brain, and even this has disappeared within 20 minutes. Since the duration of effect is many hours, the drug must cause some residual change in brain chemistry. This change seems mainly centred upon the serotonin (5HT) system, although noradrenaline (another important chemical messenger) is also profoundly affected. As Huxley remarked, following the line proposed by the Cambridge philosopher C. D. Broad, the result seems to be an interference with the filtering and integrating function of the brain, so that the mind's eye is overwhelmed with a cornucopia of unfamiliar material. It also has a 'dehabituating' effect: the familiar regains its power to generate a fresh sense of novelty. It is interesting to note that sensory deprivation in a dark, soundproofed float tank greatly reduces the psychedelic potential of LSD, and totally blind people do not experience visual hallucinations or Leary's so-called 'magic theater'.

There is no physical dependence syndrome or withdrawal symptoms after ceasing regular use. Psychological dependence (see Chapter 13) is very rare.

The 'fight and flight' mechanism of the sympathetic nervous system is mildly stimulated. This may result in dilation of the pupils, modest increases in blood pressure and heart rate, trembling, dizziness, loss of appetite, a small increase in body temperature, and sleeplessness. Death due to toxicity or overdose is almost unknown, and people have shown full recovery from documented doses as large as 100 000 micrograms.

Medical uses

LSD is not recognized as having any place in modern therapeutics.

Recreational use

Despite the passing of the psychedelic era, surveys do not at all indicate a falling-off of use. In America in 1974, the proportion of college students who had ever used LSD was reported to be 23%; the figure for a similar group in 1982 was 21% (see footnote, p. 3). The number of new initiates to hallucinogens in America has remained remarkably steady over the last decade, averaging 613 000 new users each year. Seizure rates in Britain were low in the early 1980s, but later in the decade perked up sharply from 295 (84 000 doses) in 1986 to 1772 (295 000 doses) in 1990. This re-emergence coincided with the development of the 'acid house' music scene. Most of this LSD was apparently made on the west coast of America and then routed to England via Holland. More recently, the 1996 British Crime Survey suggests that 14% of young people under the age of 24 have tried LSD and 12% magic mushrooms. These figures hide a large gender difference: the proportion of young men who have tried LSD or mushrooms is 21% and 17% respectively, while for women the figures are 9% and 7%. UK seizure rates in the last few years do not reveal a consistent trend but are certainly not declining: 380 000 doses were captured in 1995 and 1268 people found guilty of selling or possessing LSD.

PCP was widely abused in North America in the 1960s, but went into a decline as its toxic potential was appreciated on the street. It has re-emerged since the 1970s and is once again widely available. Although rarely described as a drug of first choice, it remains a popular stand-by when other, more desirable substances are in short supply, and finds its way covertly into other street drugs as a cheap, active adulterant.

Fortunately, the use of PCP has never really caught on in the UK. It sometimes crops up as a contaminant of MDMA (Ecstasy) on sale in British nightclubs, and people who say they have only smoked cannabis have sometimes tested positive for PCP, suggesting that the American practice of boosting indifferent hash may be catching on here.

In years gone by, illicit LSD was often available as a clear liquid in small bottles wrapped in foil to protect the precious elixir from the light, or absorbed into sugar cubes. There were also bits of impregnated paper (blotters), tiny tablets (microdots), gelatin sheets, and powder. An average dose was around 250 micrograms of LSD. Although often quite pure, it was sometimes contaminated with toxic by-products, or more rarely adulterated with atropine or amphetamine. Currently, LSD is usually sold in Britain from sheets of impregnated paper squares of various sizes and adornment, costing roughly £3 for a single dose. LSD content is variable but tends to be rather modest in comparison with previous years, averaging around 100 micrograms. There are periodic scares when it is announced in the press that LSD-impregnated stickers or transfers are being sold to children, presumably in the hope of widening the customer profile. It is unclear whether this is of genuine concern or an elaborate hoax, but the drug's profile would not lead one to anticipate a successful outcome to this sort of criminal marketing strategy.

Possession or consumption of magic mushrooms (usually Liberty Cap) is not illegal in the UK, as long as no attempt is made to process the fungus in any way which extracts its active ingredient (psilocybin) or heightens its potency. Those who lack the energy or initiative to hunt them out personally can buy enough dried mushrooms (which *are* illegal) for a mildish trip (around 20) for a few pounds. They are occasionally sold ground up as a brown powder or pressed into tablets. Of course, the buyer can never be at all sure what the powder or tablets contain. At the very least, there will be unease at the possibility that the picker may have selected unwisely or indiscriminately from the 3000 or so varieties of fungus which grow wild in the British Isles. A handful of these species are extremely poisonous, and it would be reassuring to see the seller sample his own wares. Occasionally, 'mescaline' is also available as a dark-brown powder, but this is likely to be heavily adulterated if indeed it contains any genuine material at all. In the US, it will probably turn out to consist largely of PCP. Those who sample Morning Glory seeds obtained from garden centres in the UK risk toxic side-effects since they are routinely doused in fungicide.

The expectations and mood of the user and the setting in which the drug is taken have a profound influence on the experience that results, as Timothy Leary pointed out. There are many hundreds of subjective accounts in the literature; a good selection can be found in Grinspoon and Bakalar's *Psychedelic Drugs Reconsidered* (1979). Typically, things get underway about 20 minutes or so after an oral dose. After an initial sharpening of perception, visual distortion, and a sense of detachment, apprehension, elation, or fear are the first signs of take-off. Thoughts begin to follow strange pathways, sparking off rapid shifts in mood. After this the shape of the experience becomes almost infinitely variable. Time seems to stand still.

Regular attitudes or viewpoints dissolve, and the familiar and hackneyed become novel, fascinating, or terrifying. Not only do hallucinations, illusions, and distortions of sight or sound tantalize or terrify, but one sense may seem to blot out all the others, or they may blend together so that a voice is felt or music experienced as a visual sensation. When the eyes are closed, swirling colours or images fill the mind (the 'magic theater'). Memories long suppressed spring into consciousness. Body image may be grossly distorted, or boundaries between the self and the external world seem to evaporate. Objects sometimes seem to loom immense or shrink away, with loss of perspective: a subject standing on Primrose Hill in London felt she could reach out and touch the Post Office Tower several miles away.

This psychedelic phase, with its twists and turns, its dread and delight, its mixture of pain and wonder, ebbs and flows in intensity. After a few hours there is a gradual drift into a more relaxed, sensual phase. Every random thing or event has a meaning, a subtle significance. Gradually this magical aura recedes and small windows of ordinary reality gradually obtrude and expand until all that is left is the memory of the journey.

PCP ('angel dust, hog') is usually smoked, although some people stir it into a drink, others snort it, and the lunatic fringe injects it. Many Americans take it inadvertently when it is sold as mescaline or psilocybin, cut into other drugs as a filler, or sprayed on to indifferent cannabis to give it a bit more bite. In a recent screen of attenders at an American drug clinic, only 14 out of 100 people whose urine tested positive for PCP were aware that they had taken it.

Whichever way it is absorbed, PCP gives quite a jolt to the system. For the infrequent user 10 mg is an active dose, but regulars find they need bigger and bigger amounts to get the same effects. Within 15 minutes or so a warm, relaxed feeling gives way to dreamy euphoria, with or without hallucinations, lasting for several hours. Tingling in the limbs precedes a numb feeling and insensitivity to pain, whilst coordination and self-concern are greatly impaired. These effects gradually pass off to be replaced by a lingering sense of irritable depression.

Most users of psychedelics allow weeks or months to elapse between trips, but some have runs of a few days at a time. Occasionally, one comes across people who have been in the habit of using lots of acid regularly for long periods, and they may seem to have only a rather tentative grasp on reality. However, they are generally easygoing and affable, and such investigations as were done in the 1960s and 1970s suggest that their intellect and brain functioning remain pretty well unimpaired. The sort of compulsive use that may be associated with stimulants or opiates is almost unknown. These are not 'addictive' drugs – it just isn't that sort of experience.

Unwanted effects

Death from overdose is incredibly rare, if indeed it ever occurs. People are on record as surviving vast unintended overdoses, and fatal cases usually seem to involve other drugs as well as LSD. Physical collapse following toxic doses also seems very uncommon. There is the occasional report of fits following a huge intake. Death resulting from accidents sustained under the influence of LSD are well documented, especially when the drug has been given to someone unawares. These may be related to lack of self-concern, impaired performance of tasks requiring concentration and coordination such as driving, the acting out of fantasies such as a feeling that one can fly, or simply a sense of omnipotence and invulnerability. Reports of people going blind as a result of staring into the sun while stoned seem largely apocryphal. There is no good evidence that LSD damages chromosomes or the unborn baby but taking it during pregnancy would not be wise.

The most distinct risk is that one will have a 'bad trip'. As we have seen, any encounter with LSD is likely to have some frightening or unpleasant moments, but most people find most of their trips rewarding overall. Sometimes, however, terror or distress dominate the whole experience. A bad trip is much more likely if the setting is unsuitable, if there are no sympathetic and trusted friends at hand, or if the pre-existing mood was a negative one.

A strong conviction that the mind is breaking up, that one is losing control, that irrevocable madness is impending may lead to intense agitation and panic. Thoughts may flow toward suspiciousness and a sense of being persecuted, which then shapes subsequent hallucinations. The destruction of mental defence mechanisms can unleash profound feelings of hopelessness, emptiness, or futility. Occasionally, such feelings may find expression in self-harm or suicide, or more rarely outwardly directed violence and even murder. Religious or other delusions may lead a person to mutilate themselves in a ritualistic or symbolic way, for example by emasculation or eye-gouging, but again this is very rare. Most people recover from bad trips in a day or so, but occasionally it drags on rather longer than that. It has been estimated that between 1 and 1.5% of regular LSD users will seek professional help at some time as a result of a bad trip.

Much more serious are the prolonged psychological disturbances which can follow the use of psychedelics. These consist either of prolonged mental illness with delusions and hallucinations (psychosis), or persistent anxiety or depression. Some idea of the prevalence of these problems can be obtained from studying the reports of large-scale studies carried out when use of LSD in psychiatry was legal. Figures are variable, but prolonged psychosis seems to have occurred in between one and 10 patients per 1000 exposed, and from 0.5–1 per 1000 experimental subjects. Bearing in mind the large numbers of people who regularly take LSD, this is by no means a negligible risk. Hallucinogens are certainly more clearly associated with psychotic illness than any other recreational drug. Suicide was reported in 0.3–0.7 per 1000 patients. Major complications with LSD occurred in just over 2% of psychiatric patients who received the drug.

When prolonged psychosis does occur, it usually resembles schizophrenia in its pattern of symptoms, though wide swings of mood are sometimes more prominent than would be usual in that condition. Most people gradually recover in the course of a few days or a week with symptomatic treatment only, but some remain ill for weeks or months. It remains an open question as to whether these drugs are capable of inducing a long-term psychosis in a person who was previously completely normal. The current consensus is that this happens very rarely, if at all. In most reported cases of illness persisting more than a week or so after the last exposure to the drug, it is possible to demonstrate vulnerability factors in the shape of pre-existing psychological abnormality, or a family history of psychotic illness. The outlook for these chronic psychoses is not dissimilar from schizophrenia itself; that is, a fairly high likelihood of further attacks. One suggestion is that some individuals have a latent genetic vulnerability acting through a defect in a particular brain system. Further exposure to the drug would be very unwise for someone who has reacted in this way. Persistent anxiety and depression usually responds in time to standard treatments, and again the drug's relation to causation is uncertain.

'Flashbacks' are sudden recurrences of psychedelic experiences occurring when no drug has been taken. About a quarter of LSD users experience them at one time or another, and some find them quite pleasant ('free trips'!). Most people are rather frightened and disturbed by the experience, and may think they are a sign of impending madness.

Flashbacks may last for seconds or hours, and usually come on in association with tiredness, stress, or the use of another drug such as cannabis. They may be sparked off by the sight, sound, or smell of something or somebody associated in the individual's mind with LSD use in the past. A number of complicated neurological explanations have been put forward, but none are entirely convincing. In most people, the experience seems to bear a close similarity to a panic attack. There is no connection at all with mental illness and flashbacks usually become less and less frequent, disappearing completely within a few weeks or months of abstinence. Occasionally, they coalesce into an almost continuous experience lasting weeks, months, or even longer; the label *post hallucinogenic perceptual disorder* has been attached to this phenomenon.

PCP is a much more toxic substance in overdose, and there are many reports of delirium, coma, brain damage, and death. Muscle stiffness, difficulty in walking and speaking, and constant drooling from the mouth may result from damage to particular parts of the brain by impurities arising during illicit manufacture. Memory may be permanently impaired. The combination of a strong sense of invulnerability and omnipotence, insensitivity to pain, impaired judgement, and reduced tolerance of frustration is fraught with danger for the user and those who may come into contact with him or her. Unpredictable sudden violence or self-harm are by no means uncommon. Various forms of psychotic reaction are reported, usually brief in duration but occasionally becoming longstanding.

the inhalants

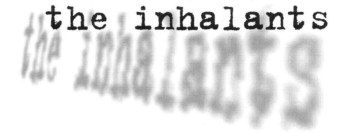

Historical background

It is clear from cave drawings in Australia and Mexico, and from the writings of Greek and Persian scholars, that humans (and some animals) have not ignored the opportunity to inhale mind-altering gases or vapours which occur in nature. Mystics, including the Delphic Oracle, used such emissions, along with other artifices such as fumes from perfumes and burning spices, to induce visions and enhance contact with the spirit world.

Modern recreational enjoyment of inhalants has its roots in the 19th century. At this time, pain relief in surgery relied upon alcohol, opium, cannabis, or even, for some unfortunate patients, concussion or partial suffocation. Sir Humphry Davy, writing at the very beginning of the century to deplore this state of affairs, was the first to propose the use of nitrous oxide gas as an anaesthetic and painkiller. He also extolled with eloquence the experience of inhaling the gas for pleasure, describing how one could summon up exciting visions without untoward effects upon sleep or appetite. He introduced this pastime to a number of his affluent friends, and their enthusiasm was sufficiently unbounded for them to toy with the idea of setting up a 'nitrous oxide tavern'.

A landmark event in the history of anaesthesia took place in 1844 with the painless removal of a molar tooth from the mouth of one Dr Wells, who had prepared himself for the ordeal by breathing nitrous oxide in the manner recommended by Sir Humphry. Ether was first tried in 1846 and chloroform the following year. These early efforts were rather hit and miss, not least because of the potential toxicity of these last two compounds, and there was some strenuous opposition on religious grounds. Despite this, the practice of anaesthesia gained ground quite rapidly. The royal seal of approval was given by Queen Victoria, who was delivered of her eighth child in 1853 with the aid of chloroform.

News of the recreational possibilities of these substances quickly spread among the upper classes, and nitrous oxide or chloroform parties became quite the thing during the remainder of the century. Medical people were particularly active in these pursuits because of their ready access to the necessary pharmaceuticals. There will always be doctors who give way to temptations posed by proximity to power-ful mind-alterers, with varying degrees of discretion. Abuse of newer anaesthetics such as trichloroethylene and halothane sporadically comes to light, sometimes through the tragic consequences of their very high potency. Nitrous oxide still makes an appearance at medical student parties from time to time, and has very occasionally been available to the general public at rock concerts, conveniently packaged in balloons.

Petrol sniffing was first reported in the newspapers in 1942, but it wasn't until the late 1950s that the recreational use of solvents first mounted a wider stage of public awareness, as the practice became increasingly popular among teenagers throughout America. (A solvent is a chemical whose task it is to keep a product in solution or inactive until it is released from its packaging, at which point it evaporates completely and frees the product to achieve its purpose). This new wave of sniffers were typically young, poor, deprived people, often from ethnic minority groups, who could not afford alcohol or other intoxicants.

At the same time, another form of inhalant was becoming increasingly popular in show-business circles, and soon afterwards within the gay community on America's West Coast. This was the pungent amyl nitrite, a volatile liquid which had been introduced into medical practice as early as 1867 for the relief of pain in heart disease (angina), a benefit brought about by its ability to dilate blood vessels. It underwent something of a resurgence for this indication in the 1960s when it was available over the counter in pharmacies. It came in small gauze-covered glass ampoules or 'vitrellas' (poppers) designed to be crushed between finger and thumb to release the vapour. Apart from the usual inhalant 'high', poppers soon got the reputation of enhancing the joy of sex.

Amyl nitrite was made a prescription-only medicine in 1969, and its place in the pleasure market largely taken by butyl-, octyl-, and isobutyl nitrite. Virtually the only remaining legal source of amyl nitrite these days is within emergency kits for the treatment of industrial cyanide poisoning. Isobutyl nitrite was and still is widely available in small bottles as a 'room odorizer', though trade names such as *Rush*, *Locker Room*, *Bullet*, *Thrust*, and *Lightning Bolt* leave little doubt that the manufacturers have more than an inkling of the true appeal of their products. Between 1973 and 1978, more than 12 million such bottles were sold in American discotheques, pornography shops, and hardware stores.

Volatile substance abuse, called 'glue sniffing' rather misleadingly since it actually involves deep inhalation, was being reported throughout the British Isles by 1970. As indicated by the historical perspective above, it is clear that inhalant abuse has always been endemic on a small scale throughout the world whenever opportunity has arisen. Some occupations apart from medicine have carried a special risk because of the ready availability and daily contact with volatile substances. These include shoe making, carpentry, printing, carpet laying, dry cleaning, painting and decorating, and hair styling. It was in the early 1970s that British public interest was first aroused on any scale and, as has been the case with other illicit drugs and activities, this publicity undoubtedly contributed crucially to the rapid expansion of the practice. In the UK, the habit spread most rapidly among teenagers in the larger towns, especially those in Scotland, Northern Ireland, and Northern England. By 1980, surveys indicated that as many as 15% of people aged between 14 and 17 in both Britain and the US had used inhalants at some time.

Alongside these alarming reports came the awareness that this could be a risky pastime. More than 300 solvent-related deaths had been reported in the US by 1972, and in 1978 alone 1800 American adolescents required emergency medical treatment as a result of solvent abuse. Nearly 300 deaths were recorded in Britain between 1971 and 1983, and by 1990 this figure had passed the 1000 mark. More than 80% of solvent-related deaths occur in teenagers, with 60% of them less than 17. The youngest fatality on record was only 10. Deaths are much more common in boys than girls and peak at 15–16 years. In the early 1980s, three teenagers were dying weekly in the UK as a direct result of solvents, but the mortality has been steadily reducing over the past 10 years to a yearly average of around 50. The reason for this is unclear, and may or may not be related to a high-profile public health campaign which began in 1985, and passage in the same year of the Intoxicating Substances Supply Act which made it an offence to supply someone under 18 with a substance the supplier knows, or has reason to believe, will be used to 'achieve intoxication'. It must be said that successful prosecutions have been few and far between.

Legal restrictions against solvent misuse have been enacted in several states of the US, but have not proved helpful. In Britain, politicians made the sensible decision not to travel this route on the grounds that it would not deter use, might increase the hazard by pushing the habit further underground, and encourage resort to more toxic substances. Since the early 1980s, solvents have been regarded as 'drugs' in the eyes of the law where driving impairment is concerned.

Preparations available

Some examples of everyday products containing volatile solvents are glues and adhesives (toluene, benzene, xylene, acetone); cleaning fluids (trichloroethylene, tetrachloroethylene, carbon tetrachloride); aerosols (fluorocarbons, hydrocarbons); petrol (hydrocarbons); rubber solution (benzene, n-hexane, chloroform); typewriter correcting fluid (trichloroethylene); paint (toluene); varnish and lacquer (trichloroethylene, toluene); nail polish and its remover (acetone, amylacetate); dyes (acetone, methylene chloride); fire extinguishers (fluorocarbons); and 'room fresheners' (butyl and isobutyl nitrites). The solvents themselves are usually relatively simple hydrocarbon compounds.

The average home contains at any one time at least 30 different products capable of producing intoxication on inhalation.

Scientific information

A typical solvent such as toluene is rapidly absorbed when the vapour is inhaled, and peak blood levels occur within a few minutes. It enters the brain very quickly and also has a high affinity for fat stores throughout the body. For this reason, toluene disappears from the blood within six hours of the last inhalation but may reappear days later as it is gradually released from these stores. Blood levels do not accurately mirror brain concentrations. A small proportion of absorbed toluene evaporates away through the lungs, but mostly the body has to get rid of it by breaking it down in the liver, then excreting it in the urine as hippuric acid. The highest acceptable concentration in the air for industrial workers is 100 parts per million; 'sniffers' can exceed this level many hundredfold. Once the toluene level in blood reaches the modest level of 0.5 micrograms per gram, it can easily be smelt on the breath.

Solvents probably achieve their intoxicating effect through a similar action to alcohol and inhalational anaesthetics. The permeability of nerve membranes to electrically charged chemicals (ions) passing in and out of the cell is altered by an effect on the gating mechanism operated at receptor sites for chemical messengers such as GABA and glutamates. The balance of these ions across the membrane determines whether or not the nerve is receptive to transmitting an impulse. Tolerance to the intoxicating effect occurs on repeated exposure.

Recreational use

Surveys carried out over the years, including the 1996 British Crime Survey, suggest that the prevalence of sniffing ('huffing') by youngsters aged 14–17 has remained fairly constant, with between 5% and 10% having inhaled a volatile substance at some time. The latest indication is that use of nitrite 'poppers' might be slightly higher than this. Among young adults use of poppers is more than twice as prevalent among males, more than a quarter of whom have tried them. This probably reflects their growing popularity on the club scene. Similar figures are reported from the US.

Although individuals from deprived backgrounds, ethnic minorities, and inner cities are over-represented in most samples, solvent inhalation (with the exception of petrol) occurs among people from all social backgrounds. The prevalence seems to ebb and flow in different areas and at different times, a finding consistent with the social nature of the practice. There is some indication that it is more widespread in the summer months. Epidemics in closed societies such as boarding schools and prisons are reported from time to time.

The commonest age to huff for the first time is between 12 and 14 and sniffers under 11 are rare, though the youngest ever reported was only four. As with most illicit drug use, almost everyone's first exposure is initiated and supplied by a friend rather than a stranger. Reports vary, but the practice is generally said to be more common among boys than girls; certainly it is true that many more boys suffer fatal consequences or require medical treatment.

Almost three-quarters of those who try sniffing only do so once or twice, a further 20% huff for a few weeks or months, and only about 10% persist long term. Heavy users are likely to be abusing a range of other substances as well as solvents, and are much more likely to be suffering from psychological problems or a seriously disrupted home life.

A young adolescent who inhales solvents at any time is 10 times more likely to try other illegal drugs in the future than non-huffing peers, and three times more likely to inject a drug at some time. There is also a strong link with delinquent behaviour of one sort or another.

The extent of use of the volatile nitrites is difficult to quantify, but it is clearly considerable. Millions of bottles of butyl nitrite are sold quite legally each year in Britain and the US.

Inhalants have a limited place as 'party drugs'. When taken on the dance floor they may provide a brief blast of energy, but unpleasant dizziness or nausea is always possible. There are dangers in combining physical exertion with huffing solvents, as will be described below. Volatile nitrites may be used specifically for sexual enhancement by both hetero- and homosexuals.

Since the average home contains such a range of solvent-containing products, the would-be sniffer has plenty of choice. Typically, a globule of suitable material such as glue or rubber solution is dropped into an empty crisp packet or small plastic bag which is then held over the mouth and nose so that the fumes can be deeply inhaled ('huffed') 10 or more times. This is very frequently a group activity, and the bag is passed round from hand to hand. 'Sniffing' is not a term which accurately conveys the vigour of the technique.

Alternatively, a volatile liquid can be inhaled directly from the container, or poured on to a rag or coat-sleeve for easier or more surreptitious access. Sometimes the user may seek to enhance the effect by enclosing the head completely, for example under the bedclothes or within a larger plastic bag. Suffocation or over-dose are all too possible in such circumstances.

Small brown bottles of butyl nitrite or similar are easily available from some hard-ware stores, sex shops, and gay clubs in Britain and America, costing a few pounds or dollars. If kept in the fridge with the cap firmly applied between episodes, a single bottle will provide several highs before completely evaporating.

Gas lighter fuel (butane) can be sprayed into a balloon or bag before inhalation, but all too often the plunger is pressed against the teeth and the contents projected straight down the throat. Aerosols, for example spray paints, are usually inhaled indirectly, but it is impossible to avoid absorbing droplets of paint (or whatever dissolved material the product contains) along with the solvent vapour.

Euphoric effects come on extremely rapidly with a distinct 'rush'. The user feels exhilarated and excited, 'high', disinhibited, and powerful. This is often accompanied by blurred vision, slurred speech, a buzzing in the ears, and marked clumsiness. Time seems to pass slowly. Interesting visual illusions or hallucinations sometimes occur, and can often be 'steered' or harnessed in an enjoyable way. Inhibitions disappear, and during sex orgasm is, or at least seems, prolonged and intensified. As with all psychoactive drugs, the user's expectations and the nature of the environment shape the experience very considerably.

These peak effects usually last only for a few minutes or so, and are followed by a more relaxed sense of well-being for half an hour or more. Some seasoned users have remarked that the intensity of the pleasurable effects increases with subsequent exposure, contrary to experience with most euphoria-producing drugs for which the opposite is normally the case. Tolerance (increasing resistance to the euphoric effects leading to consumption of ever-larger doses) is likely to occur in regular sniffers.

Unwanted effects

During the high, most users feel a bit dizzy and lightheaded, are aware of their heart pounding rather quickly, and look a bit flushed and flustered. About a third report an unpleasant headache, there may be buzzing in the ears or episodes of double vision, nausea is not uncommon, and vomiting may occur. Some experience chest or abdominal pain. An observer may note quivering eyeballs (nystagmus) and enlarged pupils. Irritant fumes may cause coughing bouts, sneezing, and streaming eyes. If the concentration of vapour is intense, there may be disorientation, drowsiness, and even unconsciousness at very high doses.

After the high has passed, there usually follows a hangover period characterized by lethargy, depression, irritability, restlessness and agitation, poor appetite, and altered sleeping pattern. The user may experience chills, aches, and pains. The mood swings unpredictably, and memory and concentration can be impaired. Parents of regular sniffers sometimes notice that their child seems more secretive or suspicious, that hobbies and established interests are being abandoned, that patterns of friendship are altering, and that school performance is deteriorating. Regular users at times develop spots or ulcers round their mouths or noses ('glue sniffer's rash'), cracked lips, and seem to suffer from a perpetual cold, sore throat, or bronchitis. They may exude a characteristic odour, spill marks are sometimes evident on clothes (especially cuffs) or around their room, and smelly bottles, bags, or rags may be left lying about. Regular, heavy huffers, or first-timers who have completely misjudged the dose, occasionally require hospital admission if they become very confused, have fits, or lapse into complete unconsciousness. Recovery is usually rapid (within a few hours) and complete.

One study did demonstrate that secondary school children who sniff solvents perform less well on tests of vocabulary, IQ, and impulsivity. However, when measures of background social disadvantage were taken into account, the difference disappeared. Also, the performance deficit did not correlate with the amount or frequency of sniffing. The authors concluded that there was no evidence of neuropsychological impairment in this particular sample of glue-sniffing adolescents.

In the very large majority of sniffers for whom the activity is a one-off or transient phase, no long-term harm ensues. People who do suffer harm are much more likely to be those using large amounts over prolonged periods, with other drug use and risky or deviant behaviour contributing to the picture. Unfortunately, there are the occasional tragic exceptions to this rule: approximately 10% of solvent-related deaths occur in children sniffing for the first time.

The use of butane gas or aerosols is particularly risky, and in recent years these substances seem to account for between half and three-quarters of all deaths. Lighter fuel sprayed directly into the mouth may cause the throat to swell massively and result in suffocation. Aerosols deliver many other toxic chemicals as droplets in the vapour, and have a particular propensity to cause the heart to beat irregularly or stop altogether.

Probably as many as half of the deaths associated with glue sniffing are caused indirectly. The combination of disorientation, clumsiness, a sense of invulnerability, and lack of self-concern is obviously a dangerous one. Any alcohol taken at the same time greatly increases the risk. Injury from accidents, suffocation with the plastic bag or as a result of throat damage, sudden fire or explosion when people mix sniffing with smoking cigarettes, or choking on vomit whilst semiconscious or comatose form part of the sad catalogue.

Most of the other acute deaths result from irregular beating and decreased efficiency of the heart. Many inhalants exert a direct effect upon the heart's muscle and nervous mechanisms, and the heart is made much more sensitive to the effects of adrenaline released in response to exercise or emotion; a sudden scare or abrupt physical exertion can provoke a potentially fatal disruption of the heart's rhythm. For this reason, it is essential not to threaten or over-react to intoxicated sniffers. The sensitivity of the heart is greatly increased by reduced oxygen levels in the blood, as when air is rebreathed in a plastic bag.

There is a small risk of long-term damage to the liver or kidneys in heavy, chronic sniffers. Toluene and benzene can depress the manufacture of blood cells in the bone marrow leading to anaemia, sometimes irreversible. Benzene use is thought to be associated with increased risks of cancer and leukaemia. The brain is also vulnerable to structural damage which can cause people to tremble, slur their speech, become clumsy and lose their balance, or develop memory problems. There may be injury to the nerves of sensation in the limbs, giving rise to 'glove and stocking' anaesthesia. A part of the brain particularly concerned with balance and coordination (the cerebellum) is particularly at risk from toluene. Occasionally, the optic nerve (which relays messages from the retina of the eye to the brain) can be affected, leading to progressive blindness. Additives such as lead in petrol may contribute greatly to the toxic potential.

Inhalation of solvents by pregnant women is dangerous because these chemicals freely cross the placenta into the baby's circulation. The absence of any conclusive evidence of damage to the unborn baby in these circumstances may simply reflect a lack of appropriate research.

Heavy use of solvents is more common in people with demonstrable psychological problems, and was found in one survey to be the major factor in 3.5% of psychiatric referrals of under-16-year-olds to one London psychiatric hospital. It seems likely that these problems predate the solvent use rather than result from it and there is no evidence that solvent misuse directly causes mental illness. The sort of person who is seeking to blot out unpleasant emotions or thoughts is likely to be a solitary, daily user of larger and larger quantities, who is a regular attender at general practices or hospital out-patients with repeated social or medical crises.

Intermittent and even quite regular sniffers will not be troubled by a withdrawal syndrome on stopping, apart from the hangover described above. Very heavy regular users, on the other hand, may experience a cluster of symptoms and signs similar to those suffered by people dependent on alcohol: trembling, sweating, and agitation, sometimes progressing in those who do not receive treatment to disorientation, hallucinations, delusions, and fits.

ecstasy and other 'party drugs'

chapter 9

The club scene

It seems that multiple drug use is very much the norm among *habitués* of dance clubs throughout the developed world. Among a sample of Australian 'ravers', 90% had used LSD at some time, 76% Ecstasy, and 69% amphetamine. At or around the last rave attended, half had smoked cannabis and a third had consumed both amphetamine and LSD.

A group of Scottish dance club attenders interviewed had each consumed an average of 11 different drugs. Over 90% of the sample had taken alcohol, cannabis, LSD, and Ecstasy at some time, and 70% had also tried cocaine, amphetamine, and psilocybin (as magic mushrooms). Drug use within the past year was as follows: alcohol 96%; cannabis 96%; Ecstasy 87%; tobacco 86%; LSD 79%; amphetamine 77%; cocaine 59%; nitrite 'poppers' 51%; psilocybin 47%; temazepam 39%; diazepam 26%; codeine 19%; heroin 11%; ketamine 7%; solvents 6%; and buprenorphine 6%. Each drug had its place, either in the preparation for the outing, the partying itself, or handling the come-down. The authors of the report identify Ecstasy, nitrites, and amphetamine as 'primary dance drugs' and alcohol, psilocybin, LSD, ketamine, and cocaine as secondary.

In trying to understand the effects, both wanted and unwanted, of Ecstasy and other party drugs, it is essential to keep in mind the fact that they are generally being taken as one among other drugs, declared or covert.

Ecstasy

Historical background

Methylenedioxyamphetamine (MDA) was synthesized in 1910, then lay dormant until 1939 when it underwent testing in animals. It was launched in 1941 as a treatment for Parkinson's disease, without any great success. Gordon Alles, discoverer of amphetamine, wrote about his experiences with MDA in the 1950s, and perhaps it was this work which suggested some military potential to the organizers of the US chemical warfare research programme. MDA (the 'love drug') became available on the streets from the mid-1960s, and was subsequently brought under the control of the American Drug Abuse Prevention and Control Act (1970) and the British Misuse of Drugs Act (1971).

Methylenedioxymethamphetamine (MDMA, Ecstasy) was created in 1912 and patented by the pharmaceutical company E. Merck two years later. It too underwent toxicology studies courtesy of the US military in the 1950s, and was available, quite legally, for recreational use from around 1970. This non-medical use grew steadily, and seems to have had a particular focus in Texas and California. In the UK an amendment to the Misuse of Drugs Act was introduced in 1976 to outlaw all amphetamine-like compounds, but in America the drug continued to go from strength to strength. One Californian laboratory alone produced 10 000 doses monthly in 1976, 30 000 monthly in 1984, and 500 000 in 1985! This enormous expansion may have been related to the easing of the cocaine epidemic and some eulogizing publicity for MDMA in journals such as *Time* and *Newsweek*.

In 1976, reports were appearing of the successful use of MDMA as an adjunct to individual, marital, and group psychotherapy. Leo Zeff, a psychologist who had used LSD in therapy sessions 10 years earlier, found that it helped people to communicate their feelings more effectively and tolerate criticism. It was also said to be helpful in the treatment of drug and alcohol abuse. A number of publications appeared in the psychiatric literature over the next few years, most of which were highly favourable in their conclusions about the drug's benefits.

At the same time, concern in official quarters about MDMA's abuse potential was growing, and the American Drug Enforcement Agency (DEA) began to investigate the possibility of bringing it under legal control in the early 1980s. Counterarguments were put forward by psychiatrists and others and the debate looked set to run and run, but in 1985 the DEA abruptly terminated the discussion by invoking the Comprehensive Crime Control Act to bring MDMA under Schedule 1 control (the toughest restriction available). Appeals brought a temporary reprieve, but DEA lawyers were able to argue that the reports of clinical success were of insufficient scientific rigour to justify their conclusions. MDMA was restored to Schedule 1 control in 1988, where it still resides. Ironically, it seems that the publicity surrounding these protracted legal disputes must have been partly responsible for a spectacular increase in the non-medical consumption of the drug. The ban in 1985 also led to a flurry of 'designer drugs', chemical variants on the theme which did not fall within the scope of the law, one of which was methylenedioxyethamphetamine (MDEA, 'Eve'). This loophole was plugged in 1986 by the Controlled Substance Analogue Enforcement Act, which proscribes drugs similar in structure or psychological effect to those already banned.

Ecstasy took off in Britain in the mid-1980s through its association with the 'acid house' music phenomenon from which the rave culture and modern club scene have evolved. There are no reliable prevalence surveys, but it seems likely that it has been a familiar commodity to many hundreds of thousands of young people over the last decade.

Preparation and distribution

More than 1000 variants on this chemical theme have been synthesized, but the most important of these currently in circulation are MDMA, MDA, and MDEA. The compounds are structurally related to both amphetamine and mescaline. Most of the MDMA now entering Britain is probably routed via The Netherlands. The drug is classified as Class A and Schedule 1 within the terms of the Misuse of Drugs Act (1971).

Black-market MDMA comes as a powder, tablets, or capsules of various shapes, colours, and sizes with whimsical names such as Dennis the Menace, Disco Biscuits, Big Brown Ones, Burgers, M25s, Pink Scuds, Bug-eyed Billies, and California Sunrise. Quality control is variable, with MDA, LSD, and amphetamine turning up in confiscated samples and anecdotal reports of adulteration with many other substances. Occasionally there is no MDMA present at all, but the usual content of a tablet is between 75 and 200 mg, retailing at around £15 or less. At some nightclubs in Amsterdam it is possible to break off a tiny piece of tablet and have it submitted to an on-the-spot purity screen, but the scene in Britain has not yet reached this pitch of sophistication.

Scientific information

Hallucinatory amphetamines produce, as the term suggests, a combination of amphetamine-like stimulation and mild sensory distortion, but their particular characteristic is to induce in a diverse range of user types a general feeling of empathy and goodwill towards all mankind. The term 'entactogen' has been coined in an attempt to convey the essence of this experience, not exactly a word which lends itself to the sound bites of journalists or politicians.

Animal studies indicate that the most important actions of these drugs are mediated through effects upon serotonin (5HT), one of the brain's chemical messengers. MDA and MDMA both cause a massive release of serotonin, and then seem to inhibit its synthesis so that the brain becomes temporarily depleted. Serotonin is thought to play an important role in regulating mood, sleep, aggression, hunger, and sexual activity. The primary, sought-after effects of MDMA seem to be related to the initial flood of serotonin through the brain, and the residual hangover to the subsequent depletion.

Animals given MDMA show increased mobility, body temperature, heart rate, and salivation. Patterns of behaviour are different from those characteristically seen with stimulants or hallucinogens. Convulsions are induced by high doses.

It has been established in animal experiments that MDMA and MDA have a toxic effect on serotonin-bearing nerves, some of which actually die off. Levels of

serotonin and its metabolites, and chemical markers of new serotonin production, remain low for weeks or months. After several months some evidence of
regeneration is evident, but it seems likely that at least a part of the damage is
permanent. The degree of damage is related to the size and frequency of the doses
but animal species vary considerably in their susceptibility. Monkeys, for
example, are much more vulnerable than mice. They sustain damage at doses as
low as 2 mg per kg of body weight twice daily, a level that is worryingly close to
doses typically taken recreationally by party-goers.

The implications of these findings for humans is uncertain for two reasons.
First, it is difficult to extrapolate from animal work in the absence of even the
most basic pharmacological information or confirmatory experiments in human
volunteers. Only one preliminary investigation has so far been conducted. In this
study, an apparent malfunctioning was discovered in the serotonin systems of
volunteers who said they were heavy MDMA users in comparison with non-
MDMA-using control subjects, but the difference was not statistically significant
and requires confirmation. Another difficulty is that subjects such as these may
well have used a variety of other drugs, and unrecognized contaminants within
illicit MDMA may themselves be highly toxic.

Secondly, the functional or practical significance of this nerve damage is unclear.
In other neurotransmitter systems there is evidence of 'neuronal redundancy'.
Perhaps we have been endowed with many more nerves and brain cells than we
actually need to function adequately, in which case the loss of a few thousand may
be neither here nor there.

Bearing these reservations in mind, there is more than enough evidence of toxicity in animals to underline the urgent need for research to clarify the effect, if
any, on the serotonin system in humans. Most people would be keen to hang on
to as many brain cells as possible, given the choice.

MDMA gives positive results in animal models of dependency, but there is no
evidence of physical dependence in humans, and compulsive use or 'addiction'
seems very rare.

As a result of their legal status, almost nothing is known about the human
pharmacology of MDA and MDMA. Only one relevant investigation in a single
subject is on record, dating from 1976. This indicated that the effect of an oral

dose became apparent within 30 minutes, peaked between 60–90 minutes, and had disappeared after four hours. The experience was described as '… an easily controlled altered state of consciousness with emotional and sensual overtones'. MDA is reported to be longer acting and a 'rougher ride' than MDMA. It is supposedly less euphoriant and more amphetamine-like, and had a reputation on the street of being less well tolerated by women than men; for example, dormant pelvic infection might be induced to flare up.

The amphetamine-like effects cause stimulation of the sympathetic nervous system, the so-called 'fight or flight' mechanism. Heart rate and blood pressure go up, blood is diverted to the muscles away from the guts and other maintaining mechanisms, the body's chemical processes speed up, and more oxygen is absorbed through the lungs.

Medical uses

The legal restrictions in both the US and Britain prevent doctors from prescribing it in any circumstances.

Recreational use

Formal surveys of illicit MDMA use are few and far between. Seizure rates increased from 399 in 1990 to 1735 in 1991, and continued to rise year on year in the 1990s. Perhaps more significantly, the quantity seized has gone up quite startlingly from a few kilograms in 1990 to more than 710 kg in 1995 (equivalent to at least 3.5 million tablets). The number of people found guilty of MDMA-related offences has increased from 559 in 1991 (1% of all drug-related convictions) to 3281 in 1995 (4%). The 1996 British Crime Survey suggested that 9% of 16–19 year-olds had tried Ecstasy, but surveys in some schools have indicated a much higher prevalence amongst teenagers (see footnote, p. 3). It is estimated that more than 500 000 people in Britain have used the drug at least once.

The author is not aware of any very recent surveys from the US, but a survey at Stanford University in 1987 suggested that 39% of students had used MDMA at least once. Of these, about half had taken it less than six times, a third between six and 10 times, and 12% more than 10 times. MDMA is also widely used in Europe and in Australia, despite its high price and low average purity, with only 30% of tablets containing MDMA as the main ingredient.

The drug is almost always swallowed, but may occasionally be snorted into the nose or, rarely, injected into a vein. There are two distinct classes of user. By far the most numerous are young, energetic nightclubbers and 'ravers' who take it for the pleasure of the high and the enhanced sense of togetherness. Many of these, as indicated above, will also be regular users of a range of other drugs, including amphetamine, LSD, and cannabis, which can hardly fail to modify the profile of effects. The other, much smaller group is made up of more spiritually inclined people in their thirties or beyond, perhaps exploring a 'New Age' philosophy of life, or seeking personal insights alone or within a relationship.

As with all drugs, the effects of MDMA depend to a large extent upon the characteristics of the taker, and the setting in which it is taken. It is hardly surprising that the experiences of a middle-aged, middle-class psychiatrist who takes MDMA in his living room with professional colleagues and a string quartet on the CD player might contrast starkly with those of an unemployed adolescent raving the night away in a disused aircraft hanger with a thousand others dancing to a sound system producing more decibels than a jumbo jet.

There are some common strands, however. Half an hour after taking a tablet, both the psychiatrist and the raver would have noted an increased sense of alertness, possibly accompanied by a dry mouth, skin tingling, and an awareness of the heart beating faster. A sense of closeness and empathy with other people gradually appears. A change in the quality of light perception (luminescence) usually occurs, and some people may experience actual visual hallucinations. The jaw often feels tight, sometimes with involuntary grinding of the teeth (bruxism).

Reports differ on the effects upon sexual behaviour. Concern has been expressed that MDMA and variants might release inhibitions and lead to an upsurge in promiscuous, 'unsafe' sex, alarming to moralists and those concerned about the spread of HIV infection in the heterosexual population. The drug certainly seems to enhance the sensual enjoyment of sex, but whether or not it increases sex drive remains unclear. The amphetamine-like component of the drug's activity may cause erectile failure in men, and inhibit orgasm in both sexes.

Some American psychiatrists have reported their personal experiences with Ecstasy. More than half described enhanced powers of communication, feelings of intimacy, improved 'interpersonal skills', and euphoria. Most also experienced enhancement of the senses (for example, increased musical appreciation), reduced fear and sense of alienation, increased awareness of emotions, and suppression of aggressive impulses. Some said that the experience had caused them to rethink their priorities in life, whilst others felt that their social functioning had been significantly improved. It is worth noting that a quarter of these people combined the use of MDMA with cannabis or tranquillizers.

In a sample of recreational users in Australia, the majority had taken MDMA several times rather than once only. More than half also smoked cannabis, and a significant minority were also on nodding terms with amphetamine, LSD, and amyl nitrite ('poppers'). A quarter had used cocaine at some time, but tranquillizers or opiates were restricted to a tiny minority. Alcohol consumption was modest and, consistent with other reports, seemed to interfere with the enjoyment of MDMA. These people were aware of the reported risks to physical and mental health, and were concerned about possible impurities and the lack of research on the compound. The vast majority took the drug orally, experiencing an effect usually lasting around five hours or so and a hangover which extended over the next 24 hours or more.

There is consistency in the reports from this and other groups that the most rewarding effects come from the first exposure, with diminishing returns for most people thereafter. Increasing the dose ('stacking') may enhance the 'rush' and also the likelihood of hallucinations, but more often it just increases the ratio of unwanted to wanted effects. These individuals reported positive experiences from the drug on almost every occasion they took it, but they also seemed to accept that some unpleasant side-effects were almost inevitable.

Those who had also experienced amphetamine and LSD had no difficulty in distinguishing the effects of the three drugs. Ecstasy was most clearly associated with intimacy, easygoing acceptance of others, and sensual euphoria. Amphetamine was seen primarily as alerting and energizing, with enhanced confidence and self-esteem, while for LSD the emphasis was on enlightenment, insight, and open-mindedness.

Anecdotal reports from ravers and clubbers mirror these reports of empathy, energy, and a sense of inner peace. Many of the small-scale dealers at street level share the ideological values of their customers, and the sense of an in-group looking out with weary contempt at the bewildered 'squares' – teachers, parents, professionals – is reminiscent of the earlier hippy generation. The importers and sellers higher up the pyramid take a more robustly commercial view of the situation. As with other illicit drug markets, the size of the profits precludes any of the finer feelings and more than compensates for the larger penalties associated with Class A drug dealing (see Chapter 12).

Unwanted effects

Certain pre-existing diseases, of which a person may be unaware, increase the likelihood of unpleasant or dangerous reactions to MDMA. People with any of the following would be well advised to steer clear of it: diabetes, liver disease, high blood pressure or heart disease, epilepsy, glaucoma, hyperthyroidism, or any form of mental disorder. Prescribed medicines may interact with it. Pregnant women would be wise to avoid it; the lack of direct evidence of toxicity to the unborn baby may simply reflect the lack of appropriate research, and there is always the risk of toxic adulterants in black-market drugs.

There are anecdotal reports that MDMA inhibits the immune system in some way, so that users become more susceptible to colds and other infections. This must remain speculative pending scientific confirmation. As with all street drugs, there is always the risk that you may not be taking MDMA at all, or that there is contamination with cheap but toxic hallucinogenic substitutes such as phencyclidine (Chapter 7) or damaging by-products of incompetent manufacture.

MDMA produces a lot of unwanted effects, including clumsiness, incoordination, and poor concentration which may lead to accidents; drowsiness or restless agitation; fear or anxiety sometimes escalating into panic attacks or a sense of loss of control; depression; a racing heart, dizziness, or fainting; nausea and vomiting; headaches; and persecutory feelings or unpleasant hallucinations.

Most people experience hangover effects which last for a day or two. These usually consist of tiredness, lethargy, irritability, depression, or see-sawing emotions. The muscles may ache and feel stiff, especially around the jaw after all that tooth-grinding. For many people with jobs, these residual effects limit the use of Ecstasy to Friday or Saturday nights. A recent study showed that weekend use in one small group of young people was associated with memory impairment and a dip in mood mid-week approaching the sort of severity seen in clinical depression. Flashbacks have been reported.

There are well-documented records of serious physical and psychological reactions to MDMA. Whilst many of these seem to have occurred in people predisposed in some way or taking large doses of other drugs as well as MDMA, it is clear that idiosyncratic reactions to modest doses do occur, though with extreme rarity, and that these may prove fatal. Generally, such limited information as does exist indicates that serious side-effects correlate poorly with blood levels of the drug. The amphetamine-like effect may overstretch the heart and circulatory system, especially if there is unrecognized narrowing of the arteries or other pre-existing disease, so the heart beats inefficiently or stops completely. Fits have been reported, and blood pressure changes may be enough to cause a stroke. Interactions with other illicit or prescribed drugs (for example, antidepressants of a particular type) can prove fatal. An association with liver damage has been suggested.

A rare but particularly serious physical reaction is a vicious rise in body temperature associated with damage to muscle fibres and blood clotting inside arteries and veins. This can lead to liver or kidney failure, coma and convulsions, and death. There is a convincing theory that the environmental conditions to be found in nightclubs or at parties may increase the risk of this reaction. These places may be very hot, and with energetic dancing and a lack of water or soft drinks dehydration can easily occur. External heat, vigorous physical activity, and dehydration may combine with the direct effects of the drug to bring about a rapid increase in temperature to the point at which internal tissue damage occurs. It is therefore essential that at each venue there should be adequate ventilation with access to water and soft drinks, rest areas, and cool retreats where people can 'chill out'.

On the other hand, overdoing the water may cause a loss of salts from the body and Ecstasy may itself heighten this effect leading to overhydration or 'water intoxication', and at least one death has been attributed to this. The best advice is to sip water regularly rather than gulp it in huge amounts, and try to include some isotonic drinks and salty snacks.

Although these risks are undoubtedly genuine, it is important to keep them in perspective. Deaths and serious reactions are very rare indeed in relation to the huge amounts of the drug which have been consumed over the years. Some of the deaths attributed to MDMA, and other serious but non-fatal reactions, may be due at least in part to pre-existing physical disease, other drugs, or adulterants in the black-market supplies.

Serious psychological reactions to MDMA can also occur. These usually take the form of prolonged anxiety or depression, but a few cases of persistent psychotic illness with hallucinations, delusions, and loss of contact with reality have been reported. In almost all of these cases, an important contribution from pre-existing mental disorder, or the regular use of other street drugs clearly associated with the risk of psychosis such as amphetamine, cannot be ruled out. Again, these reactions seem few and far between when viewed in context of the millions of doses consumed worldwide. Treatment is symptomatic with antipsychotic medication and psychological support. No information on outcome is available for these patients, many of whom will later be diagnosed as schizophrenic.

Gammahydroxybutyrate (GHB)

GHB was developed in the US as a possible anaesthetic and premedicant for surgery, but its authorization for medical use was removed in 1990 because of unwanted effects. It is still available there as a health food product advertised for its sleep-enhancing and weight control activity at a recommended dose of around 2.5 grams. Though not approved as a food or drug in the UK, it is not currently restricted under the Misuse of Drugs Act. GHB is increasingly popular as a euphoriant on the club scene, and among body-builders as a muscle-bulking agent.

GHB probably acts as an inhibitory chemical messenger (neurotransmitter) in the brain, and it has structural similarities to naturally occuring neurotransmitters such as GABA and glutamic acid. It is rapidly absorbed by mouth, reaches peak levels in blood within an hour, and is broken down quite rapidly to carbon dioxide.

It was not much use as an anaesthetic because it doesn't have much of a painkilling effect but does have a propensity to cause fits. On the other hand, its action in increasing slow-wave (deep) sleep might give it a role in the treatment of the sleep disorder narcolepsy, and there is evidence from animal experiments that it can alleviate withdrawal from alcohol and opiates.

GHB ('GBH') is available on the street in the form of powder, capsules, or more usually in small bottles containing 40 ml or so of colourless, odourless liquid containing up to 20 grams of drug and costing around £15. It is popular among body-builders because slow-wave sleep is associated with the secretion of growth hormone. It is taken by clubbers for the euphoria and alcohol-like intoxication which can be quite long-lasting.

Unwanted effects, which can also be persistent, include dizziness, nausea and vomiting, muscle weakness, visual problems, agitation, hallucinations, fits, and coma. The ratio between a euphoriant and a toxic dose is very small. A withdrawal syndrome consisting of cramps, anxiety, and insomnia has been reported following heavy regular use. It may interact with MDMA to produce psychosis, amphetamine to cause fits, and alcohol to bring about dangerous respiratory depression. It seems to antagonize the effects of cannabis. No deaths caused by GHB alone have so far been reported, but there is no information as to what dangers may result from long-term use.

Ketamine

Ketamine (Ketalar, 'special K') is used in medicine as an intravenous anaesthetic, but its application is limited by a high incidence of hallucinations. It also increases muscle tone, speeds up the heart, and increases blood pressure.

It is available on the street in the form of powder, tablets, capsules, or liquid costing up to £20 for a single dose, and can be taken orally, snorted, or injected.

It produces hallucinogenic and painkilling effects which are similar to those of PCP but is shorter lasting, and probably less toxic. Users feel depersonalized or cut off and remote from their surroundings. Nausea and vomiting, clumsiness, limb numbness, visual impairment, and slurring of speech are all quite likely to occur, so accidents are always possible. It would be very easy to take a bit too much and lose consciousness, with a risk of inhaling vomit. The effects on the heart are worrying. There is no information on the possible consequences of long-term use.

chapter 10

anabolic steroids

Historical background

The effects of testosterone on muscle growth and development were first reported in 1938, and the following year the idea that this might have some relevance to improving sports performance was first mooted. Derivatives were used by the German military in World War II to enhance aggression among new recruits. Body-builders began to give public endorsement to various brands of anabolic steroid in the 1940s and 1950s and they were openly used by Olympic weight-lifting teams at that time. Since then, millions of pounds have been spent by official sporting bodies in an attempt to eliminate their use, but with only limited success.

Preparation and distribution

The only anabolic steroids listed in the 1998 *British National Formulary* are nandrolone ('Deca-Durabolin') and stanozolol ('Stromba'). However, many others are available illicitly, some of which are manufactured in 'underground' laboratories and may therefore be of dubious purity. Names which often crop up include Dianabol, Anadrol, Anavar, Parabolin, Finajet, Sustanon, Premastin,

Primabolin, and Testosterone Cypionate. Price tends to hover in the region of £20 for 100 tablets.

Anabolic steroids are categorized as 'prescription-only medicines' under the Medicines Act (1968), and fall into the same category of restriction as the benzodiazepines (excluding temazepam) under the Misuse of Drugs Act (1971) in that they are illegal to supply but not to possess. In the US it is unlawful to import, sell, or supply them without a licence, and unauthorized possession is a criminal offence. Medical indications are now largely restricted to a particular form of life-threatening anaemia, the severe itching associated with certain types of jaundice, and the rare condition of hereditary angio-oedema. In the past they were used in a much wider range of conditions, including osteoporosis (bone thinning), metastatic breast cancer, testicular deficiency, and as an aid to recovery from burns, surgery, or trauma, but alternatives with better side-effect profiles are now generally preferred. They are effective as male contraceptive agents, but are far too toxic to be marketable for this indication.

Scientific information

The term 'anabolism' is derived from the Greek *anabole* which means 'a raising up'. In physiology it refers to the building up in the body of complex chemical compounds by the bringing together of clusters of simpler ones, and particularly the creation of proteins from collections of amino acids. An androgen is a substance which stimulates the male genital organs, and all anabolic steroids have some androgenic effect.

The most important androgen is testosterone, and when secreted at puberty this hormone produces a growth spurt and stimulates development of the masculine sexual equipment and general appearance. In females and prepubescent boys the testosterone levels in plasma are generally less than 60 mg per 100 ml, while those in adult men are usually more than 10 times greater than this. In animal studies there is a clear link between testosterone levels and aggression, but this link has not been so clearly demonstrated in humans.

Anabolic steroids increase the proportion of protein laid down as tissue, especially in the muscles. They also stimulate the growth of bone but at the same time hasten the process (epiphyseal closure) which terminates the extension of the long bones in the arms and legs. This can result in a stunting of growth if they are taken by children or adolescents.

Volunteers given test doses describe euphoric effects, increased energy, and sexual arousal, but also irritability, mood swings, and raised feelings of hostility.

Anabolic steroids are taken by male and female athletes because they increase lean muscle mass and strength if taken alongside intensive exercise and a high-protein, high-calorie diet. They also stimulate production of red blood corpuscles, thereby increasing the oxygen-carrying capacity of the blood and enhancing the capacity for intensive training. The androgenic component seems to boost competitiveness and determination.

Recreational use

Among gym attenders and competitive athletes, surveys suggest that up to 10% of males and 2% of females use them regularly, and this is likely to be a marked underestimate given the risks of sanctions such athletes face if steroid use is revealed. Among such users, there is great resistance to giving them up despite a clear awareness in most cases of the risks to health that are involved. Athletes are on record as saying that serious illness in the future or even a premature death would be an acceptable price to pay for sporting excellence now. Nor is the law an effective deterrent: 87% of those interviewed in one survey said they would continue to use steroids even if possession was made illegal and large fines or imprisonment were in prospect.

The average age of first use is in the mid-twenties but household surveys indicate that 2% of 16-year-olds sampled in the UK and US admit to having used them. Among regular steroid users the profile of other illicit drug use is comparable to that of the general population.

They are usually taken by mouth, though injection is by no means uncommon, and are easily obtained at gyms and weight-training clubs. Athletes often consume them in cycles of three months on alternating with three months off, and doses way beyond recommended maximums are the norm. There are many other performance-enhancing drugs which are likely to be taken in addition, including clenbuterol (promotes muscle growth and fat metabolism), growth hormone (not detectable on urine testing), human chorionic gonadotrophin (stimulates secretion of testosterone), diuretics such as spironolactone or frusemide (for muscle shaping), and thyroxine (promotes fat metabolism). For sprinting and other 'explosive' sports stimulants such as caffeine or amphetamine may be used, and erythropoietin boosts stamina by enhancing the oxygen-carrying capacity of the blood. When extra steadiness is required, beta-blockers such as propanolol may be effective. Corticosteroids, anti-inflammatories, and even opioids are used to suppress the pain that comes from excessive exercise, and female gymnasts have been known to take endocrine agents to delay the inconvenience of puberty. Diuretics are used by boxers and jockeys to lose weight – artificially, since this is only due to a temporary voiding of fluids – just before a fight or a race. Among the various possible permutations, there are several which are capable of bringing about dangerous drug interactions.

Although most steroid use is in the context of enhancing sporting performance, some young people take them simply for the euphoric and confidence-boosting effect. Injecting in this context is not unusual, and the majority of needle-exchange clinics have steroid injectors amongst their clientele.

Unwanted effects

Anabolic steroids produce a wide range of unpleasant or dangerous effects, most of which are dose related, but there have been no long-term studies which could quantify this risk in young, healthy people. In one cross-sectional survey, less than a fifth of users escaped with no unwanted effects at all, while two-thirds had experienced two or more at some time. The commonest effects described by this sample were shrinking testicles, menstrual problems, raised blood pressure, and nosebleeds.

The most obvious cosmetic problems in men include a puffy face and spotty skin, enlargement of the breasts, and a bulkier penis offset by shrinking testicles and a propensity to impotence. Women risk hair loss and masculinization. Cracking headaches, nausea, and vomiting are common.

In regular users blood pressure is increased alongside fluid and electrolyte retention, giving a risk of strokes. Raised fat levels in the blood could contribute to heart attacks and furring of the arteries (atherosclerosis). Liver damage may result in jaundice (stanozolol is particularly dangerous in this regard) as may a particular form of inflammation (peliosis hepatitis), and there is a considerably raised incidence of liver cancer. Sex drive is often boosted but fertility declines in both men and women as a result of suppression of sperm production and motility and disruption of the menstrual cycle. The immune system may be impaired, and it is possible that injectors who share equipment are more than usually vulnerable to infection with HIV or hepatitis B and C. In adolescents, growth and pubertal changes are inhibited as a result of direct effects on growth mechanisms of bones in the arms and legs and suppression of hormones such as gonadotrophin. Large doses can produce diabetes and the hormonal disorder acromegaly.

Anabolic steroids can induce a wide range of unpleasant psychological symptoms in as many as one in 10 users. Depression, confusion, chronic fatigue, psychosis, emotional instability, grandiose delusions, and impulsive aggression have all been described. The phenomenon of 'roid rage' is particularly associated with the more androgenic agents or with large doses ('stacking'), and the 'steroid defence' has been used in a number of rape, assault, and homicide cases in the US. Sleep patterns are often interrupted, and memory and concentration may suffer. Some cases of addiction have been reported.

All in all, a tremendous price to pay for a heartbeat of extra pace, a few more ounces on the squat-thrust, or an admiring glance on the beach.

chapter 11

tranquillizers and sleeping pills

Barbiturates

Historical background

Insomnia is a difficult phenomenon to tie down because individual variations in the requirement for sleep vary so widely, but the need for that 'balm of hurt minds, great nature's second course, chief nourisher at life's feast' has preoccupied mankind from hunter-gatherer days. In modern Britain, up to 15% of men and 25% of women visiting their family doctors will be complaining of inadequate sleep. Herbal potions, opium, and alcohol have all served as sleeping-draughts in their time. In the middle of the 19th century, the sleep-inducing property of bromide was discovered, and its derivatives became very popular. It was not until the 1930s that recognition of the toxic effects on nerves led to their disappearance.

The coming-of-age of organic chemistry permitted many pharmaceutical innovations before the turn of the century, many of which are still in use today. Examples from the sedative field include paraldehyde and chloral but the most significant in this domain was barbituric acid (named by its originator after 'a charming lady named Barbara'), and the subsequent marketing of barbitone in 1903. Phenobarbitone quickly followed, and quite soon there were more than 50 'barbiturates' on the market. These were prescribed more and more widely for insomnia and anxiety and later, in combination with amphetamine, for depression. Cases of dependence were reported in Europe as early as 1912, but it was not until 1950 that the possibility of becoming physically dependent upon barbiturates was fully acknowledged.

For many years, the morbidity and mortality associated with barbiturates was mainly confined to the large numbers of people receiving legitimate prescriptions, and those members of their households who had access to the bathroom medicine cupboard. In the late 1950s, young people who had discovered the delights of amphetamine also discovered that barbiturates were just the thing for bringing the pace of life back down to a controllable tempo after partying with speed. Heavier users of stimulants came to realize that combining them with barbiturates mellowed out the sharp edges of the high and eased the crash which eventually has to be faced at the end of a binge. Heroin users found that their ready availability and low price made them an invaluable fall-back when supplies ran short, and dealers cut them into street opiates as a cheap alternative to the real thing. Oblivion seekers found they had access to the ultimate lift-shaft.

This rapid growth in non-medical use of barbiturates by young people was facilitated by the huge amounts then being manufactured for the legal market. In 1960, one billion tablets were dispensed from pharmacies in Britain. Drug combinations containing barbiturates found a special niche within the street scene. Purple Hearts (Drinamyl), a combination with amphetamine, were all the rage with hipsters and party-goers. Mandrax (methaqualone – not a barbiturate but very similar in profile – plus diphenhydramine) arrived in Britain in 1965, and by 1968 was the most widely prescribed sleeping tablet. Although withdrawn in the 1980s, methaqualone still retains a select but enthusiastic band of black-market devotees.

By the late 1960s, there were more than 2000 barbiturate-related deaths each year in Britain, with some well-known pop musicians among them: Brian Jones, Jimi Hendrix, Janis Joplin, even Elvis Presley. At least a third of the heroin addicts attending a major drug dependency unit in the US were also regularly injecting barbiturates, and more than half of London's opiate addicts had injected the stuff within the previous year. On the broader stage, these drugs were second only to coal gas as the instrument of death in suicide, accounting for 8000 deaths yearly in Britain.

These sombre statistics did little to stem the enthusiasm of doctors or their insomniac and anxious patients. British doctors wrote 16 million prescriptions for barbiturates in 1964. Five hundred thousand people were reckoned to be taking them legitimately, with almost a quarter of these dependent upon them. It was only the appearance and ready availability of a safer alternative, the benzodiazepines, that stemmed the tide. The barbiturates went into a rapid decline during the 1970s, and their use in medicine became highly restricted. There was a small upsurge in illicit use in the early 1980s, and they retain a limited though toxic presence within today's street drug scene.

Scientific information

The barbiturates can be divided into three categories based on their duration of action. Short-acters such as thiopentone are never prescribed to patients outside the operating theatre or intensive care unit, are of no interest to recreational users, and will not be considered further. Long-acting drugs, which include phenobarbitone and allobarbitone, hang around in the bloodstream for many days and so rapidly accumulate in the body if taken regularly. Blood levels of the medium-acting group (consisting of pentobarbitone, quinalbarbitone, butobarbitone, and amylobarbitone among others) halve every 30–40 hours. All are absorbed well by mouth and are gradually broken down by the liver. This drug-neutralizing function of the liver becomes generally overactive through having to deal with the barbiturates, and this can result in reduced effectiveness of other drugs as they are disposed of more quickly. Examples include the contraceptive pill, blood thinning agents, and steroids.

Resistance develops to the sleep-inducing and tranquillizing effect but less so to the depressant effect on breathing, which may lead to accidental overdose with fatal consequences. This resistance generalizes to other brain depressants such as alcohol.

Barbiturates facilitate the brain's inhibitory chemical messenger, gamma amino butyric acid (GABA). Messages pass along nerves in the form of waves of electrical depolarization. There is an electric charge across the resting cell membrane of the nerve because of differences in concentration of various chemicals across it, and these differences are maintained by active transport mechanisms. GABA presides over one such mechanism by regulating the flow of chloride ions across the membrane. Barbiturates interact with the GABA receptor complex on the membrane to increase the flow of chloride through its channel, increasing the polarization and making the membrane less susceptible to depolarization. The chloride channel then seems to remain locked open for some time, causing prolonged depression of the cell.

A small dose of barbiturate produces a sense of calmness and relaxation that is comparable to a couple of pints of beer. It is an effective sleeping draught to start with, though likely to induce a hangover effect and sluggishness the following day. Rapidly diminishing effectiveness on regular use (tolerance) may lead to an escalation of intake to the point that depression of breathing becomes a risk. The ratio between therapeutic and toxic doses is small, and clumsiness, slurred speech, and unsteady gait may become apparent at quite modest levels of consumption. People taking barbiturates are notoriously accident prone.

The barely detectable depression of breathing, even at therapeutic doses, makes the user vulnerable to bronchitis and even pneumonia.

Medical uses

Apart from the use of short-acting compounds in anaesthesia, the only current medical indications in Britain are for epilepsy and 'severe intractable insomnia in patients already taking barbiturates'. Available preparations are amylobarbitone (Amytal), butobarbitone (Soneryl), quinalbarbitone (Seconal), and a mixture of amylobarbitone and quinalbarbitone (Tuinal).

Recreational use

There are virtually no statistics available on today's recreational use of barbiturates. More than a third of heroin addicts presenting recently to a drug dependency unit in Oxford said they had used barbiturates in the past two years, but none would admit to using them currently. A survey published in 1987 suggested that 15% of addicts used barbiturates regularly, and more than half of these people injected them on some occasions.

They are not easily accessible to street drug users nowadays because only limited quantities are manufactured, but are still prized by a small minority of oblivion seekers. Many of these people will be prepared to grind up tablets or dissolve the contents of capsules and inject the resulting sludge into a vein. Pill injecting is a risky business at the best of times, but with barbiturates it is particularly dangerous. Others will swallow them if they happen to become available to mitigate the less welcome effects of stimulants, fend off opiate withdrawal symptoms, or get some hard-to-come-by sleep at the end of a day's hustling. Heroin addicts sometimes inject barbiturates unknowingly when dealers cut them into their 'gear' to give inferior material a bit more punch.

It is the medium-acting drugs that are most favoured on the black market (pento-, amylo-, quinal-, butobarbitone). Alcoholics have traditionally used these to suppress withdrawal symptoms. The combination of barbiturate and amphetamine has an appeal which transcends the current lack of a ready-formulated product. It seems that the stimulant's effect on energy, confidence, and strength, and the depressant's suppression of fear and anxiety combine to produce a particularly desirable high. The shortage of barbiturates makes it much more likely that the infinitely safer benzodiazepines will fulfil this role, and opiates are another alternative.

Unwanted effects

Mild toxicity, apparent at quite modest doses, is characterized by clumsiness, quivering pupils (nystagmus), slurred speech, and emotional instability. Alcohol and other brain depressants will potentiate these toxic effects. Minor side-effects include skin rashes, growth of hair in the wrong places, and swelling of the gums. Larger doses may result in depression of breathing, pneumonia, inefficiency of the heart and circulation, and kidney failure. Any of these can have a fatal outcome. Confusion may progress to delirium or coma, sometimes after a lag period of several days.

Long-term users often exist in a state of chronic impairment with symptoms of mild toxicity ebbing and flowing. They will exhibit unpredictable emotional states, switching between euphoria, depression, or irritability with little warning or provocation. Behaviour may be disinhibited and impulsive, and if influenced by a feeling of persecution dangerous aggression can result. Social deterioration is often apparent.

When tablets or the contents of capsules are ground up, mixed in water, and injected into a vein, the resulting suspension is highly irritant. Local tissue damage may be intense, and injury to the vein, or even worse to the nearby artery or nerve, can threaten the viability of the limb. Because of the rapid destruction of superficial veins, intravenous users may be forced to go for the large veins in the groin or neck, with disastrous consequences.

Sudden withdrawal of barbiturates will produce anxiety, agitation, trembling, stomach cramps, and sleeplessness. The sufferer may vomit, develop circulatory disturbances, or a fever. Without treatment, disorientation may be accompanied by false or illogical beliefs and hallucinations. There is a serious risk of fits, and these can be very difficult to bring under control. Because of the potential seriousness of the barbiturate withdrawal syndrome, the procedure should be conducted in hospital or under close medical supervision.

There are a number of drugs which are not actually barbiturates but are very similar in their effects. *Ethchlorvynol* (Placidyl) is a tranquillizer with a characteristic mint-like aftertaste, whose action comes on about 30 minutes after swallowing it, peaks at 90 minutes, and goes on working for between four and six hours. A hangover the next day is the usual sequel when it is used as a sleeping pill, and facial numbness is not uncommon. The profile of unwanted effects is very similar to that of the barbiturates.

Glutethimide (Doriden) enters the brain with particular rapidity, but is broken down in the body rather slowly. Apart from the usual barbiturate-like effects, it blocks the chemical messenger acetycholine quite powerfully. In the graphic phraseology of a 1940s article, this can make you ' … hot as a hare, blind as a bat, dry as a bone, and mad as a hen'. More prosaically, it can also cause loss of calcium from the bones or anaemia.

Meprobamate (Miltown) is an effective muscle relaxant and tranquillizer, and in 1957 became the most widely used sleeping pill in the US because of effective marketing as a safer alternative to the barbiturates. It soon became a great favourite with opiate addicts for intravenous use. Its popularity waned as its true toxic potential emerged: fatalities were reported after as few as 15 tablets.

Although *methaqualone* (Qaalude) was withdrawn from legal supply many years ago, it is still prized on the black market. It is manufactured illegally in South America and elsewhere, and is usually available on the streets of London and New York if you have the right contacts. It is famed for its ability to produce a dreamy 'dissociative high' without sedation, an effect similar to that described following heroin. Unfortunately, this state is not compatible with taking good care of yourself and the drug has been associated with a number of deaths resulting from lack of attention, clumsiness, or disinhibition. There is also the possibility of rare but serious toxic effects, including nerve damage, life-threatening anaemias, and fits.

Benzodiazepines

The benzodiazepines are phenomenally successful drugs prescribed in vast quantities throughout the world. In 1977, more than 8000 tons were consumed in North America alone, and 30 million prescriptions were filled in the UK. They form the major part of a worldwide anti-anxiety and antidepression drug market worth more than $2 billion yearly. Most people who take them do so perfectly legally, but there is a wide overlap between the licit and illicit arenas. There are no illicit manufacturers, the extensive black market being supplied entirely by diversion from legal supplies. It is legal to possess benzodiazepines without a prescription, but illegal to sell them or even give them away.

Historical background

Extensive research in the 1950s fuelled by growing awareness of the toxicity of barbiturates led to the synthesis of chlordiazepoxide in 1957. This was shown to have a 'taming' effect in animals and increased exploratory behaviour, eating, and drinking which had been suppressed by new or frightening experimental conditions. It was unveiled as Librium in 1960, and was soon followed by diazepam (Valium) in 1963. Both products were marketed aggressively by their manufacturer, Hoffman La Roche, and prescription sales accelerated rapidly as more variations on the theme appeared and the barbiturates were swept aside.

Repeat prescriptions became commonplace, a process aggravated in Britain by the fact that the vast majority of benzodiazepines were and are prescribed by hard-pressed family doctors who are confronted daily by an army of men and women attending their surgeries to demand treatment for sleeplessness and worry. Since their zenith in the mid-1970s a slow decline has been noted, more recently reinforced by limited prescribing lists established by health authorities so as to reduce the local NHS drug bill, recommendations from the Committee on Safety of Medicines, and publicity campaigns in the media. Even so, the prevalence of use remains impressive. Averaging across Western nations, around 15% of adults use benzodiazepines each year, and 3% use them daily for a year or more. In the UK as recently as 1985, three and a half million adults had been on benzodiazepines for more than four months and one in 50 visiting a general practitioner had been taking them continuously for more than a year. The typical long-term user is a female over 50 with multiple, chronic health problems who is frequently to be seen sitting patiently in her GP's waiting room.

Since the mid-1970s there has been growing concern at the prevalence of benzodiazepine dependence and misuse, and questions as to their continuing efficacy when used long term. This has led to a gradual decline in prescriptions, a process which will no doubt gather momentum as more lawsuits are brought against doctors and pharmaceutical companies by individuals who feel they have been turned into addicts. Although many doctors now limit their prescribing to carefully selected patients for no more than a few weeks, there are still those who argue that the reaction against them has been excessive. They draw attention to the impressive safety profile on the one hand, and the high prevalence of anxiety disorders (around 10% of the North American population) on the other. They point out that alternative medication for these people is less safe, and that non-drug treatments may be unacceptable, unavailable, or ineffective. There is some epidemiological evidence that when benzodiazepine availability is reduced, self-medication with more toxic depressants, such as alcohol, increases.

Scientific information

In 1975, it was realized that benzodiazepines work by enhancing the effects of gamma amino butyric acid (GABA) in the brain. In 1977, a specific receptor site for benzodiazepines was discovered within the GABA complex on cell membranes of nerve cells. This suggests the existence of some naturally occurring substance in the body which has a similar effect to these drugs. Barbiturates, and possibly alcohol, have an effect at the same site.

The way that GABA inhibits nervous activity by controlling the flow of chloride through a specific channel in the cell membrane has been described above in connection with the barbiturates. Since GABA is very widely distributed throughout the brain and spinal cord, the effects of the benzodiazepines are diffuse throughout the nervous system. Inhibitory transmission in the spinal cord results in muscle relaxation.

Benzodiazepines are not particularly powerful in animal dependency models, but greatly reduce the suppressive effects of punishment on animal behaviour. There is no evidence of nerve damage in long-term dosing in animals or humans. Like most sleeping pills, they alter the pattern of 'rapid eye movement' and 'slow wave' phases of sleep. The pattern bounces back in the opposite direction when they are discontinued, giving rise to 'rebound insomnia'.

All benzodiazepines are well absorbed by mouth, and most are broken down in the liver to active and inactive metabolites, some of which may be very long-acting. There is a wide range of compounds on the market, and the use to which they are put depends to a large extent upon how rapidly they disappear from the bloodstream. They are categorized on this basis as short-acting (temazepam, oxazepam, loprazolam), medium-acting (lorazepam, alprazolam), and longacting (nitrazepam, flunitrazepam, chlordiazepoxide, diazepam, clobazam, flurazepam, ketazolam). Unfortunately, the blood level does not always reflect brain levels and so may be misleading. There is a complicated chemical interrelation between the drugs. For example, one of the metabolites of diazepam is temazepam, which in turn has oxazepam as one of its breakdown products.

Medical uses

Benzodiazepines are still widely prescribed for sleeplessness and anxiety. Other indications include supplementation of anaesthesia, muscle spasm or cramps, and epilepsy. From the pharmacological point of view, they are remarkably benign drugs with virtually no adverse effects outside the nervous system. Breathing can be depressed by enormous doses, but a fatal outcome from benzodiazepine alone is extraordinarily rare. In combination with other brain depressants such as alcohol, the danger is much greater. They cross the placenta and do seem to be associated with a small increase in the incidence of birth defects. When taken late in pregnancy, they may produce the 'floppy infant syndrome'. As with all drugs, they should be avoided in pregnancy if at all possible, especially in the first three months. They enter breast milk and can make the baby sleepy.

The most commonly prescribed drugs are temazepam (seven million prescriptions in the UK each year), nitrazepam (four million), diazepam (four million), and lorazepam (two million). In 1996 the UK government responded to the serious abuse problems of temazepam by increasing the regulatory controls which apply to it and banning the prescription of the capsule formulation by doctors within the NHS.

Recreational use

Non-medical use of benzodiazepines has been documented since the 1960s, and in 1985 they were used in this way by 4% of the US population, a very similar figure to that obtained in the 1996 British Crime Survey. In other countries, surveys have indicated that in some areas as many as 10–15% of adolescents have used them recreationally (see footnote, p. 3). Most of this use is by mouth, but tablets and the contents of capsules are occasionally ground up and snorted into the nose. Temazepam seems to be increasingly popular among young people on the club scene. Intravenous use is rare except among those already accustomed to using other drugs by this route.

A recent survey suggested that about half the benzodiazepines obtained on the black market were taken with a view to obtaining a 'buzz' or high. Other important reasons included the need for sleep or rest, to limit the unwanted effects of stimulants or hallucinogens, to gain confidence to carry out criminal activities or other stressful tasks, and to boost the effects of opiates, especially heroin or buprenorphine (Temgesic). Almost half of those questioned thought tranquillizers made them more violent and disinhibited, and many thought their memory was impaired by them.

A lot of people seem to find that a handful of Valium or temazepam takes away all the worries of street life for a while. Adolescents sometimes take them as an alternative to 'Special Brew' or solvents. At modest doses, the effects are very similar to those of alcohol, but increasing resistance to the euphoriant and sedative effects mean that some people get up to massive amounts with no visible signs of intoxication: the equivalent of 20 or 30 times the manufacturer's recommended maximum dose of diazepam taken daily is by no means unusual. Such an intake is quite simple to maintain because the drugs are so cheap and easy to come by. Tablets can be obtained from enterprising pensioners whose repeat prescriptions for insomnia generate a useful supplement to their income, from alcoholics who prefer alcohol to the Librium or Chloral they are prescribed for withdrawal symptoms, or from the medicine cupboard of a hard-pressed parent. As prescribing has slowly declined, so the seizure rate by police of illegal stockpiles has increased in recent years. The most popular recreational benzodiazepines are temazepam, diazepam, lorazepam, and flunitrazepam, and these all form part of the regular currency and barter of street life.

Amongst attenders at drug dependency units (DDUs), benzodiazepines are rarely drugs of first choice, but a large majority use them from time to time, often in huge doses. A survey in Oxford indicated that 81% of heroin addicts had used them in the previous year, and 27% were using them daily at presentation. Other surveys have suggested an even higher prevalence than this. The price on the black market is variable, but always cheap: even on a bad day, £1 will buy three or four diazepam or temazepam tablets. Surveys from the US and Australia demonstrate that this is not a problem limited to the UK.

Awareness that the intravenous use of benzodiazepines, especially temazepam, was becoming a significant problem grew from the mid-1980s. It tended to be focused in particular areas of the country, and did not necessarily reflect a shortage of more conventional merchandise such as heroin. By the end of the 1980s the practice had become more widespread, with up to a third of injecting addicts admitting to it. One survey suggested that as many as 70% of injecting drug users had injected temazepam at some time. The manufacturers of temazepam did not welcome the publicity they were getting, and in 1989 reformulated their liquid capsules as a hard gel in an attempt to make them uninjectable. Determined addicts found they could overcome this hurdle by warming the gel and using larger needles. Not surprisingly, this practice carries with it terrible health risks, since the gel tends to harden up again in the blood-stream and can easily block vessels.

Several independent surveys have indicated that injecting drug users who also use benzodiazepines show higher levels of psychological and social impairment and are harder to treat. In comparison with other injectors, they are more likely to share equipment, use multiple drugs, and inject more frequently; to be infected with hepatitis C; to be of low educational status and unemployed; to be more criminally active; and to have fewer friends.

Recently, a sinister version of the 'Mickey Finn' has been reported in connection with flunitrazepam (Rohypnol, 'roofies'). This drug, a particularly powerful and long-acting benzodiazepine, dissolves rapidly in fluids and is then tasteless and colourless. Hundreds of reports, mainly from the US but increasingly from the UK and elsewhere, suggest that many women have suffered rape and other sexual abuse after being rendered helpless by roofies slipped covertly into their drinks. Disinhibition or semi-consciousness results, and the victims have little or no memory of what happens subsequently. In 1998 the manufacturer of Rohypnol (which is barred from prescription in the NHS) altered the formula-tion to reduce its solubility and included a blue dye which is released when the tablets dissolve.

Unwanted effects

Physical risks associated with the benzodiazepines are mainly by-products of depressed mental functioning, for example clumsiness, forgetfulness, or disinhibition leading to self-neglect or accidents. As mentioned above, depression of breathing can occur with massive doses, or more easily if other depressant drugs are taken at the same time. Very rarely, abnormalities in liver function crop up which are reversible if the drugs are withdrawn.

Injecting benzodiazepines is associated with all the usual risks of this practice: septicaemia, hepatitis, HIV, and other infections; blockage of veins, damage to nearby arteries or nerves which can lead to loss of the limb; and abscesses or ulcers at the injection site. The newly formulated hard-gel temazepam 'eggs' are particularly likely to damage veins or lead to blockage of vessels. Injecting tranquillizers seems to have a particular association with a self-destructive, chaotic, deviant lifestyle. People whose lives have taken this course are more likely to share injecting equipment, have unprotected sex, and take more accidental and deliberate overdoses.

Many people take benzodiazepines for months or even years on end and find it very hard to contemplate doing without them. Is it worth the bother of battling to give up what is after all a cheap and relatively non-toxic drug? The answer is that for most people, chronic use does carry definite disadvantages. There can be problems with concentration and memory; depression, tiredness, and apathy; clumsiness and accident proneness which has particular significance for drivers; disinhibition; and instability of mood. The ability to cope with everyday problems is impaired. From time to time, withdrawal symptoms may emerge due to altered sensitivity to the regular dose. The elderly are particularly prone to all these effects. With toxic doses, confusion and memory deficits worsen and control over bodily activity deteriorates.

Physical dependence on benzodiazepines is now well recognized and may become apparent after as little as six weeks or so of regular ingestion. Symptoms overlap with those related to psychological dependence (see Chapter 13), and will be considered together. The withdrawal syndrome has to be distinguished from re-emergence of the pre-existing anxiety state. The proportion of people reported to experience a withdrawal syndrome after coming off long-term benzodiazepines ranges from 20% to 90%, but most studies suggest that it will occur in more than half. It is difficult to predict with any confidence who is likely to suffer, but those people who might be described as 'neurotic' are particularly vulnerable, as are those with a history of dependency on other substances. Unsurprisingly, it is more likely when larger doses are taken over longer periods. Abrupt termination results in more symptoms than tapering the dose off gradually. Shorter-acting drugs cause more intense withdrawal symptoms, and are associated with greater rates of relapse. Relapse occurs in up to half of those trying to give up, but people who successfully remain abstinent for five weeks or more report lower levels of anxiety than when they were still taking the drugs.

Withdrawal symptoms come on after a day or two of abstinence in the case of short-acting compounds such as temazepam or lorazepam, but can be delayed for a week or more following more slowly metabolized drugs such as diazepam. Patients complain of anxiety, restlessness and irritability, heightened sensitivity to noise and other environmental stimuli, twitches and shakiness, weakness and lack of motivation or energy, stomach cramps, headaches, poor concentration or confusion, sleeplessness, and a craving for tranquillizers. These symptoms vary greatly in severity, and usually last for about two weeks after the last tablet has been taken. Fits occur in up to 20% of patients withdrawn abruptly from substantial doses.

Anyone taking benzodiazepines regularly for longer than three weeks or so risks developing both physical and psychological dependence. This is particularly like-ly in people suffering chronic stress, or those with rather a passive nature, a past history of dependence on other drugs or alcohol, poor coping skills, impulsivity, or subject to rapid and unpredictable mood swings.

There are a number of drugs which are not actually benzodiazepines but have a very similar effect. *Chloral hydrate* (or chloral betane, 'Welldorm') is marketed as a sleeping tablet. It is rapidly absorbed by mouth and the blood level halves in around six hours. It has a characteristic bitter taste and is irritating to the stomach, and so should be avoided by indigestion sufferers or anyone with a history of ulcers. It is dangerous for those with severe heart, liver, or kidney disease. Breast-feeding mothers who take it will make their babies sleepy. Chloral is widely available on the black market.

Chlormethiazole (Heminevrin) is another sleeping pill, and is structurally related to vitamin B_1 (thiamine). It is broken down rapidly in the body, with blood levels halving every four hours. It has similar contraindications to chloral, and should be avoided during pregnancy and by breast-feeding mothers. It seems to cause sneezing and itchy, red eyes. It is often prescribed to alcoholics to relieve their withdrawal symptoms, and potentiates the toxic effects of alcohol in those who continue to drink. Chlormethiazole spills liberally on to the black market from this and other sources.

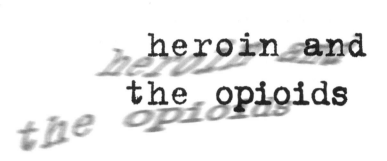

heroin and the opioids

Historical background

The opium poppy has been one of mankind's greatest friends. For thousands of years, ordinary people have eased their lives through the power opium has to soothe and sedate, and this folk-knowledge found its expression in the great pharmacopoeias of the Egyptians, Sumerians, Greeks, Persians, and Romans.

Each age, including our own, has spun its myths around the drug. Theophrastus defined its medical applications in 320 BC but the Ancient Greeks also knew that when the goddess Demeter discovered the poppy's secret she forgot all her sorrows. What else could Helen of Troy's nepenthe have been but opium?

Today, the need and desire for opium and its derivatives remain as great as ever. Strict international legal control of supply has opened the door to a worldwide, multi-billion dollar crime network whose malign influence has seeped into every part of society, and whose windfall profits are built upon the exploitation and misery of millions.

Although opioids remain central to pain control in Western medicine, thousands of hospital patients and others suffer needlessly because of the unspoken fear of inducing dependency. Heroin addiction has become a terrible scourge of our times, but has this resulted primarily from the properties of the drug itself or the way that society has reacted to it?

From its roots in the ancient world, knowledge of opium was borne along the arteries of commerce. Arab traders introduced it into India in the seventh century AD, and to the shores of China a couple of hundred years later. Another messenger was the common soldier. Opium found its way to Europe in the pouches of returning Crusaders at the start of the new millennium.

Paracelsus (1490–1541), the first European to recommend the targeting of specific symptoms with specific remedies (for which he has been called the 'father of modern pharmacology') invented a mixture of opium, alcohol, and spices which he called laudanum ('worthy of praise'). With minor modifications to the formula, laudanum was to soothe and torment millions of Europeans over the next 400 years.

Although the possibility of addiction was recognized from the earliest times, nobody seems to have worried much about it until relatively recently. Perhaps it was in 18th-century China that the first high-profile problems can be detected. At this time, the British thirst for quality tea was already highly developed and the Chinese produced the best product available. Unfortunately, Britain was rather short of anything that these sophisticated people might wish to trade for it. The solution to this dilemma came in 1773 with the conquest of Bengal, which gave the British a monopoly in Indian opium. The East India Company set about exporting this in large amounts to China, circumnavigating quota problems with piratical zeal.

Recreational use of opium by the Chinese had hitherto not been prominent but opium smoking now caught on in a big way, and paying for these huge imports soon became a serious embarrassment to the Chinese exchequer. The Emperor made the first of many attempts to ban the habit and limit imports in 1799 but in 1839, after decades of helpless frustration, he was driven to take more active steps with the seizure and destruction of large amounts of the drug in Southern China. Lord Palmerston promptly despatched 16 warships to besiege Nanjing, and what later became known as the First Opium War was underway. It ended in 1842 with massive concessions to the British, including the ceding of Hong Kong island as a colony 'in perpetuity'. Further fighting took place between 1856 and 1860, but this simply led to more humiliation for the Chinese. By this time, there were between 15 and 20 million opium addicts in the country.

Opium was eulogized in the European medical textbooks of the 18th and early 19th centuries. Not only was it manifestly effective in relieving a tremendous range of symptoms, it was even recommended for use by those in the pink of health because of its ability to 'optimize the internal equilibrium of the human body'. In England, it became a popular home remedy comparable to aspirin nowadays, with consumption peaking at 11 pounds per thousand population in the middle of the 19th century.

Use of opium for pleasure or the relief of fears and anxiety was widespread throughout society. Everyone knows of the famous writers who were enslaved or bewitched by it: Thomas de Quincy, S. T. Coleridge, Wilkie Collins, Charles Dickens, Elizabeth Barrett Browning, and many others. The ability of this and other drugs to enhance creativity remains a matter of vigorous debate to this day. Less well publicized were those politicians and members of the professions who were also awash with laudanum. But it is important to realize that opium was well within the financial reach of the poorest in the land. There were agricultural workers in the Norfolk fens who would have regarded a mug of ale without a knob of opium in it with as much enthusiasm as a modern business executive might view a gin and tonic without the ice. Of course, one could always resort to a bowl of poppy-head tea; and a selection of poppy heads was available in some English pharmacies right through to the 1950s.

What were the problems associated with this completely unregulated free availability of opium? The risk of dependency was certainly recognized, but those who succumbed were regarded with rather amused tolerance for the most part. It is interesting that this tolerance was generally restricted to opium 'eaters' ('drinkers' would be a more appropriate term, since laudanum or patent medicines were by far the commonest form in which the drug was available). Opium smoking seems always to have been regarded as a rather vile alien indulgence.

Opium-containing medicines were widely used as child-calmers, and the mortality associated with this became a major concern in the middle of the 19th century. Most at risk were the small children of those women whose labours fuelled the industrial revolution. Inflexible working hours meant leaving children unattended for long periods. Oversedation in such circumstances could easily have fatal consequences, and recorded cases (likely to be a considerable underestimate) were running at around 80 each year. In the population at large, fatal poisoning with narcotics made up about a third of all poisoning deaths.

This growing concern, along with a certain measure of professional self-interest, led to the introduction of the Pharmacy Act in 1868, which restricted sale of opium and its derivatives to registered chemists but had little or no impact on the volume of sales. This only began to decline significantly towards the end of the century as public perception of the drug became less favourable. This period saw a number of lawsuits against patent medicine manufacturers, and a rapid decline in the popularity of these products. The Act was made rather more restrictive in 1908.

Opium was brought to North America by the early European settlers, and quickly became familiar to most households as in Britain. With characteristic energy and enthusiasm, entrepreneurs were quick to see the commercial possibilities; America's first opium-containing patent medicine appeared as early as 1796. The dangers of excess were recognized just as quickly and were laid out in some detail in the Dispensatory of 1818 but, as in Europe, the drug soon became absolutely central to mainstream medicine. A prominent American physician wrote in 1846 that 'opium is undoubtedly the most important and valuable remedy of the whole materia medica'.

Laudanum could be bought for a few cents an ounce, and Americans took to patent medicines even more enthusiastically than the Europeans had. The foundations of some collosal modern fortunes were laid in those unrestricted times, and by the end of the century more than 50 000 products were on the market. Poppies were cultivated throughout the land, and business was booming. Opiate addiction at that time was said to be much more common in women, possibly because social restrictions limited their access to alcohol.

Two 19th century advances laid the foundation for the scale of problems we face today. First, the active ingredients of opium were identified, paving the way to the creation of immensely potent synthetic opioids. Second, the technique of intravenous injection was perfected.

In 1805, a German pharmacist's apprentice called Sertuerner isolated a chemical from raw opium which he initially called *principum somniferum*. Later, he hit upon the snappier name of morphine, after Morpheus, Greek god of dreams. This chemical was found to make up 10% of the weight of opium, and to be 10 times more potent. Isolation of codeine followed in 1832, thebaine in 1833, and papaverine in 1868. In 1874, di-acetyl morphine was synthesized but was not marketed by Bayer until 1898. For many years after this it was considered a highly effective remedy for morphine addiction, and its trade name was derived from the German word *heroisch*, meaning powerful.

The architect Christopher Wren was one of the first to experiment with injecting substances into the bodies of both animals and humans. In the early days, a blob of material would be placed on the skin, and repeatedly jabbed with a quill or something similar. Then someone hit upon the idea of inserting a hollow tube into a vein and later in the 17th century there were even attempts at blood transfusions. The outcome of these early experiments was extremely disappointing, particularly for the recipients. Interest was revived in the 19th century, and in 1858 a Scottish surgeon adapted an instrument which had been designed to drain blood from birthmarks to deliver a dose of morphine as closely as possible to the point of pain. This device became known as the hypodermic syringe. Administering drugs by injection very rapidly transformed medical practice, and the face of addiction too.

Despite the widespread use of opium and its derivatives in 19th century America, the practice of opium smoking remained socially unacceptable as in Britain. This was largely due to the negative attitude of the native population towards the Chinese immigrants who had been brought over in large numbers to work on the railroads in the 1850s. When a deep recession arrived soon after this with large-scale unemployment in its wake, these hard-working foreigners were deeply resented. Their habit of opium smoking became symbolic of a perceived degeneracy and debauchery. In an age of almost totally unrestrained drug and alcohol use, opium smoking was made illegal in San Francisco in 1875.

It is often said that the American Civil War with its widespread misery and suffering gave a huge boost to opioid usage, and it is true that morphine addiction became known at the time as 'the soldier's disease'. Certainly, vast amounts of opium and morphine were issued to soldiers on both sides in their field packs, but the effect on addiction prevalence remains controversial.

Attempts to regulate the booming patent medicine business and its outrageous marketing techniques were very slow in coming to the US. Not until 1906 did the Federal Pure Food and Drug Act require the ingredients to be specified on the label. Public concern mounted rapidly in the early years of the 20th century, and action to stem misuse of opioids suddenly became a vote-winner for politicians. In 1909, importation of smoking opium became illegal, and America was instrumental in bringing about a series of international conferences on narcotic abuse, first in Shanghai then at The Hague. In 1912, it was agreed that the participating countries (by then numbering more than 30) should go away and enact domestic legislation to restrict the use of opioids to medical indications on prescription from a doctor. In the same year, the importation of opium into the US was banned.

Accordingly, the Harrison Act entered the statute books in 1914. There then followed a lengthy debate as to whether the maintenance prescription of opioids to confirmed addicts by a physician constituted acceptable medical practice. In 1919, the Supreme Court ruled that it did not, thereby setting in motion a punitive response to drug addiction which remained firmly in place until the AIDS epidemic forced a change of policy in the 1980s.

The public alarm which made possible these legal and political moves is understandable given the size of the problem at the time; it was conservatively estimated that there were at least 275 000 opioid addicts in the US in 1920. In Britain, the situation seemed to be very different. Despite the massive use of opium and morphine throughout the previous century, opioid addiction was not a particularly visible problem in the early years of the 20th century. The British were in no great hurry to fulfil the agreement to legislate that they had made at The Hague. This may not have been totally unconnected with the fact that Britain produced most of the world's supply of morphine at that time.

This *laissez-faire* approach was quickly abandoned during the First World War when it became clear that British soldiers on leave in London were keen to get hold of drugs which might make life in the trenches a bit more acceptable. There was a roaring London black market in cocaine, but the fashionable shops were getting in on the act too. Harrods, for example, sold morphine and cocaine kits complete with syringe and spare needles labelled 'A Useful Present for Friends at the Front'. An order came from army big-wigs forbidding the supply of drugs to soldiers on active service lest their efficiency or will to fight be impaired, but this merely fuelled the black market. The order was then given teeth by the introduction of Defence of the Realm Act Regulation 40B in June 1916. This primarily targeted cocaine, but restricted opium as well for good measure.

After the war, there were some lurid stories in the newspapers of drug-soaked debaucheries in the night clubs of London's West End. The sordid death of a well-known actress and the subsequent high-profile prosecution of her dealer gave the Home Office the opportunity to press for immediate civil legislation. This was unsuccessfully resisted by the fledgling Ministry of Health, and in 1920 the DORA 40B was enacted with many extra restrictions as the first Dangerous Drugs Act.

For a few years it looked as though the British response to drug problems would follow the penal route chosen by the Americans. But in 1926 a government-sponsored committee chaired by the President of the Royal College of Physicians was asked to examine the logic and practicalities of this course. The Rolleston Committee recommended that addiction should be regarded as an illness requiring treatment, rather than a crime demanding punishment. Long-term maintenance on a prescription of opioids was recommended for those addicts who were unable to give up but who could lead a 'useful life' when so maintained. The 'British system' for the treatment of opioid addiction thus came in to being.

Whether this admirably humane approach would have found support if addiction had been other than a thoroughly middle-class affair has often been questioned. It is certainly true that there were very few working-class opioid addicts known to doctors in the Britain of the 1920s and 1930s. Most came from the professional classes, and for some reason morphine injecting was particularly prevalent among respectable housewives. This stable, almost complacent state of affairs remained in place right through to the 1960s when it was suddenly and rudely disturbed.

In the United States after the First World War, the situation was very different. The visible plight of large numbers of opioid addicts led many doctors to hope that the Harrison Act would not be vigorously enforced. Addiction clinics were set up, and large numbers of patients maintained. The Narcotics Division within the Bureau of Prohibition had other plans. In 1922, agents began a clamp-down on the clinics, and initiated prosecutions against addicts, doctors, and pharmacists. At first, many physicians were prepared to contest these prosecutions in the courts, but after a number of careers had been ruined the heart went out of the fight and by 1925 the medical profession had withdrawn from the addiction field. By this time heroin had also been banned from use in medicine, and its legal manufacture in the US ceased completely.

Half a million opioid addicts were thus abruptly cut off from their drug supply. The racketeers who had already grown fat on the proceeds of bootleg whisky couldn't believe their luck. Supplies of opium were cheap and easy to come by, morphine and heroin were simple to manufacture in backstreet laboratories. The bad guys were not slow to respond to the demands of their desperate customers, and the black market in drugs was soon consolidated nationwide. When prohibition of alcohol was repealed in 1933, the mobsters were unconcerned. By this time, undreamed-of profits were being achieved in the most lucrative criminal enterprise of all time. Since the 1920s, no world event has ever seriously interfered with the flow of heroin into North America.

American addiction rates probably fell during the Second World War and for a time thereafter, but rose steadily in the 1950s as the Mafia reopened trade routes from Turkey and South East Asia. In particular, there was tremendous demand from urban Black and Puerto Rican communities which the Mob was only too pleased to meet. The penal response became more savage in an attempt to reverse the trend. The 1951 Bogges Act had already defined minimum mandatory jail terms for possession with no possibility of parole in some cases. In 1956, the Narcotic Control Act doubled maximum sentences, and made it possible to award dealers the death penalty.

By this time, it was becoming noticeable that the average age of American addicts was falling steadily: in the 1930s, less than 20% of male addicts were under 30 years of age, but by 1962 more than half were in their twenties.

Observing this trend with concern, the British government decided to review the situation in the UK. The Brain Committee's first report in 1961 was immensely reassuring. Nothing had changed since the 1920s, just a small number of well-behaved professional types plodding along quietly on their scripts, and a handful of bohemian addicts in Soho and West Kensington.

Barely was the ink dry on the parchment when it became obvious to anyone visiting a jazz club or a coffee bar in West London that things were changing fast. The Brain Committee was hurriedly reconvened, and its second report had to concede that there was a growing problem requiring drastic practical measures. The recommendations included restrictions on who could prescribe heroin and cocaine, compulsory notification of opioid and cocaine addicts by doctors to the Home Office, and the establishment of special drug dependency units. The Misuse of Drugs Act was passed through Parliament in 1970.

Why had the drug culture suddenly exploded? Economic stability meant money in people's pockets, better international communications were leading to the emergence of a powerful and independent youth culture, and a number of established addicts escaping the repressive policies of their own countries arrived in England to take advantage of the British system. This hitherto relaxed and restricted philosophy was being reinterpreted by a small number of London doctors in a way which was to have a profound effect on the local drug scene.

In an attempt to keep their demanding patients out of the clutches of criminal suppliers who were imagined to be lurking on every street corner, or more occasionally for simple monetary reward, these doctors were prepared to prescribe truly awesome quantities of heroin, cocaine, or injectable amphetamine to their young clients. One infamous doctor prescribed at least 600 000 heroin pills (for injection) to addicts in 1962. It was apparently not unusual for her to give an addict as many as 900 pills on a single occasion, and be prepared to replace them a few days later if they were reported 'lost'. She went on a lecture tour of Canada to describe her philosophy; not surprisingly, a number of Canadians decided to return to the Old Country. Some 'drug doctors' held their surgeries in pubs or station buffets. When the restrictions on heroin prescribing were introduced, some were undeterred or simply switched their addicts to other drugs. One who was later struck off the medical register is said to have prescribed more than 25 000 ampoules of methamphetamine in one month alone. By 1967, there were 2000 known heroin addicts in the UK.

The irony is that there was virtually no criminally organized black market in Britain at that time. Almost all drug seizures up to the end of the 1960s were of pharmaceutical heroin, cocaine, or amphetamine – overspill from this orgy of prescribing.

In both the UK and America there seems to have been a further upsurge of heroin use as the hippy movement degenerated, in the wake of an outbreak of methamphetamine injecting which swept the big cities. Heroin was one way of coming down from this switchback ride of a drug. A sordid scene centred on Piccadilly Circus in London, and other places conveniently close to all-night chemists. Two peaks of prevalence seem to have occurred from 1968–1972 and 1974–1976: at these times, the drug was unusually plentiful, of relatively high quality, and cheap. Heroin use became endemic in provincial cities during the 1970s and 1980s. Street dealing seems to have become associated with more and more violence. It is an unwelcome and recent change in Britain that some inner-city areas have become virtual no-go areas to law-abiding citizens at certain times.

In periods of relatively short supply, 'designer drugs' tend to become more prominent on the streets, especially in America. These are chemical variations on a theme, and the opioid versions have frequently been based upon fentanyl, a synthetic compound 200 times more potent than morphine. Alpha-methyl fentanyl appeared on the streets in 1979 as 'China White', so-called because of its similarity in appearance to Chinese heroin of a particular type. Within 10 years, backstreet chemists had come up with at least 10 variations of this basic drug, and it is estimated that a quarter of California's heroin addicts used a fentanyl variant at some time. One potential advantage for the user of these drugs is that they do not show up in standard laboratory tests for heroin. The high potency of China White caught some people on the hop: at least 100 overdose deaths were associated with it.

Analogues of pethidine (meperidine) also crop up from time to time. Between 1982 and 1985, methyl-phenyl-propionoxypiperidine (MPPP) and another drug with a long chemical name (MPTP) were marketed as 'synthetic heroin'. Unfortunately, there was a toxic by-product of manufacture which resulted in more than 500 people being permanently brain-damaged, yet another example of the lack of quality control in the world of criminal chemistry.

Heroin pills designed to be vaporized by gentle heating in special jars became very popular in the Far East after the First World War. Seizure rates give some indication of the level of use, increasing from 200 000 pills in 1928 to over four million in 1937. Attempts to import the pills to the US failed to create a market there. In Hong Kong the practice went into a temporary decline but picked up again in the 1950s and remains the commonest route of consumption in that part of the world. Smoking remains an uncommon route for heroin consumption in the US, but has caught on in a big way among certain populations in the UK since its introduction in the early 1980s.

Preparation and distribution

International gangsters continue to enjoy the billion-dollar bonanza that illicit heroin provides. Mafia, Camorra, Triads, Yardies, even the Hell's Angels, there's more than enough profit for all of them. The source material comes from the countries which form the 'opium crescent' – Turkey, Iran, Afghanistan, Pakistan, India, Nepal, Bangladesh, Burma, Thailand, Laos, and other countries of South East Asia. Mexico also contributes, especially to the US scene. Sources, routes of supply, and location of refinement plants change according to the exigencies of law enforcement successes, weather, demand, and the activities of rival gangsters.

Raw opium is obtained from the seed capsule of the poppy, *Papaver somniferum*. When this is slit after the petals have fallen, a white juice oozes out which soon thickens and darkens to a tar-like substance with a bitter taste and pungent smell. This is scraped off and boiled in water for several hours, then strained and evaporated to a thick paste called prepared opium which can be rolled into balls or squashed into bricks. Active ingredients, including morphine, codeine, papaverine, and thebaine, make up about a quarter of this material by weight, and medicinal opium has to contain a minimum of 10% of morphine by weight. When smoked, up to half of the material is left behind in the pipe as a charred powder. This 'opium dross', rich in carcinogens, is usually recycled by boiling it up with the next batch of raw opium.

It is estimated that more than 5000 tonnes of illicit opium was prepared in 1996, an entirely typical year. About a third is consumed as opium, the rest is converted into heroin. Smugglers much prefer the latter since it is odourless and much less bulky.

Street heroin reaches the user by what amounts to a massive pyramid-selling operation. The importer has contact with a number of distributors who connect with people who will buy a few pounds in weight, who in turn sell to others in ounces. These ounce dealers are often users themselves. The next level consists of street users who can afford to buy several grams at a time and then parcel them out in smaller and smaller quantities, right down to the lowly £10 bag or wrap. The drug becomes more adulterated (cut, stepped on) at almost every point of this journey. So most heroin users are also dealers at some level, even if the profit simply goes towards funding their own habit.

Substances which have been identified in street heroin range from the relatively harmless – mannitol, glucose, lactose, and sucrose; the not so harmless (especially to the intravenous user) – caffeine, ephedrine; and the potentially lethal – talcum powder, flour, brick dust, Ajax, barbiturates, and strychnine.

Heroin base (diamorphine not attached to a hydrochloride salt) vaporizes at a much lower temperature and is therefore preferred for smoking or 'chasing' (see below), and is often mixed with barbitone or caffeine which both increase the diamorphine content of the vapour. Brown heroin is more likely to contain a proportion of base than white.

Prepared opium for smoking seems to be making something of a comeback in the West, and is usually presented as a material resembling treacle, or compressed into tablets or sticks. It gives off a pungent odour recognizable at a dozen paces by those in the know. In some parts of the world, arsenic is still added to prepared opium in the belief that it is an effective tonic and aphrodisiac. Pharmaceutical preparations of opium for medicinal use are still available.

A small number of patients receive pharmaceutical diamorphine on prescription as a white powder in 'dry amps', since diamorphine decays quite quickly in solution. These appear on the black market from time to time. Most addicts on prescription receive methadone as a green, rather sticky mixture, or less commonly in ampoules for injection. This will cost around £10 for 100 ml of mixture or £5 an amp on the street corner. Pharmaceutical morphine does not seem very popular with addicts unless formulated with the antivomiting drug cyclizine, but Palfium and Diconal tablets are highly sought after. Various milder opioids all have some black-market value, and proprietary cough medicines containing small amounts of morphine or codeine come in handy to fend off withdrawal if street supplies run short. Buprenorphine is particularly fashionable in some parts of the country.

Scientific information

Terminology for the derivatives of opium can be rather confusing. Narcotic (derived from the Greek word meaning stupor) is a misleading term because it does not reflect the principal activity of the drug. Some people use the term 'opiate' for those drugs directly obtained from opium, and 'opioid' for all other morphine-like compounds. For simplicity, the author uses the latter term to represent all drugs, natural or synthetic, with a morphine-like action.

It had first been suggested in the 1960s that the opioids might act through binding with specific receptors in the nervous system, and several were identified soon after. The function of these receptors in nature was clarified by the discovery of the 'brain's own opiates' in 1975. It became apparent that certain peptides (basic building blocks of protein made up of strings of amino acids) are produced by the body in response to pain and modulate its perception. They achieve this by acting as short-lived chemical messengers in the brain and elsewhere, modifying and shaping the effects of serotonin, dopamine, and noradrenaline. These peptides were given the collective title 'endorphins' and several have been isolated, including met- and leu-enkephalin, dynorphin, and the rather unimaginatively titled peptide-E.

The opioids latch on to 'receptors' on nerve cells where the endorphins would normally roost and influence the function of the nerve, either by altering the flow of chemicals across the cell membrane and hence its electrical polarity, or by modifying the release of other chemical messengers. The picture is further confused by the fact that different opioids vary in the way they affect a receptor. Some stimulate it and produce a positive effect (agonists); others sit on the receptor and block it without turning the system on (antagonists); a third group are capable of bringing about either of these outcomes (partial agonists). Sometimes, it is difficult to predict which effect will predominate in this third group. For example, if buprenorphine (third group) is given to a heroin (first group) addict, it may either intoxicate the person or induce a withdrawal reaction.

Opioids exert a mainly inhibitory effect within the brain and nervous system, with a wide range of results. Perception of, and concern about, pain is reduced; the pupils are constricted; drowsiness or sleep is induced with larger doses; anxiety, panic, and fear are inhibited, as is the 'fight and flight' mechanism; the cough reflex is suppressed; breathing is depressed; and body temperature is reduced.

Sex hormones are reined in, whilst prolactin and growth hormone are increased. Peripheral blood vessels relax and blood pressure falls, the guts slow down, the muscles loosen, and the sphincters tighten. In short, the organism slows up and a state akin to brief hibernation ensues.

Most opioids are not very effective when taken by mouth because the liver neutralizes most of the dose before it can reach the brain. An exception to this is methadone (synthesized in 1941 by German chemists) which also lasts much longer in the body. It takes 24 hours or more for the level in the blood to fall by half, compared with four hours for most other opioids. These properties have led to methadone being the most widely prescribed substitute opioid for addicts in treatment.

There is no evidence that opioids directly damage the unborn baby but they do cross the placenta, so neonates may be slow to breathe, or show withdrawal symptoms if the mother was taking them regularly. They also enter breast milk and may sedate the infant.

Medical uses

Some of the more commonly used opioids are listed below. The roughly equivalent dose to 10 mg morphine (a fairly modest painkilling dose) is given in brackets: diamorphine (heroin, 4 mg); codeine (120 mg); hydromorphone (Dilaudid, 1.5 mg); hydrocodone (10 mg); pethidine/meperidine (Demerol, 100 mg); dextromoramide (Palfium, 7.5 mg); dipipanone (Diconal, 10 mg); methadone (10 mg); buprenorphine (Temgesic, 0.4 mg). The main uses of opioids in medicine today are in the treatment of severe pain, premedication for surgery, suppression of cough and diarrhoea, and for the alleviation of a particular form of heart failure in a hospital setting.

After an adequate dose by intravenous or intramuscular injection (at least 10 mg for an average-size adult), morphine is effective against pain within minutes and lasts for three or four hours. It is well known that many patients suffer needlessly in hospital because of a fear amongst doctors of inducing addiction. In fact, this is vanishingly rare in patients treated for pain: approximately one in 100 000 treatments in one series.

Opioids are very safe drugs in ordinary medical practice, except in overdose when depression of breathing may be life-threatening. If recognized, this can easily be reversed by injections of the opioid antagonist naloxone. Since this has a very short duration of action, it may have to be given repeatedly until the opioid has worn off. The danger of fatal respiratory depression is greatly increased if other brain depressants such as alcohol, tranquillizers, or antidepressants have been taken as well. People with lung complaints or liver disease are particularly vulnerable to this dangerous effect.

Repeated doses may be associated with increasing resistance to many effects of the drug (tolerance), necessitating larger doses to achieve the same result. Some effects, such as constipation and pupillary constriction, do not exhibit tolerance.

Recreational use

Current estimates are that around 500 000 Americans and between 100 000 and 150 000 Britons are dependent upon injected opioids (see footnote, p. 3). It is important to note that this is the number of *visible* opioid users. They are visible either because they have presented to doctors or others requesting help, or have come to the attention of the police; by definition, they are 'problem drug users'. Research indicates that a larger number of opioid users remain invisible. As many as 1% of the adult American population will admit to having used opioids recreationally at least once, and the 1996 British Crime Survey gives an identical figure. One study suggests that as many as three million Americans may use opioids from time to time, only about 10% of whom could be described as being addicted. These intermittent, non-dependent individuals have been called 'chippers'. It is probable that only 10–15% of opioid addicts are in contact with the health services at any one time.

Four times as many opioid addicts were notified to the British Home Office in 1990 than was the case in 1980, though this may just indicate greater diligence on the part of doctors, and the number has increased by a further 75% over the past five years. Heroin was the primary drug in nearly three-quarters of these cases. In 1997, the legal requirement for doctors to notify opioid addicts was cancelled and the Home Office register terminated. The amount of heroin seized has risen consistently over the years, increasing from 494 kg in 1991 to 1395 kg in 1996; and 4263 people were convicted in the UK in 1995 for opioid-connected offences, with heroin as the key drug in 99% of these cases. Average purity of seized material was 43%, and prices remain static at about £80 per gram. American street heroin only costs about $80–100 a gram but it is generally much less pure, containing as little as 3–5% diamorphine.

Opioid use is common among convicted criminals, most of whom have a record which antedates their drug use. One study revealed that 28% of the inmates of a Scottish prison were intravenous drug users prior to their incarceration. Eight per cent had injected drugs at least once in prison, and of these three-quarters had shared injecting equipment. Heroin is not difficult to come by in prison, but injecting equipment can be in short supply. Ex-prisoners say that dozens of inmates will sometimes share a single needle and syringe – a truly terrifying prospect in the era of HIV and hepatitis C.

Heroin is by far the most sought-after opioid throughout most of the world, though opium remains dominant in Asia. British street heroin (known as gear, smack, skag, H, junk, brown) usually consists of an off-white or brown powder, although it may occasionally be granular in consistuency. It has a bitter taste, which may be artificially heightened by the addition of quinine. The powder can be snorted up the nose, smoked in a cigarette, vaporized off heated foil ('chasing the dragon'), or dissolved and injected ('fixed'). Most of the people who seek help with drug problems either inject or chase.

Chasing involves heating some powder on creased silver foil and inhaling the fumes through a tube of rolled foil or, for those with less steady hands, the outer case of a match box. Chasing is quite a skill. The amount of heat applied has to be just right so as to get the heroin to liquefy and run along creases to avoid charring. At the same time the tube has to be manipulated to follow and inhale the wisp of vapour that resembles a dragon's tale. Opening up the foil tube reveals smoke deposits which can be vaporized in their turn to minimize waste. The rush (sudden wave of euphoria) achieved by this method is almost as good as that obtained by injection. On the other hand it is less economical since some of the smoke is lost into the atmosphere, and demands better-quality heroin. Quite apart from this, some people find that the act of sticking a needle into themselves becomes an essential part of the reward process.

The availability of heroin with a high content of diamorphine base, and therefore better for chasing, seems to be increasing. Chasers tend to be younger and less likely to be experiencing legal or medical problems. They constituted more than two-thirds of all 'invisible' heroin users in a recent Oxfordshire survey.

Injectors usually mix the powder with water in a spoon, heat the mixture and add a little acid in the form of lemon juice or citric acid to get it to dissolve, then draw it into the syringe through a small piece of cotton wool (or a cigarette filter) to get rid of the larger chunks of undissolved matter. This is a particularly important part of the operation when one is injecting ground-up tablets which contain large amounts of chalky material. When times are hard, junkies will boil up their 'cottons' to extract every last bit of intoxication or comfort from their investment. The next step is to apply a tourniquet ('tie off'), locate a vein, and 'shoot up'. Many people have the habit of drawing blood back into the syringe once or twice ('booting') to ensure that all the material has been absorbed.

There are thousands of first-hand descriptions of the opioid experience in print. Here is one from a 19th-century physician who was a frequent indulger:

> 'A sensation of fullness is felt in the head, soon followed by a universal feeling of delicious ease and comfort, with an elevation and expansion of the whole moral and intellectual nature which is, I think, the most characteristic of its effects ... the intellectual faculties are raised to the highest point compatible with individual capacity. It seems to make the individual, for the time, a better and greater man. The hallucinations, the delirious imaginings of

> alcoholic intoxication are, in general, quite wanting.
> Along with this emotional and intellectual elevation, there
> is also increased muscular energy; and the capacity to act,
> and to bear fatigue, is greatly augmented.'

The modern chaser or injector will experience a powerful rush of pleasure, perhaps amounting to ecstasy, as the drug washes over the brain. This subsides into a delicious, relaxed, dreamy, cocooned feeling as anxieties and fears melt away. The user's head may droop and his eyes close as he goes 'on the nod' or 'gouches out'. The body feels heavy and warm. If problems come into the mind at all, they are suffused with optimism and confidence that all will turn out well. Unless over-dosed into unconsciousness the mind remains active, though it may appear otherwise to an observer. Nausea and vomiting may occur, especially in inexperienced users. Diconal has a more 'wiring' stimulant effect. The best high of all is said by some to be produced by a mixture of heroin and cocaine in the same syringe – the famed and potentially lethal 'speedball'.

Many addicts are quite blasé about their experience with heroin, and downplay the ecstasy angle considerably. After a while, they say, you are taking the drug just to 'stay straight'. Others tell you they are either stoned or 'clucking' (withdrawing) with no happy medium. Emotions are suppressed in the regular user who is detached and insulated from all cares and worries. Instead of the usual array of problems that life presents, the addict must face only one – where's the next hit coming from?

Unwanted effects

When used medically, opioids are remarkably safe drugs. Unwanted effects are for the most part minor and include nausea and vomiting, reduced appetite, constipation, drowsiness, and apathy. Much more rarely patients may experience dry mouth and sweating, allergic reactions, difficulty in urinating, or problems due to spasm of various tubes leading from the liver to the intestines or the kidneys to the bladder. For the great majority of patients with serious pain, the beneficial effects vastly outweigh the nuisance of any side-effects that do occur. Recreational users, naturally, may also experience these effects from time to time.

In overdose, of course, the opiates are anything but safe. Depression of breathing can easily lead to a fatal outcome if not recognized and treated, drowsiness may progress to unconsciousness, and the blood pressure may fall so low that vital organs are starved of oxygen. Some opioids have particular risks in overdose; for example, pethidine can induce fits.

The uncertain strength and purity of street drugs make accidental overdose an ever-present hazard. It is thought that three out of four regular injectors have experienced this at least once, and four out of five have been present when someone else has seriously overdone it. This is particularly likely if other depressants such as alcohol or sedatives have also been taken. Unfortunately, there is a reluctance to summon help in such circumstances and well over half the deaths among heroin addicts are due to overdose, accidental or otherwise. Onlookers often attempt a home-remedy approach with cold showers or injections of amphetamine or cocaine, and 80% of those with a fatal outcome are already dead when the ambulance arrives. A typical victim would be a man in his late twenties with many years of heroin use under his belt, but about one in five fatalities occur in non-addicted users.

The number of people asking for help with opiate addiction steadily increased through the 1980s: 61 689 presented to British drug dependency units in 1989 compared to 13 905 in 1985. It is a condition with a considerable mortality, with 2743 deaths in America directly attributable to opioid abuse in 1989, which accounted for 38% of all drug-related deaths (cocaine accounted for 50%). Most studies suggest an annual mortality among injecting opioid users of between 1% and 3%, which represents a six- to 20-fold excess in mortality rate.

It is difficult to use opioids without becoming addicted to them. Undoubtedly some people do manage it, but little is known about them because they mostly remain invisible to services. Those who are coping successfully with their lives do not need the help of doctors or social workers. It is therefore unwise to build a picture of a typical opioid user based on those who stagger through the doors of drug dependency units or pester GPs incessantly for prescriptions. This would be as misleading as trying to understand social drinking on the basis of conversations with a group of skid-row alcoholics.

So what do we know about these non-addicted opioid users ('chippers')? First, we have no real idea how many there might be. It has been suggested that there may be more chippers than addicts, and certainly most dependent users say they know people who can use heroin intermittently. Population surveys suggest that far more people experiment with heroin than ever become addicted or require treatment. It must be the case, therefore, that many people are able to experiment a few times and avoid going on to regular use. What is less certain is whether it is possible to use intermittently for long periods without becoming hooked. Are such intermittent users simply in a transitional state on a path to either giving up or becoming addicted?

Research suggests that intermittent use is determined more by an ability to build the drug into a social ritual than by personality factors or family background. For example, a person may limit heroin use to a particular time and place, and separate it completely from family life and the social circle this includes. On the other hand, common sense dictates that the more heroin (or any other drug) is able to compensate for deficiencies or disadvantages that distress a person, the more difficult it is going to be for that person to relinquish the drug or use it sparingly.

How do chippers differ from addicts? Most retain jobs, homes, and families. They are unlikely to be involved in criminal activities, except a minority who take part in some drug dealing, usually on a small scale. Most restrict their heroin to once or twice a month, with 20% using less frequently and 20% using weekly. Around one in five give a history of addiction at some time in the past.

Knowledge gained from observations of heroin use by American servicemen in Vietnam is relevant to this discussion. Heroin was accessible and cheap, and large numbers of GIs snorted, smoked, and even injected it during their active service. Moreover, with a purity of over 90% (compared with 5–10% on the streets of New York), this was highly potent material. Despite this easy availability of high-quality heroin, most of these individuals never became hooked and did not use it on leave in the US, or when their tour of duty finished. Of those that did become addicted in Vietnam, only 20% ever used in the US. Even among those who did go on to use back home, only about 12% were addicted there and only 1% were still using the drug a year after their return.

Even intermittent users of street heroin expose themselves to considerable immediate risk, however, especially if they choose to inject it. Variations in diamorphine content may result in accidental overdose and people who have either not developed the tolerance that comes from daily use or have lost it by cutting back on their intake for one reason or another may actually be more vulnerable to this. This risk was confirmed by a study which compared morphine content of the hair of individuals who had died of heroin overdose with that of active heroin addicts and a sample of ex-addicts (hair analysis gives a measure of average drug intake over several months). Morphine content from the hair of the fatalities was similar to that of the ex-addicts and very much lower than that of the addicts who were still using. Poisoning by adulterants and impurities is always possible, and life-threatening infections can fulminate in the bloodstream (septicaemia) or take hold within the heart, liver, lungs, bones, or brain. Local skin infection leading to abscesses is commonplace. Sharing needles or syringes is one of the most important ways in which infectious hepatitis and the human immunodeficiency virus (HIV) which leads to AIDS are passed on.

Opioids cause both psychological and physical dependency. The former involves an intense desire for the drug (craving), and a reorganization of one's life around ensuring a regular supply. The latter refers to the physical symptoms which appear when the drug is no longer available. Once addiction is established, people will go to extraordinary lengths to maintain their habit. Consideration of the rights of others or the consequences to their own life and well-being tends to go out of the window.

You have to work at building up a physical dependence on heroin as it is not something which develops after a few fixes. People vary considerably in their vulnerability, but a couple of weeks at least of daily use are likely to be needed. The usual pattern is a gradually increasing frequency of intermittent use over many months, with a blithe confidence that, despite everybody's warnings, 'I can handle it'. Tolerance to the drug's effect, and the consequent steady increase in dose, starts the process rolling. The early signs of dependence, often confused with a particularly stubborn headcold, are explained away somehow. The realization of addiction comes with a jolt as insight breaks through. At this stage the person has to decide whether to seek help or increasingly embrace the 'junkie' lifestyle. At any one time in America, there are likely to be around 200 000 people receiving treatment for opioid addiction, and a further 100 000 in prison for opioid connected offences.

Even when addiction has taken hold, it is clear from historical analysis and some modern case histories that as long as a regular supply of pharmaceutically pure drug is available, and the personality of the addict is adaptive, a productive lifestyle remains entirely possible. For example, there are a number of documented cases of doctors having long and sometimes highly distinguished medical careers whilst addicted to huge doses of intravenous morphine or heroin. Indeed, one famous example asserted that his illustrious achievements would have been impossible *without* morphine, which he believed increased his stamina and capacity for hard work.

When an addict is denied heroin for one reason or another, a predictable withdrawal syndrome develops. Roughly eight hours after the last dose, the person is aware of increasing anxiousness, restlessness, and irritability. There is intense desire for another hit or chase. The victim yawns, stretches, sweats, and the eyes and nose begin to stream, with frequent sneezing. Cramping pains in the abdomen gather momentum, nausea comes on in waves, and the sufferer may be embarrassed by uncontrollable diarrhoea. Trembling, deep aching in the bones and muscles, terror, and insomnia complete the wretched picture. The skin is pale, clammy, and covered in goosebumps ('cold turkey') and the legs twitch and thrash in the bed ('kicking the habit'). Very rarely, there may be fits or a confusional state with delusions and hallucinations.

These unpleasant but not life-threatening symptoms are at their height for two or three days then gradually pass off over the next couple of weeks, although sleep disturbance and a feeling of not being quite right sometimes persists for many weeks. Onset and recovery can be delayed if the addict has been taking regular methadone because of this drug's long duration of action. Although the syndrome is certainly unpleasant, most addicts have a disproportionate fear of 'clucking' and their whole life is organized around ensuring at all costs that it doesn't occur. Unfortunately, the exigencies of street life mean it will have to be faced on numerous occasions in an average addiction career.

The lifestyle of an addict often involves poor nutrition and living conditions, and a general lack of self-concern. Women may be driven to exchange sex for drugs, or to take up prostitution to support a habit or keep a family together. It can be very hard for addict parents to give their children the physical and emotional nurturing they need, but many somehow manage to achieve this. Some could benefit from seeking assistance and support from their local drug service, but hesitate to do so for fear that their children will be taken away from them. In fact, this occurs very rarely. These days, doctors, nurses, and social workers will be concentrating on providing the sort of practical help which will enable these parents to cope more effectively with the problems of family life.

It is not surprising with all these hardships that addicted intravenous users have a high incidence of physical and mental health problems. Quite apart from the risks of overdose and poisoning, they are susceptible to accidents and serious infection. If a group of addicts is followed up for 10 years or so, around 15% can be expected to have died. A study in Rome showed that the death rate among male addicts was 10 times higher than among men of the same age in the general population; for women, the ratio was 20 times.

Heroin suppresses ovulation and makes pregnancy less likely, but if conception does occur special problems can arise. The addict lifestyle is hardly conducive to a relaxed pregnancy or good antenatal preparation. Poor nutrition can cause anaemia and increased susceptibility to infection. The strain of coping alone can lead to depression with a risk of self-harm.

There is no evidence that opiates cause direct damage to the fetus, although impurities in street heroin pose a threat. The main danger is premature delivery of a low birth-weight baby, and there is some increase in the risk of perinatal mortality. It is essential that the mother receives coordinated care and support throughout the pregnancy, and that steps are taken to get her off street drugs whilst avoiding withdrawal symptoms (which may cause miscarriage). This is usually achieved by switching her to methadone, and then either withdrawing this very cautiously or maintaining her at the lowest dose consistent with resisting the temptations of the black market. If the birth takes place while the mother is still receiving methadone or taking street opioids, specialist attention from a paediatrician is needed because the baby is likely to exhibit withdrawal symptoms such as irritability, twitching, diarrhoea and vomiting, or repeated sneezing during the first few days of life. The onset may sometimes be delayed for days or weeks if the mother was taking methadone. Usually the syndrome responds to simple measures such as gentle handling, demand feeding, and possibly swaddling, but tiny doses of morphine or chlorpromazine are sometimes required. If the mother has been taking large doses of opioids up to delivery, the baby may not breathe adequately or may develop fits. With appropriate medical management the immediate prospects are excellent, but the lifestyle of an addicted mother may prove hazardous to the physical and mental welfare of the developing child.

Psychiatric symptoms are common among opioid addicts presenting to drug units, but true psychiatric illness is unusual. The symptoms usually disappear spontaneously when the immediate problems related to the addiction are alleviated. True mental illness when it does occur usually antedates the addiction.

Dependency upon drugs is often the least of the problems bedevilling those who present to a drug unit. These are people who are likely to have experienced a disrupted and deprived childhood, possibly with physical or sexual abuse, and their emotional or behavioural problems usually predate the reliance upon drugs. To attribute their difficulties solely or even mainly to opioid addiction, or to hold them up as a dreadful warning to those who question the merits of the current drug laws, would be misguided.

part three

chapter 13

the nature
of addiction

Definitions

Addictus – a citizen of ancient Rome who had built up debts that could not be repaid and was therefore delivered by the courts into slavery under his creditor. That heroin and cocaine are potential slave-masters few would question, but are alcohol and tobacco to be feared in the same way? And what about tea, or sugar, or gambling?

Any individual's opinion as to the meaning of addiction is bound to be coloured to a large extent by the dominant attitudes within the culture he or she inhabits. Since these attitudes are by no means consistent across time, nation, or even quite small sub-groups within society, the concept is certain to be a slippery one. Just like our beliefs about the drugs themselves, it is based on value judgements rather than any serious grip on 'the facts'.

Being 'addicted' is to be caught up in the following sequence: an increasingly pressing desire to carry out some activity; growing anxiety and ever-increasing mental preoccupation if this is resisted or prevented; a sudden and highly rewarding elimination of tension and desire as the act is carried out; as the glow of satisfaction wears off, a resumption of the cycle all over again. It will immediately be recognized that most biological drives conform to this sequence: eating, drinking, sleeping, and having sex. But leaving aside natural functions essential for life, there are quite a lot of human activities which fulfill the addictive sequence but do not involve the ingestion of any substance. People can get over-involved in all sorts of activities from train-spotting to hang-gliding, stamp-collecting to jogging, and suffer as a result. There are people whose work compulsion is as devastating to family life as any heroin habit. All of these out-of-control behaviours can be managed in the same way as dependence on drugs or alcohol.

Obtaining consensus as to what constitutes a 'drug' is by no means easy. A pharmacologist might define it as any substance capable of modifying one or more of the functions within a living organism. Many people have difficulty in seeing their enjoyment of alcohol and tobacco in the context of drug use, let alone the oceans of caffeine-containing drinks consumed every day. Yet in Britain 200 years ago, people generally viewed coffee as a substance with a powerful (and sometimes highly undesirable) psychoactive effect, and its regular users were often looked upon with disapproval; rather similar, in fact, to the way cannabis is seen today. Myths come and go. Caffeine is now disregarded as a bland nonentity whilst cannabis is feared and vigorously suppressed.

Many definitions of addiction have been written, and there are some common strands. There is an ever-growing preoccupation which increasingly gets in the way of the ordinary priorities in life, such as family, work, and leisure pursuits. With this comes a sense of compulsion, a feeling of being driven to do something that at least in part one would prefer not to do. Routines become increasingly focused upon ensuring a ready supply, consumption becomes less dependent upon what is appropriate to the time and place and less inhibited by concern for consequences. More may be required to achieve the desired effect as tolerance develops.

If addiction is easy enough to define, explaining it is a good deal trickier. A desire to move away from rather woolly psychoanalytic concepts has led to a focus on the two independent elements of physical and psychological dependency. These concepts lend themselves to scientific research, and can prove a focus for treatment strategies.

Physical dependence can be diagnosed if a consistent pattern of bodily symptoms and signs, the 'withdrawal syndrome', develops when the drug is withheld. This phenomenon is characteristic of drugs whose primary effect is to inhibit or depress brain function, and these include alcohol, tranquillizers and sleeping pills, and opioids. Psychological dependency is manifested by a powerful preoccupation and intense longing for the drug (craving) touched off or modified by elements of the environment (cues) which have become associated in the person's mind with pleasant or unpleasant drug-related experiences. A cue could be a room, a smell, a person, a word, a syringe, almost anything.

Explanations

So far, we have only got as far as labelling what is observed. In trying to arrive at explanations, it must be accepted that there are no established truths, only more or less convincing theories. What is clear is that the old 'disease' concept of addiction has to be abandoned. The essence of this proposal is that an abstinent addict is merely in remission, so any further exposure to the offending drug would inevitably bring about immediate relapse into compulsive drug use. Reality is more complicated than this. Every clinician knows once-dependent drinkers who have evolved back into social drinking, or former speed-freaks who can now take it or leave it. Moving in and out of dependency on opioids during an addiction 'career' is more the rule than the exception. Community studies of cocaine users show that the commonest natural history in those who never seek treatment (and would thus still be 'invisible' if they had not been uncovered by field research) is to escalate consumption gradually to a peak, then decrease to a much lower level which may be maintained for a considerable period.

Explanations of addiction generally fall into three categories: biological, psychological, and socio-cultural.

Biological factors

Biological theories concentrate on the many ways in which drugs and their breakdown products (metabolites) can interfere with the transmission of chemical or electrical messages in the brain and nervous system, or alter the balance of neurological function.

The discovery of the endorphins (the brain's own opiates) in the 1970s brought home the possibility that drugs may compensate for an inborn or acquired chemical deficiency. These endorphins are chemical messengers made in nervous tissue and released in response to painful, frightening, or satisfying experiences (e.g. sexual intercourse). They turn off aversive (unpleasant) messages and mediate reward. Intuitively, it is highly desirable to have an abundant supply at your disposal. If you are deficient in endorphins and happen to be exposed to opioids, or short of dopamine and exposed to amphetamine, it seems logical to suppose that you will be particularly sensitive to the rewarding or aversion-reducing effect. We know from research into depression that people can be naturally low in certain chemical messengers (for example, serotonin), and that this may increase their susceptibility to suicide. Perhaps this deficiency could be genetically programmed, an idea which finds some support in animal experiments. This finding has prompted the suggestion that some addicts may be no more to blame for their state than diabetics. Just as a diabetic needs insulin to maintain normal functioning, perhaps the endorphin-deficient junkie needs heroin and the dopamine-starved cocaine snorter must have his stimulant.

Biological systems are programmed to restore themselves to their original state when perturbed (known as homoeostasis). When the balance is upset by an external agent such as a drug, compensatory mechanisms cut in to restore the status quo. These might include activation of feedback mechanisms, alterations in receptor numbers or sensitivity (see below), and release of other chemicals which exert an opposing effect to the interloper.

Messages in the brain cross the gaps (synapses) between nerves by means of chemical messengers (neurotransmitters), which are manufactured and stored in the end of the nerve and released by changes in the electrical charge which is actively maintained across the nerve membrane. They pass into the gap, latch on to receptors on the other side, and cause changes in the permeability of the membrane. As a result of this, electrically charged chemicals are allowed to move in or out of the cell, which reconverts the impulse to an electrical wave. There are also receptors on the proximal side of the gap (pre-synaptic receptors) and when the messenger combines with these, further discharge from the nerve is inhibited.

So the greater the flow of chemicals into the gap, the greater the activity of these pre-synaptic receptors in inhibiting further release. This sort of mechanism is called a 'negative feedback loop'. Perhaps heroin could induce a long-term shortage in endorphins by such an action, and cocaine a persistent impairment of dopamine function. Maybe it is this secondary deficit state which drives drug-seeking behaviour.

The number of the various receptors, and their sensitivity, are not fixed. They can be influenced by drugs themselves, or by the effect these have on naturally occurring brain chemicals. If a drug produces a push in one direction, the brain may increase its output of a chemical which is directly oppositional. This chemical merry-go-round finds tangible manifestation in a wide variety of symptoms, behaviours, or emotions.

Withdrawal syndromes may be due to the chemical imbalance left behind as a drug wears off. For example, one of the effects of opioids is to suppress the activity of noradrenaline in the brain. If an opioid such as heroin is taken regularly over a long period, the noradrenergic system becomes distinctly lazy. As the drug wears off and the restraint is removed, it springs back into life with a vengeance. Indeed, the effect is very much like the release of a spring in that there is initially an overshoot. The system becomes hyperactive for a while before settling back to its pre-drug level, and this period of hyperactivity gives rise to many unpleasant symptoms.

Of course, the chemical messenger which is boosted or suppressed by a drug may express itself through psychological rather than physical manifestations. Drugs such as cocaine and amphetamine which are not so obviously associated with physical dependency are certainly capable of inducing very powerful mental effects on withdrawal. These are just as closely related to chemical changes in the brain as the 'cold turkey' of opiate addiction.

But what if these homeostatic mechanisms fail, either due to the slow recovery rate of suppressed systems or some sort of permanent damage within nerves as has been noted in animal studies with amphetamine, cocaine, and MDMA? An example of the former mechanism may be found in the case of the benzodiazepines. Some people who try to give them up after years of repeat prescriptions find that distressing symptoms persist for months, if not years.

Some researchers believe this may be due to long-term changes in the cell membrane receptor complexes associated with a particular inhibitory chemical messenger, gamma amino butyric acid (GABA). Dependency could then be explained as a manifestation of the need for a drug simply to restore normal physiological harmony, just to feel normal. Both this concept, and the inherent deficit model, suggest that the logical response to addiction is long-term replacement therapy.

A fascinating discovery of the 1980s was the identification of a brain pathway concerned with the mediation and experience of pleasure and the drive to seek novel experiences. Pleasurable activities are associated with the revving up of a particular bundle of dopamine-containing nerves originating deep within the roots of the brain and projecting widely through a blob of cell bodies called *nucleus accumbens* to parts of the brain concerned with emotion, pain interpretation, memory, and reasoning (the ascending ventral-tegmental dopaminergic system, VTDS). If a tiny electrode is implanted into the VTDS of an animal, and the animal is then given the opportunity to stimulate itself electrically by repeatedly pressing a bar, it will choose to do this with tremendous enthusiasm and persistence in preference to other rewarding activities such as eating, mating, or sleeping. Indeed, the animal will press the bar many hundreds of times to achieve a single stimulus and, given free access, is likely to go on pressing the bar until exhaustion or even death supervenes. Many drugs capable of producing addiction turn out to have a powerful stimulatory effect within this pleasure pathway. Perhaps craving might be the result of activation of memories of past stimulation of the pathway induced by exposure to environmental cues.

One of the most potent drugs in stimulating the pleasure pathway is cocaine, but there is a price to pay. Animal experiments suggest that it may permanently damage the system so that it remains depleted of dopamine. This might account for the clinical observation that some long-term cocaine users experience a prolonged reduction in their ability to obtain pleasure from life after giving up the drug. Ironic indeed if it turned out that pursuit of the ultimate pleasure led to the destruction of the means of experiencing it.

Recently it has become clear that nicotine has a direct effect on the reward pathway, where the depression in reactivity on stopping smoking is every bit as great as that seen in opioid and cocaine withdrawal. Small wonder then that newly abstinent smokers feel so wretched. It has also been observed that nicotine receptors in the pathway rapidly become desensitized and unresponsive, but that this effect is itself very fleeting with sensitivity fully restored after a few hours of abstinence. This may explain why for many smokers the most pleasurable cigarette is the first of the day.

An interesting phenomenon that can be explained by the existence of a pleasure pathway is called priming. Exposure to a small dose of an addictive substance can spark off a full relapse into addiction in abstinent subjects, an observation that formed a major plank in the now-unfashionable disease theory of addiction. Priming can be demonstrated in previously addicted but currently drug-free animals trained to bar-press for reward. A small micro-injection of morphine delivered into the VTDS will immediately reinstate compulsive bar-pressing to obtain cocaine. The theory is that anything which tickles up the pleasure pathway will spark off a 'positive appetitive state' with subsequent drug-seeking behaviours. Note that it does not have to be a dose of the favoured drug; anything which twitches the VTDS will do. An obvious implication concerns the possible role of everyday drugs such as caffeine and nicotine which may be capable of this 'tickling-up' process. Coffee or tobacco could then be covert factors in inducing relapse in abstinent heroin or cocaine addicts. Recent work suggests that the tickling-up effect in the VTDS can also be induced by environmental cues associated in the addict's mind with previous drug use.

Of course, the role of the VTDS can only offer a partial explanation of addictive behaviour in humans, most of whom do not respond to cocaine in the same way as experimental animals. Most reasonably well-adjusted humans who snort cocaine a few times do not go on to sacrifice everything to the drug. The ability to think abstractly, to weigh up cost–benefit analyses, to defer reward, and to place social obligations alongside the satiation of basic appetites usually provides an effective counterbalance against primitive messages from the pleasure pathway.

What about drugs that are clearly addictive but appear to have little activity in this pleasure system, such as benzodiazepines (tranquillizers)? There is some evidence of the existence of a separate brain system which could underlie the mechanism for the relief of distress as distinct from the appreciation of reward. It makes sense that drugs which are able to neutralize punishment (depression, fear, pain, anxiety) might be every bit as addictive as those which magnify pleasure.

Another recent discovery may prove important in explaining the extraordinary addictive power of cigarettes in the absence of anything much in the way of a pleasurable sense of intoxication. Mono-amine oxidase type B (MAO(B)) is an enzyme which breaks down dopamine, which as we have seen is closely associated with the appreciation of pleasure. Brain levels of MAO(B) have been found to be 40% lower in regular smokers than non-smokers, a reduction which reverts to normal after a period of abstinence. The cause of this suppression is not nicotine itself, but some as yet unidentified component of tobacco smoke. This induced deficit does not seem acutely rewarding in itself, but a longer-term effect may be to increase the 'pleasure tone' within the brain. It might also be an additional priming effect (see above) which could enhance the reward from other enjoyable activities or euphoric drugs. Could this be one explanation of the strong link between smoking and heavy drinking, and the fact that illegal drug use is much more common in smokers? If so, tobacco, not cannabis, could turn out to be the true 'gateway drug'.

A final example of the role of biology concerns the way in which the body transports and breaks down drugs. It is well known that people differ greatly in their reaction to alcohol. Some can down vast quantities and never even pay the penalty of a hangover, whilst others get a crashing headache after a half-pint of shandy. One reason for this discrepancy is the individual variation in the balance of breakdown products (metabolites) emanating from the liver and other disposal mechanisms. If a person happens to be physiologically programmed to produce lots of acetaldehyde (an unpleasantly toxic metabolite of alcohol) but less good at moving it rapidly on to the next stage in the metabolic process, the unpleasant symptoms which result will ensure that the overall effect of toping will be most unrewarding. Such a person would be extremely unlikely to progress to excessive drinking and addiction. On the other hand, an unusually efficient metabolism might necessitate the consumption of large amounts simply to get as mildly tipsy as one's less well-endowed companions. Since it is known that the enzyme systems that drive these metabolic processes are genetically determined, it might be expected that such characteristics might run in families and this indeed turns out to be the case. Genetics are not the only possible explanation for this observation, however, as will be explained below.

Psychological factors

Psychological models can be subdivided into psychoanalytic, behavioural, cognitive, and personality theories.

Psychoanalytical explanations Psychoanalytical explanations vary according to the school of thought – Freudian, Jungian, Kleinian, and so forth – to which the theorist belongs. Put very simply, the basic concept is that observed behaviour is the result of an interaction between external events and repressed or unconscious mental processes of which the subject remains unaware, unless and until they are revealed and interpreted by psychoanalysis. Merely tinkering with the surface behaviour, in this case drug dependency, is a waste of time. Even if you succeed in getting rid of it, the internal conflicts remain and will re-manifest in due course either in the form of relapse, or by the appearance of some other 'neurotic' activity (symptom substitution). There are various more specific explanations of addiction. Some analysts believe that addicts are regressing to unfulfilled phases of psychosexual development. Others refer to defects in personality structure such as a poorly developed 'super-ego' or retention of 'infantile thought processing'. There is talk of the search for a form of satiation that was never achieved in early childhood, of oral fixation, or anal regression. The drug user may be seen as 'fundamentally suicidal'. Attempts have been made to explain why particular individuals may be drawn to particular drugs. Heroin users, for example, experience '… a need for the ego to control feelings of rage and aggression, emotions that relate to the anal stage of psychosexual development'. The 'weak ego structure' of such an individual leads them to seek quiet and lonely lives, hence the attraction to narcotics.

There was a time when such ideas underpinned the treatment philosophy of many drug and alcohol units, but this is no longer the case. Abstract hypotheses like these do not lend themselves to scientific testing, and even analysts from within the same theoretical school often come up with completely different interpretations of the same observed phenomena. Psychodynamic treatments of addiction have not proved particularly successful, and they are very time-consuming. The psychodynamic approach can sometimes seem patronizing and judgemental. Since it hinges on the ability of some external 'expert' to understand and interpret the hidden meaning of the various behaviours and feelings, it can also have the effect of increasing the addict's sense of helplessness and passivity.

Behavioural models   Behavioural models are based upon the various forms of learning theory. Classical conditioning is familiar to most people through the efforts of Pavlov and his dogs. When a hungry dog is exposed to food (unconditioned stimulus) it salivates (unconditioned response). If a bell (conditioned stimulus) is rung on a number of occasions at about the same time the food is presented, it will be noted that after a number of exposures the dog will salivate on hearing the bell (conditioned response) even when the food is omitted. By the same process, various elements of a drug user's environment (cues) become linked to highs and lows of the drug experience. Thus a cue which has become a conditioned stimulus for euphoria may spark off positive memories of drug use, leading to craving for a repeat performance, whilst one which induces the symptoms of withdrawal will lead to drug-seeking behaviour to alleviate the misery.

Many injecting drug users find that they become extremely attached to the process of injecting, which itself becomes highly rewarding to the extent that they will sometimes inject themselves with water or other inert substances between 'live' hits. This phenomenon can be explained on the basis of classical conditioning, which also suggests a specific treatment (cue exposure and response prevention – see Chapter 14).

'Instrumental' or 'operant' conditioning is induced according to the outcome of the behaviour. Unsurprisingly, activities which have a pleasant outcome, or take away some unpleasant experience like depression or fear, are rewarding or reinforcing and are likely to be repeated.

There are a number of well-established experimental models by which one can compare the reinforcing properties of different drugs. For example, a rat or a monkey can be trained to press a bar to obtain a reward, and the number of times it is prepared to do so is a measure of the reinforcing power of that particular reward. If the reward is a small amount of amphetamine, cocaine, or heroin, a monkey will press the bar thousands of times to obtain a single dose. If allowed the choice between food or cocaine, it is likely to choose the cocaine option to the point of death. Alcohol, barbiturates, and benzodiazepines are also active in this model, but induce lower rates of bar-pressing. By comparing the number of bar presses with the results obtained from standard rewards such as access to food or water, the findings can be calibrated to the real world.

The way in which the reward is presented is also influential. You might think that a consistent, fixed relationship with the activity would be most reinforcing (i.e. compelling), with each press of the bar predictably delivering a gulp of water or chunk of food, but on this occasion common sense is misleading. It turns out in practice that the most reinforcing pattern is an intermittent, random one. This is what makes slot machines ('one-armed bandits') so amazingly addictive. Not all that surprising then to discover that these mechanical pickpockets were invented by a psychologist. He or she probably forgot to patent the idea, however.

The third form of conditioning is vicarious learning, through contemplation of what happens to others. This 'modelling' can take place after observing the behaviour of family or friends, or activities portrayed in the media. Analysis of the effect of advertising confirms that compelling images such as the 'Marlboro man' do actually succeed in associating, in this case, the act of smoking with feeling tough, fearless, and independent. Repeatedly seeing the heroes (or anti-heroes) of films puffing contendedly on cigarettes or gulping whisky has a measurably reinforcing effect on viewers of all ages. This form of learning can have a powerful influence in unforeseen directions. An infamous government-funded anti-drug propaganda programme (*Heroin screws you up*) backfired because instead of causing adolescents to recoil in horror, it provided an association between heroin and the exciting concept of rebellious youth daringly rejecting the uncool, wholesome way of life represented by their parents and teachers.

Psychologists have models to explain all of the important components of dependence, such as withdrawal, intoxication, and craving. Many of these are very convincing though complicated and beyond the scope of this book (and often the comprehension of its author). A point worth noting is that psychological mechanisms may play a vital role even in outcomes which appear at first sight overwhelmingly biological. This can be illustrated by reference to the phenomenon of tolerance. Regular, repeated exposure to most drugs of abuse leads to increasing resistance to some or all of their effects. Larger doses are required to achieve the same result, and the individual can eventually tolerate doses that would kill an inexperienced user. Pharmacologists can put forward several explanations for this, pointing to alterations in the way the body is metabolizing the drug, changes in the number or sensitivity of receptors, and homeostatic responses from brain systems with oppositional effects to those of the drug. A simple experiment illustrates that there is more to this than basic physiology. If an animal is exposed to gradually increasing doses of morphine in a completely consistent environment, it will eventually tolerate a huge dose without discomfort, as one would expect. If it is then moved to an unfamiliar place and given exactly the same dose, it will keel over and die of overdose as if it were a drug-naive animal. It has also been noted that addicted rats which have been withdrawn from opiates become rehooked much more quickly in the cage associated with the previous addiction. These observations show that what the animal has learnt to expect powerfully shapes what actually happens.

Cognitive theories   Cognitive theories focus on the way people interpret their experiences in life, and account for what has happened to them. Emotions are not seen as the product of surging chemicals or the repressed unconscious, but rather as the logical outcome of particular patterns of thinking. These thoughts are usually so fleeting and familiar that the subject is completely unaware of them, and the profound effect they are having in shaping her view of the world and herself. Cognitive therapists attempt to uncover these 'automatic' thoughts, then collaborate with the patient to see how true or useful they are.

An example of how this works in practice can be illustrated by the experience of a student who suffered frequent, inexplicable bouts of gloominess which he self-medicated with cannabis. Unfortunately, the cannabis was interfering with his ability to study and satisfy his tutors, so he sought help. Asked for the most recent example of these sudden attacks, he described being gripped by one on the way to the clinic. Going back over the journey in his mind, he was able to pinpoint the onset of the mood at a particular place on the street, then remembered that at about the same moment he had nodded to an acquaintance passing in the opposite direction without receiving any acknowledgement. Invited to imagine himself back there and examine the thoughts going through his head at that moment, he eventually came up with the following sequence: 'He's ignoring me; he thinks I'm pathetic; he obviously doesn't like me; who the hell does like me?; I *am* pathetic; nobody likes me; I'm always going to be lonely.' If this interpretation of events was true, depression would certainly be a logical outcome, but is it really the most likely explanation? Perhaps the fellow simply didn't see him. Repetitive undermining thought sequences often stem from deep-seated negative beliefs the individual has about himself. Ways in which the cognitive therapist tries to get to grips with these are described in Chapter 14.

The way people explain what has happened in the past also shapes their expectations for the future. These explanations or 'attributions' can be categorized in various ways, such as internal or external, stable or unstable, specific or general. Individuals tend to be quite consistent in the way they attribute, and this 'attributional style' has a profound effect on self-concept and confidence in achieving desired goals. Imagine three people who have all failed a maths exam. One is miserable, one is apparently unmoved, the third is delighted. How is one to account for such different reactions to the same event? The first person thinks he failed because he is stupid. This attribution is internal, stable (he will still be stupid tomorrow and next year), and general (it has implications beyond the boundaries of the current event). No wonder he is miserable. The second person blames the examiner for setting such poorly worded, inappropriate questions (external, stable, specific); the result has little bearing on his ability or future. The third believes that he is destined to be a great painter (internal, stable, general) and that maths is a complete waste of his time; this result will finally convince his parents that a career in engineering, though secure, is not for him. Most 'normally' functioning individuals adopt a 'self-serving attributional bias' most of the time, giving themselves the credit when things are working out well but blaming external agencies (luck, the government, God's will) when they are not.

A self-defeating attributional style can lie at the heart of the helplessness expressed by many dependent people. Telling myself 'I've got a disease, it's not my fault, there's nothing I can do about it' is likely to be a self-fulfilling prophesy in that it gives me licence to sit back and wait for someone else to come along with a magic pill or some other passive cure. The subtle, undeclared advantages of continuing an apparently self-destructive behaviour are sometimes overlooked in the face of disadvantages which seem horrific to the observer but, perhaps contrary to what he says, have little genuine impact upon the subject. How desirable, all things considered, the 'addict' *really* regards a particular outcome, such as abstinence, is not always easy to ascertain for patient or therapist, and will obviously influence the likelihood of reaching that outcome (which may be much more attractive to therapist, employer, and spouse than the 'addict' himself). The author has put 'addict' in inverted commas here because some attributionally minded theorists regard the whole concept of addiction as a myth, preferring to see it as a form of behaviour which can be explained entirely in the context of attributions, learning, and interpersonal relationships.

Let us take as an illustration a journalist whose addiction to heroin has cost him his job and his marriage, and who now presents at a drug unit with a massive abscess on his leg from a dirty injection. He begs to be admitted for detoxification and rehabilitation, and convinces everyone that at last he has reached rock bottom and is absolutely determined to achieve an abstinent lifestyle. On the fifth day of his admission when he is through the worst, he suddenly announces he can't take any more and discharges himself. Within half an hour of leaving the ward, he has scored a gram of smack and is 'on the nod' in a lavatory at the bus depot. The medical team, the wife, the employer scratch their heads, and wonder at the mystery of addiction.

The difficulty here is that all these people are looking at the 'problem' from a completely different perspective to the 'addict'. They think of the pain and fear of illness, the loneliness and squalor of life in a bedsit away from the family home, the waste of a promising career. The 'addict' knows that heroin will kill the pain and take away all thought of illness. Worries about long-term risk are always displaced by immediate reward, be it ever so slight and fleeting – think of the cigarette smoker! Family life carries a ton of responsibility and frustration as well as reward and satisfaction. Being in the office at 8.30 a.m. every morning of the week, meeting a deadline for an article on New Labour's policy on the single European currency, running on the treadmill. Nobody expects a junkie to be tidy and polite, confident and cheery in the face of hassle or boredom, considerate and unselfish. How easy to let it all blow away, to compress all these obstacles and cares and worries into just one question: where's my next fix coming from? It's only when this last dilemma can no longer be answered, when the energy and organization and deviousness have ebbed away, when the will to duck and dive is finally sapped that the addict throws himself, temporarily, on the mercies of the 'caring' professions.

Two other largely cognitive ideas seem important in explaining dependency: self-efficacy and self-esteem. The former is the degree to which a person believes that she possesses the skills necessary to achieve a desired outcome. Many distressed heroin addicts, for example, can accept that giving up would be highly desirable but do not really believe that they could tolerate detoxification, manage their emotions without the cocoon of opium, or resist temptation to use again if by some miracle they did manage to pack it in. Tackling such beliefs in treatment is influential to outcome.

Self-esteem can be defined as the sense of contentment and self-acceptance that stems from a person's judgement of her own worth. People arrive at this sense by self-appraisal in a number of areas: perceived competence and ability to persevere in valued tasks; an estimation of worthiness and significance in comparison with others; perceived attractiveness to, and approval by, other people; the ability to like oneself in the absence of support from others, or in the face of active criticism and disapproval; and an idea of the value of existence in general. Many therapists in the drug and alcohol field regard low self-esteem as an important causative or maintaining factor, and essential to target in some way during treatment. If you don't like yourself, why should you care what happens in the future?

Personality theories The idea that there may be such a thing as a clearly defined 'addictive personality' carries little weight these days. Apart from the lack of any convincing research evidence that such a consistent entity exists, there was an uncomfortably pejorative feel to many definitions. By and large, personality labels do not actually explain anything, they just lead in circles. Bob murdered his mother because he is a psychopath; he is a psychopath because he murdered his mother. Experts love labels, but the trouble is that those labels can be extraordinarily undermining to their recipients.

Then there is the problem of teasing apart cause and effect. When confronted with an addict of 10 years' standing who seems to have a maladaptive or unpleasant personality, how can you be sure that this is not the effect of all that drug use rather than its cause? A more fruitful approach is to analyse the ingredients (traits) which come together to make up a personality to see if any tend to make an individual more likely to try drugs or become dependent upon them.

In studies of normally functioning adolescents, the only trait which is consistently associated with an increased likelihood of experimenting with drugs is that which relates to sensation seeking or risk taking. Those children who climb highest in a tree, ride their bike the fastest down a hill, or swim the furthest out to sea are also the most likely to try whatever drugs are going. Deviant children, those who are bunking off school and committing petty crime, also have a much higher prevalence of drug use.

Attempts have been made to pigeon-hole drug users according to some particular trait or motivation. One classification separates them into pleasure seekers, conformists (responding to peer pressure), experimenters, and self-therapists. Intuitively, it is the latter group that will be more vulnerable to dependent use. As remarked elsewhere, the more a drug is able to offer a particular individual, the more it overcomes or camouflages a deficit or weakness, the harder it will be to relinquish. Shyness, low self-esteem, poor self-confidence, boredom, fear, anger, loneliness – it is hard to go back to all that once you have found a way to push it out of sight. The more 'normal' a population exposed to a drug, the less will be the casualty rate in terms of dependent use. In the recent cocaine epidemic in the US, the proportion of individuals who became compulsive users was estimated at between 10% and 15%, a figure similar to that found with alcohol. In the population attending an average drug dependency unit the proportion would be vastly higher. This may be explicable in terms of the higher prevalence of psychological disorder or maladaptive personality traits in this latter group, or in more sociological terms.

Socio-cultural factors

Here the primary considerations are the effects of a person's family in shaping attitudes and behaviour, the nature of society itself, and the manner in which the individual and his peer group relate to these social conditions.

The family, the circle of friends, and the neighbourhood networks are crucial in both starting and maintaining drug use. It is under the influence of these structures that the individual's attitudes to drugs develop, and the first initiation characteristically takes place with a good deal of social ritual in the heart of the peer group. At the beginning of a drug career, the source of supply is almost invariably from within the immediate social circle.

Compulsive, self-destructive drug use is much more common among groups in society that are poor and deprived, and people from this sort of background are greatly over-represented amongst those seeking help from the average drug and alcohol unit. These are people with little prospect of adequate education or material advance, whose families are disrupted, who are daily exposed to a wide range of deviant or criminal behaviour, who have little to occupy their time, and who have no reason to admire the values of the affluent classes glimpsed on the street or through the television tube. It would hardly be surprising if they sought an internal escape from such a bleak reality. Yet we know from observations on American GIs in Vietnam that a simple proportionate model of drug use and addiction, that is to say that x individuals exposed to a drug will result in y addicts, doesn't work. Here, there were a number of environmental reasons that encouraged the use of heroin: the normal cultural and moral restraints were absent; familiar close interpersonal relationships were disrupted; the surroundings were alien, hostile, and frightening; heroin was cheap and easily accessible; and the immediate peer group regarded heroin use as socially acceptable and even desirable. So a large number of people used heroin, very pure material and in large amounts, and around half of these became dependent. The first point to note is that this is a much lower proportion than would be predicted from studies on a drug unit or inner-city populations. Then the fact that a considerable majority of those who did become dependent stopped using heroin immediately they returned home demonstrates that once all these sociological parameters were reversed, the 'addiction' usually evaporated.

Deviant people may start and continue to use drugs simply because it is consistent with the other illegal or antisocial activities in which they are indulging. They may be more vulnerable to heavy consumption or dependency because their particular peer group does not disapprove, or actually values it. The grungy image of the classical junkie is very attractive to some, perhaps because it gives them that sense of belonging, of having a place, that their upbringing failed to provide. Certainly a history of broken homes, emotional deprivation, or physical and sexual abuse is very common indeed among drug unit attenders.

Within any society, people cluster into groupings whose attitudes and social values differ fundamentally. The average law-abiding resident of a Newcastle housing estate would write a very different essay on 'What I think of the police' than a lawyer or accountant from Tewkesbury. Within the larger groupings there are any number of sub-cultures, each with their own goals, aspirations, and values. Membership of groups has lots of advantages: shared interests, aims, and activities to talk about and pursue together; a sense of belonging, 'us against the world'; a romantic sense of risk, perhaps, of not giving a damn, of pushing the limits all the way. Becoming delinquent is not so much a matter of consciously rejecting one lifestyle but gradually learning an alternative one which seems to deliver better results, particularly in the short term. Values and judgements learned in these groups may quickly lose their influence once the group itself has been left behind. How many successful journalists, businessmen, politicians even would have frequently taken time out from their study of economics or history of art to slip into a kaftan and pass round a joint to the strains of Purple Haze or The Incredible String Band? How many readers cannot look back with some pleasure at a period of at least part-time hippiedom or punkhood before stumbling back to the path of righteousness as greater reinforcements beckoned?

Anomie (Greek for 'absence of law') was a word used by the sociologist Émile Durkheim to describe a state in which cohesion within society has been weakened to the point that individuals begin to pursue their own goals with little concern for the 'common good'. At times, this state of affairs can almost seem to become consistent with government policy. It certainly appeared that way in the Britain and North America of the 1980s, the decade of the yuppy and the 'if you've got it, flaunt it' philosophy. Margaret Thatcher went so far as to state baldly 'there is no such thing as society'. Of course, she was merely expressing her enthusiasm for individual enterprise, but what if you happen to belong to a part of society that decidedly has *not* 'got it'. What if you can fully appreciate how agreeable it would be to have it, and can also see the majority of the population at large achieving it in some degree, but no matter how industrious or creative you may be there is no chance at all that *you* are going to get it. Let us imagine an impoverished woman in a ghetto who wishes to become a lawyer or own a Mercedes, but perceives this is beyond her reach no matter how hard she strives. A person in that position has three alternatives: lower her aspirations, and aim to get a job as a servant travelling to work on a bike; rebel, and become a terrorist or a revolutionary; or retreat, perhaps by numbing herself out with drugs. A person who chooses the latter course will have little incentive to stop using drugs even if considerable problems occur as a result.

Summary

The three important theoretical models through which one can set about explaining the observed behaviour which is labelled drug addiction are the biological, the psychological, and the socio-cultural. Whilst it is true that some 'experts' attempt to provide a complete explanation based on one of these models and discount the others entirely, the evidence suggests that they are complementary. All three are likely to play their part in any individual's dependency, though one or two may be dominant for that person. How the models underpin an approach to the treatment of dependency will be discussed in the next chapter.

Perhaps the most important thing to stress in conclusion is that addiction should not be regarded as a walled-off, stand-alone 'condition'. Rather, it is a state of mind and pattern of behaviour maintained by a precarious balance of drives stemming from the individual, with his particular genes, biochemistry, and patterns of learned behaviour, and the social and physical environment.

Some individuals, for internal and/or external reasons, are bound to be more vulnerable to becoming addicted than others, but in prospective studies of large groups of adolescents it has proved very difficult to pick out the ones most at risk with any accuracy. Once dependency is established, there is no external 'cure'. Addicts have choices and must take responsibility for their actions but, as we have seen, there are immensely powerful physical, psychological, and social forces at work which can make behaviour change very difficult. Treatment can only succeed if it takes place as a collaborative venture, with the 'addict' encouraged to be the prime mover.

chapter 14

helping problem drug users

The first step on the road to obtaining help with a drug-related problem is to recognize that one exists. Not infrequently, the person most concerned remains resolutely unaware that things are getting out of hand, and it falls to friends or family to bring it to his attention. This may be the result of 'defence mechanisms', those unconscious mental devices we all use to fend off unwelcome thoughts or inner conflicts, or simply because it isn't the user that has the problem; doing badly at school or acting like a jackass at home are, in an immediate sense, problems for teachers and family rather than the rascal himself.

Of course, it is always possible that these concerned onlookers may be confusing drug use with *problem* drug use. Whilst it is true that any flirtation with a recreational substance has the potential to become problematic in one or more of the physical, psychological, legal, or social spheres, it is far from inevitable that this will come about. Many people are able to keep things under control even while using drugs quite regularly, and don't seem any the worse for the experience.

Drugs and young people

Regular use of any drug, including tobacco and alcohol, is likely to be a risky and counter-productive activity for younger teenagers who are still developing physically and emotionally. They are more vulnerable to some of the physical and mental unwanted or toxic effects, and drug use with the rituals that surround it can interfere with, or completely disrupt, activities which open up options for the future. Having options is essential for contentment, and perhaps one of the cruellest effects of a drug-fixated lifestyle is that options dwindle away to a single track, with no passing places.

There are a number of pointers which may suggest to parents that something is amiss with their child, and that this could be related to drug use. Behaviour around the house may change. An altered pattern of sleeping may become evident, with the child pounding around late at night, then showing a greater than usual reluctance to respond to the alarm clock. A previously healthy appetite may fade with resulting weight loss, or alternatively mounds of food are tucked away. A previously placid person may become moody or unpredictable, or a live-wire appear lethargic and torpid. Concentration span or memory may be diminished. The child may seem suspicious or secretive, irritable or restless, or pale, tired, and apathetic. Hobbies and interests get abandoned, friendship patterns change.

These rather non-specific clues would carry considerably more weight if there were also reports of declining school performance, or the person had actually been seen to be clumsy of demeanour and slurred of speech. The obvious clinching factor would be the discovery of drug paraphernalia around the house, for example peculiar-looking cigarette ends, powder or plant material in twists of paper, or small plastic bags, tablets, or capsules. Regular solvent inhalers often leave a highly visible trail: odd smells coming from the bedroom or on the breath; plastic bags, cans, bottles, and rags in waste-paper baskets; spill marks on clothes or bedding, faded sleeves from surreptitious sniffing; spots or sores round the nose and mouth, cracked and dry lips, chronic cough and cold.

Discovery of needles, syringes, or ampoules would indicate that problems had progressed into a different league.

How should a parent or guardian react to evidence suggestive of drug use? The most important thing is not to *over*-react, and there are several reasons for this. Firstly, many of the earlier pointers are part and parcel of ordinary adolescence and may have nothing whatsoever to do with drugs. But even if they do, it is essential not to make matters worse by going off at the deep end and further alienating the child. Quite apart from this, there are some immediate physical risks in winding up the emotional tone in someone who is actually intoxicated. A surge of anxiety or fear (or anger) can prove fatal to someone high on glue because of the effect on the heart, and could provoke a panic attack or worse in someone deep into an LSD trip.

So first, remain calm by keeping things in perspective. Remember that your off-spring is not unique, at least a third of his or her mates will have tried an illegal drug before leaving school, and that the chances of emerging unscathed are very high. The most constructive approach is to be prepared to listen to what the child says, understand the worries and conflicts he or she is facing, and help to find practical solutions to problems. Gaining the confidence of the child, improving communication, and restoring trust will enable the parent to find out the true extent of the drug use, and develop the sort of collaborative approach that can re-establish more constructive priorities.

To change direction, a person needs to see the prospects of clear benefits resulting from that change. Threats or punishment produce only short-term, superficial responses. Factual information should flow both ways since many teenagers know a lot more about street drugs than their parents or teachers (and doctors). This is why many well-meaning drug education ventures are ineffective – when some of the content is grossly overstated or at odds with what the recipients see with their own eyes, the credibility of the whole message will be lost. The most important task is to give people the information most relevant to their immediate life-goals, and instigate peer discussion. For example, horror stories about cannabis causing lung cancer or mental illness at some point in the future will probably be discounted by school students, but the fact that it can threaten GCSE outcome or selection for the football team is more likely to capture their attention.

Once this collaborative approach is established, the practical steps taken depend on the scale of the problem. There may be health issues which necessitate a check-up from the family doctor. Broadly, the aim is to boost the offspring's confidence and self-esteem by giving a sympathetic ear and practical support, whilst avoiding wading in and taking control. Getting the person to keep a diary can be a useful way of understanding problems, and it also serves to sharpen the insight of the diary-keeper. Self-monitoring of this sort has been shown to be therapeutic as well as informative in people with out-of-control binge-eating and other counter-productive habits. Various practical ways of solving a particular problem can be discussed but the responsibility for carrying these through should always remain with the young person so that the sense of personal control and self-determination is fostered.

Parents faced with adolescent drug use should be prepared to examine their own conduct and relationships for the source of their child's troubles. It may even be necessary to examine the rest of the family's use of drugs to determine whether the 'do as I say, not as I do' factor might have got a bit out of hand. A father who regularly enjoys 10 pints with his mates or a valium-befuddled mother are hardly in a strong position to castigate a son or daughter caught in possession of a few dodgy tablets or a sixteenth of hash.

Availability of treatment

In most health districts, services will be structured on a number of levels. Health authorities try to encourage family doctors to accept that problems related to drugs (and alcohol) fall within their remit, with varying success. It is essential they do because otherwise the specialist services become completely swamped and waiting lists then extend for months. Efforts are being made to improve relevant training to medical students and to include the topic in postgraduate education programmes, and the UK government-sponsored Advisory Council on Misuse of Drugs has issued guidelines for the management of such patients by GPs and other doctors.

Any big town or city should have some sort of informal walk-in centre where people can get advice and information, education about HIV (human-immunodeficiency virus, which can lead to AIDS), counselling, or referral to relevant services. Outreach work, with streetwise individuals mingling with drug users in their natural habitat giving non-judgemental support and advice, is an important component. Such workers are often highly effective at spreading the health protection message to individuals leading risky lifestyles who are not in contact with services, and who have scant regard for the advice of middle-class 'experts' or official pronouncements.

Needles, syringes, and condoms should be made easily available free of charge from street agencies and elsewhere because of the demonstrable individual and public health benefits that result from such simple harm-reduction measures: the savings in medical and social expenditure which result from preventing a single case of AIDS would support one of these agencies for a whole year.

The threat of a worldwide epidemic of HIV has transformed the political and clinical response to injecting drug use, which has been established as a major factor in the spread of the virus. Transmission to heterosexual non-injecting partners and from an infected mother to her baby are of particular concern.

A lack of drug services can be associated with frightening consequences. In Edinburgh, for example, a culture developed among drug users in which the sharing of injecting equipment was routine. The HIV infection rate in a sample of these people in 1987 was a horrifying 52%. Twenty per cent had shared needles with users in other parts of the country. A disaster of this sort has sombre implications for the population at large. In this same city, screening of a sample of people aged between 20 and 30 attending a particular general practice revealed an HIV positivity rate of one in 14 men and one in 28 women.

Research carried out in needle-exchange clinics suggest that around three-quarters of attenders have no other contact with services, so this represents a unique opportunity to provide health education to an otherwise invisible group. Although knowledge about HIV is good among the majority of attenders, about a third seem to continue sharing needles or syringes, and only a minority use a condom with any regularity. It is still difficult to convince heterosexuals that they too are at risk of acquiring HIV. There is some reassuring evidence that people will change their behaviour in response to health education. Amongst non-attenders, however, outreach work suggests that the majority continue to share equipment from time to time despite awareness of the facts of HIV transmission. There is no evidence that easy availability of needles and syringes results in an increase in injecting drug use, though this remains a theoretical possibility. Public health risks stemming from the careless disposal of used equipment is a very real concern; insisting on exchange of old for new as far as a chaotic lifestyle will permit is the best way to counter this risk.

As we approach the end of the century, it looks as if these public health initiatives have been remarkably successful in preventing an HIV epidemic among drug users in the UK. Unfortunately, the measures have been less effective in the case of hepatitis C, a potentially fatal affliction which is beginning to assume epidemic proportions among injectors.

Strategies for smokers

The recreational drug which seems to have largely escaped therapeutic attention is the most addictive and destructive of them all – tobacco. There is an almost complete absence of NHS smokers' clinics in the UK, and this omission is replicated in most other countries. Some GP practices offer advice or counselling, but most smokers who want help have to depend upon a limited private sector which often relies upon strategies of unproven value. This lack of support is particularly unfortunate given that the spontaneous quit rate is only around 5% each year, despite the fact that three-quarters of adult smokers feel uneasy about their habit from time to time and a third of them make at least one serious but unsuccessful attempt to quit each year. Only a third of smokers manage to pack up permanently before they reach 60.

Brief interventions by GPs, consisting of health education, advice, and provision of leaflets, can increase the natural quit rate by about 2% but is likely to be effective only for light smokers. If in addition the smoker is provided with nicotine substitution in the form of gum or skin patches and put in touch with a self-help smokers' group, the quit rate is pushed up 8–10% above spontaneous rates.

Unfortunately, nicotine gum and patches are not available on the NHS. The gum delivers between 2–4 mg per stick, and is usually taken for around three months after quitting then gradually withdrawn. It relies on absorption through the lining of the mouth, which is impeded in acidic conditions caused, for example, by coffee or coca-cola. Patches come in varying strengths, and to start with a delivery of 22 mg each 24 hours is usual. After a month or so, a patch delivering 14 mg daily is substituted, then 7 mg a month after that. Nicotine can also be administered by nasal spray and inhalation aerosol. These substitutes are of proven value in reducing anxiety and depression, craving, irritability, and poor concentration. They are less successful in combating insomnia and weight gain. Fear of the latter is a major barrier to giving up for many people, especially women. Very few adverse effects have been reported, especially in the case of gum. Patches sometimes cause rashes, nausea, insomnia, or vivid dreams.

The relatively few mainstream specialist clinics which exist tend to select interventions on the basis of outcome research. Smokers at different points in their love affair with the weed require different strategies, and one widely adopted approach is to separate them into four categories. A 'pre-contemplator' is some-one happily puffing away at 20 a day without any thought or concern about possible consequences. A 'contemplator' has begun to think now and again that it would be good to cut down, experiences the occasional twinge of guilt or anxiety whilst lighting up, and dreads coming across an article about lung cancer or heart disease in the newspaper (it *could* happen to me!).

A person who is taking practical steps towards giving up has reached the stage of 'active change', whilst someone who is abstinent and struggling to stay that way is at the level of 'relapse prevention'. The point of this classification is to empha-size that the therapeutic intervention must be appropriate to the stage the person has reached. There is no future in attempting to persuade pre-contemplators to give up; the aim should be to nudge them up to the next stage, to get them to begin the process of weighing up the pros and cons of the habit. As we shall see below, this concept is applicable to other addictions.

Specialists try to form a good rapport with the smoker and then boost morale, confidence, and motivation through a variety of psychological strategies. Abrupt cessation rather than steady cutting down is generally preferred. Tackling secondary issues such as unwanted weight gain, or the role of alcohol or caffeine in cementing the habit or bringing about relapse, are very important. Nicotine replacement works best for those with high levels of physical addiction, which is signalled by lighting up the first cigarette soon after waking, difficulty in refraining even when in entirely inappropriate settings, continuing to smoke even when unwell, and smoking very regularly throughout the day whatever the circumstances. Risk factors for relapse (such as a smoking spouse) have to be identified and coping strategies worked out in advance. Self-help leaflets and hypnosis have some supporting evidence, but acupuncture remains unproven at present.

A degree of scepticism, alas, must greet claims of success. Biochemical screening (of cotinine) in one study revealed that no less than a third of smokers who claimed to have given up completely were fibbing!

Strategies for drinkers

With alcohol, it is particularly desirable to nip things in the bud before serious problems have become established. No opportunities should be lost to uncover asymptomatic heavy drinkers through screening of accessible populations among whom the prevalence of alcohol abuse is much higher than in the general population, such as attenders at general practice surgeries and hospital in-patients. Examples of screening include taking the opportunity of an unrelated consultation to ask about alcohol (and smoking) habits and checking for signs and symptoms of related disorders, handing out questionnaires to vulnerable populations, or including a liver function test or other biochemical measure when blood is taken for other reasons.

At-risk individuals identified in this way are often responsive to brief interventions from family doctors or practice nurses, with reduction of intake averaging around 24% in most studies. These reductions are associated with falls in absenteeism from work, and even mortality. A typical brief intervention consists of giving clear information about risks, firm advice to cut down or abstain, a request to keep a drinking diary (to boost insight), and a self-help booklet.

The evidence in support of more specialized treatments targeted on people who have already developed alcohol-related problems is less convincing, but alcoholics in treatment generally drink less than those untreated. However, the research does not show convincingly that intensive (and expensive) in-patient regimes are more effective than out-patient or community work. Given the huge cost of alcohol problems to society ($100 billion annually in the US, for example), there is no room for therapeutic nihilism.

For those who have become physically dependent, abrupt withdrawal carries some risk and may require medical support. For milder cases of the shakes and agitation, a long-acting benzodiazepine such as diazepam tapered off over a week or so plus some vitamin supplements will be all that is required. Full-blown delirium tremens ('the DTs') is potentially life-threatening and should be treated in hospital. Sedation, intravenous fluids, electrolytes, carbohydrates and thiamine (to prevent damage to the brain which can result in severe, permanent memory loss), and skilled nursing are likely to be required.

It seems sensible to try and separate alcoholics into different types and match treatments to individuals, but so far there is little evidence that this makes much difference. 'Dual diagnosis', the coexistence of full-blown mental illness with addiction, requires a specialized approach but symptoms of anxiety and depression which very frequently accompany alcoholism usually clear up spontaneously once the addiction is sorted out. Behavioural treatments (assertiveness and social-skills training, contracting, deconditioning, outcome reinforcement, relapse prevention) work better than insight-oriented therapy (e.g. psychoanalysis). 'Controlled drinking' rather than abstinence can be a realistic goal, especially in younger, socially stable, less physically dependent people, and women seem to do better at this than men. Marital therapy may be appropriate, and attendance at Alcoholics Anonymous also helps some people. Whatever the form of treatment, long-term, low-intensity interventions usually achieve better results than intensive, short-term measures.

Disulfiram (Antabuse) and calcium carbimide have been used for many years in an attempt to prevent relapse in abstinent alcoholics. They work by inhibiting the enzyme aldehyde dehydrogenase, which results in a rapid build-up of toxic acetaldehyde in the blood if the subject drinks. Severe vomiting and diarrhoea, and potentially dangerous increases in blood pressure, then ensue. Adverse effects of these drugs are quite unpleasant, so it is hardly surprising that compliance is usually poor and the evidence for their usefulness less than compelling.

Two newer drugs look promising. Naltrexone, an opioid antagonist, has attracted interest because alcohol has been shown to stimulate certain opioid receptors in the brain. Early indications of research suggest that abstinent alcoholics given naltrexone take longer to relapse and drink less if they do relapse than people given placebo. Acamprosate is similar in structure to the soothing brain chemical GABA, and as with naltrexone it seems significantly better than placebo at preventing relapse with minimal unwanted effects.

Strategies for illegal drug users

Harm reduction philosophy

NHS specialist services are now expected to be as accessible and 'user-friendly' as possible. The aim is to provide a rapid response tailored flexibly to the needs of the individual, but in many districts it is increasingly difficult to persuade budget-holders to maintain levels of funding in the face of competing demands. This problem is further aggravated by steady removal of 'ring-fencing' around money earmarked for drug services.

Assessment of a new patient should include a physical examination and whatever further investigations are indicated. Ideally, vaccination will be offered to injectors who test negative for hepatitis B. HIV testing, with counselling before and after the test to help people cope and come to terms with whichever result is forthcoming, should be on offer.

Chemical analysis of the urine (or blood) will detect the presence of most street drugs consumed within the last few days or, in the case of cannabis, weeks. LSD is undetectable because doses are so tiny. More recently it has proved possible to measure the drug content of hair. Like examining the rings on a chopped-down tree trunk, this can give a longitudinal picture of drug use but is rather too expensive at present for routine practice. Salivary testing is in the early stages of development.

In the case of a pregnant drug taker it is most important to give the woman accurate information about the drugs she is taking, pay special attention to her general health and emotional well-being, arrange for support with practical problems, and do all that is possible to promote a stable lifestyle. Some drugs, including barbiturates, cocaine, and amphetamine, have been linked with direct damage to the fetus. If the mother feels she simply cannot give up, or has a physical dependency, the primary aim is to wean her away from black-market drugs with a substitute prescription whilst being careful to avoid inducing withdrawal symptoms which may bring on premature labour.

The philosophy which now underpins the activities of most drug dependency units is 'harm minimization'. In the old days, DDUs were orientated towards abstinence in a fairly rigid way, so that those who came asking for help but were not ready to give up drugs right away got short shrift. These days, driven largely by public health considerations, the emphasis is on making contact with as wide a range of drug users as possible, including those who intend to go on using for the foreseeable future.

Just making contact is not much use in itself if nothing else is achieved, and the minimal requirement in the 'treatment hierarchy' is risk reduction. This involves giving advice about safer sex and injecting, including instructions on how to clean used equipment effectively if fresh 'works' are unavailable. It may be possible to provide basic health care and help with housing, child care, or legal issues. Many people present with problems partly related to drug use but partly related also to the ubiquitous difficulties of homelessness or 'bedsitterland', lack of money, and dearth of prospects. Such people primarily require practical help, not 'treatment'.

The hierarchical approach should not be taken to imply defeatism. With many individuals it will be possible to substitute oral drug use for injecting, stabilize the lifestyle to the point that detoxification becomes feasible and desirable, then go on to arrange rehabilitation or strategies to prevent relapse. What the harm-reduction approach does do is to get things into more sensible proportions. In the words of the Advisory Council on Misuse of Drugs, '… the spread of HIV is a greater danger to individual and public health than drug misuse'. Even leaving HIV aside, saving money in the short term by ignoring chaotic drug users will eventually cost the taxpayer infinitely more in hospital bills, prison and probation costs, street crime, and the break-up of families. From the perspective of the late 1990s, the strategy seems to have been strikingly successful in preventing the predicted epidemic of AIDS among injectors; unfortunately, the same cannot be said about hepatitis C which is becoming absolutely rampant.

One useful initial approach to drug users is to place them in one of four categories, as described above for smokers: precontemplation, contemplation, active change, and relapse prevention. By this means interventions are chosen according to the level of awareness and readiness for change the person has reached.

Detoxification

For those who have decided that enough is enough, medical help with detoxification may be required. This is usually the case when 'downers' such as alcohol (see above), opiates, or tranquillizers have been taken in sufficient quantity and regularity to induce physical dependence. Benzodiazepine detoxification is usually best carried out at home. If the individual is dependent upon a short-acting compound such as temazepam, withdrawal symptoms are often made more tolerable by transferring to a longer-acting drug such as diazepam before beginning the reduction. Reasons for choosing hospital detoxification would include a history of serious complications during previous detoxifications or coexisting medical or psychiatric problems.

Opiate detoxification is usually an unpleasant experience feared disproportionately by addicts, but it is not dangerous to those in reasonable health and so can usually be undertaken out of hospital. Indeed, the average addict will detoxify himself from choice or necessity many times over the months or years of his habituation. Sometimes, all that is needed is brief symptomatic treatment from the GP with lofexidine, diphenoxylate, hyoscine, metaclopramide, or benzodiazepines, or a reducing dose of opioid over a few days.

Unfortunately, detoxification in the form of steady reduction of methadone or some other opioid over days, weeks, or months in the community, or symptomatic treatment of withdrawal symptoms as described above has a low success rate. Perhaps as few as a fifth of attempters successfully resist the temptation to score from the black market. So, when resources permit, addicts are often admitted to hospital for the procedure, which traditionally consists of a three-week methadone withdrawal regime. This has quite a high immediate success rate, though many relapse shortly after discharge. It is important for the patient to be aware from the start that withdrawal symptoms are usually at their height towards the end of the procedure, and may persist at some level for many weeks. Unless warned of this, it can be most dispiriting to discover that far from feeling invigorated and born-again, the hard fought for abstinence leaves one feeling like death warmed up. Small wonder that a call to that old familiar mobile phone number may seem like the best solution. Shortening or lengthening the reduction seems to increase the drop-out rate which, interestingly enough, is not much affected by the size of the starting dose.

An alternative detoxification method is the clonidine–naltrexone technique. Clonidine specifically antagonizes many of the withdrawal symptoms while naltrexone speeds up the withdrawal process, possibly by displacing the opioid from the receptors in the brain. Apart from the advantage of a briefer hospital stay of 7–10 days, quicker if necessary, with resulting financial advantages to hard-pressed services, it has been suggested that persistent withdrawal symptoms may be less prominent. Lofexidine is a more expensive alternative to clonidine and is better tolerated by some patients, but both have to be monitored carefully because of their effects of lowering blood pressure.

Results may be influenced by whether the hospital stay is in a ward which is kept locked with strict restrictions on visitors and the coming and going of patients, or operates as an open unit. The locked ward probably achieves a higher completion rate, but may also be associated with higher levels of subsequent relapse, will not be acceptable to some potential customers, and raises civil rights issues. The open arrangement is more user-friendly but is much more likely to be bedevilled by problems associated with covert use of smuggled drugs.

Compulsive users of drugs not associated with physical dependence and people with pre-existing physical or mental illness may also benefit from a short stay in hospital. Most addiction units no longer segregate alcohol and drug users, recognizing that there are more similarities than differences between them. Detoxification on its own has not been shown to have any influence on longer-term outcome. It is only useful if it forms part of some more general treatment plan.

Substitute prescribing

For those not yet ready to abstain, some form of substitute prescribing may be indicated. Doctors vary widely in their attitude to prescribing to addicts. Some regard it as colluding with dependency and won't contemplate it under any circumstances, while others take the opposite view that heroin and cocaine for injection, smoking, or snorting should be readily available to addicts if for no other reason than to undercut the black market and undermine the profits of criminals. A consensus would be that substitute prescribing forms an essential part of any service for drug users, but that if employed indiscriminately it may encourage or worsen addiction and swell the black market, as happened in the late 1960s.

Methadone is by far the most commonly used substitute opioid. Unlike heroin, it is effective by mouth and a single dose goes on working for 24 hours, a simple routine which encourages a more stable lifestyle. Unfortunately, it is every bit as addictive as heroin itself and produces a withdrawal syndrome of equal severity. It is in no sense a cure, merely an effective palliative. Methadone itself is easy to find on the black market, and 100 mg can be bought for around £10. It is salutary to remember that heroin itself was introduced in 1898 as a cure for morphine addiction.

Providing regular methadone to someone not genuinely addicted to opioids would be to create a new addict. The wise doctor sees his patient actively withdrawing before prescribing. Indeed, the correct dose is best arrived at by titrating against visible withdrawal effects such as sweating, trembling, running eyes and nose, yawning, goosebumps, and vomiting, and increasing the dose on a daily basis as required. Once an appropriate stabilizing dose has been identified, the methadone is either reduced and stopped according to a time-scale agreed between doctor and patient, or continued long term at the same level.

Methadone maintenance is now a widely accepted strategy. Research shows that patients remain in treatment much more reliably than in drug-free programmes, and that there are a number of concrete benefits which include lower levels of drug dealing and general criminality, improved physical and mental health, more stability in family life, and lower rates of unemployment. Arguments against maintenance are that it is social manipulation rather than treatment, that it colludes with dependency, and that methadone is harder to come off than heroin. Both sides of the argument have weight, but most people involved in the field have concluded that the tangible benefits for both the individual and society greatly outweigh these ethical and theoretical objections.

Prescribed doses of methadone tend to be much larger in the US than Britain, but this is made possible by a marked difference in practice between the countries. In America, methadone is always consumed at clinics under supervision, whereas most addicts in the UK collect their prescription from a community pharmacist, sometimes on a weekly or even less frequent basis. Inevitably, some will be sold on to the black market in these circumstances, so a daily pick-up arrangement is desirable unless there are good reasons why this is impractical. In Britain, methadone is usually dispensed for oral use as a 1 mg/ml mixture which most addicts are not interested in injecting because unpleasant side-effects can be anticipated and the formulation is inconveniently dilute. Exceptions to this rule seem to be becoming less uncommon. There are no apparent toxic effects when methadone is consumed orally over long periods.

A relatively small number of addicts receive injectable prescriptions of methadone ampoules, or pharmaceutical heroin from the hundred or so doctors licensed by the Home Office to provide it. Heroin, dipipanone, and cocaine are the only three drugs which require a special licence to prescribe to addicts; any doctor can prescribe any other drug by any route. Injectables are sometimes used as a short-term measure aimed at building rapport and severing links with the black market, though some patients remain happily maintained on them for months or years. Either way, it remains a controversial practice but there seems little doubt that some people who fail with more conventional approaches achieve a stable life on injectables.

The results of a famous clinical trial of the 1970s suggest that when choosing which opioid is most appropriate for substitute prescribing, it is not a matter of which is more 'effective' but a philosophical question as to which outcome is the more culturally acceptable. Intravenous heroin was compared with oral methadone. The subjects, established opiate addicts adamantly seeking injectable heroin and nothing else, were randomly allocated to the two treatments and followed up for a year by independent assessors regardless of whether or not they remained in contact with services. Three-quarters of the heroin group remained in treatment for the year of study but, of course, all were continuing to inject. Twelve per cent of this group were regularly selling some of their script into the black market. In the methadone group, 12% broke contact with services immediately on being given the disappointing news that heroin was not available to them, and after a year only 29% of the original sample remained in contact with services. However, 40% of those out of contact had given up illegal drugs. Overall, the two groups were similar at the end of the study in their average rates of illicit drug use, time spent in the drug culture, unemployment, criminality, and poor general health, but this equivalence concealed a polarization effect in the methadone group; some did unusually well in terms of illicit drug use, crime, and so forth, but a similar proportion fared very badly. So which is the better result? Only a politician can decide!

The prescribing of substitute stimulants such as amphetamine or cocaine is even more controversial, and very few doctors are willing to do it. There is no research evidence to support it, but it can prove useful for a small number of carefully selected people who can be helped to move away from destructive amphetamine or cocaine use by judicious, time-limited prescribing of dexamphetamine.

Psychological interventions

Symptoms of anxiety or depression are common in dependent drug users presenting to health services, but usually clear up spontaneously when the problems related to the addiction are sorted out. A small proportion turn out to have a genuine depressive illness, and these are amenable in the usual way to antidepressant medicines or psychological treatments.

A wide range of psychological techniques have been applied, but evidence of effectiveness is rather limited. Whilst it is clear that many of these 'talking treatments' are undoubtedly beneficial, it is more difficult to demonstrate convincing differences between them.

The cornerstone approach is counselling. A good counsellor will be an excellent listener, and the sort of person who is able to build up trust and rapport with a wide range of different clients. Having clarified what the person wishes to achieve, the aim will be to guide her towards realistic goals, then advise, educate, problem solve, and support. More than anything else, an effective counsellor will build up a confidence-enhancing and supportive relationship, collaborating with the client without compromising his or her autonomy. The effectiveness of counselling relates to the personal attributes of the individual counsellor, many of which are inherent rather than taught: natural warmth and empathy, patience, confidence and inner strength, communication skills. The sort of concrete benefits which have been recorded include reductions in prescribed and illicit drug use, arrests, and convictions. Clients maintained on methadone do better if they also receive regular counselling.

More specialized psychological treatments are of proven worth in the treatment of anxiety and depression, but because of the greater expense can probably only be justified for selected people with particular problems. Many therapists now rely heavily on the principles of cognitive behavioural therapy (CBT). As mentioned elsewhere, the idea of CBT is to uncover the self-defeating patterns of thinking which, it is argued, lie at the heart of such blights as depression, anxiety, and guilt. Various behavioural experiments are thought up to test out the predictions of therapist and client. For a simple example, let us imagine a person who concedes that his heroin use has become rather more regular recently, but is vigorous in his view that he could give it up at any time he wished. The therapist disagrees. Instead of arguing about what is, after all, a matter of opinion, she suggests a little trial: 'Just out of interest, why not see if you can manage without a hit until the day after tomorrow.' The beauty of this is that the outcome should prove useful whichever way it goes. Success would result in a psychological boost to the client, whilst failure might bring home an important insight to build upon. The therapist will also be interested in analysing with the client the rules by which he governs his life – the 'shoulds, musts, and oughts' – attitudes and beliefs, habits and rituals, in order to reflect with him on which are helpful and life-enhancing and which are not.

'Cue exposure and response prevention' may be useful for people with 'needle fixation', that is, an addiction to the act of injecting itself. This strategy consists of exposing the client to a 'cue', such as a loaded syringe, without allowing him to inject. The resulting intense agitation and craving gradually subsides over an hour or so, and the patient is kept in contact with the cue until this is complete. If this is repeated at regular intervals the subject's response to the cue diminishes ('habituates') or disappears completely. Although this approach seems quite promising, it is uncertain if the effect persists beyond the treatment setting into the real world.

'Motivational interviewing' has become fashionable in recent years. This takes as its starting point an attitude towards the client which is fundamentally different from the traditional, paternalistic view of old. Individuals are expected to take full responsibility for actions and their consequences, encouraged in the belief that they have the power to shape their own destiny, and helped in developing the skills and confidence to achieve personal goals. 'Denial', that great let-out clause for unsuccessful therapy, is seen not as an immovable character trait, but rather as a product of a confronting client–therapist interaction without genuine rapport. The therapist tries in various ways to raise the client's self-esteem and confidence, in the expectation that this improved internal concept will become more and more incompatible with self-damaging behaviour. Strategies drawn from CBT are used to challenge assumptions and experiment with new solutions.

Relapse prevention and long-term rehabilitation

Relapse prevention is all about planning ahead so as to foresee high-risk situations, and understanding how subtle lifestyle decisions may bring these about. An example would be an abstinent alcoholic deciding to keep a bottle in the house just in case an old drinking companion should call round. Risky situations, such as returning to old haunts or friendships, are either avoided or confronted with rehearsed coping responses. Coping is generally more desirable than avoiding since, if successful, it will lead to an increase in self-confidence and esteem, making future relapse less likely. Of course, the converse is also true, so the choice between avoidance and control is a tactical one.

The therapist will be aware that a small lapse may induce what is known as the 'abstinence violation effect' – 'that's it, I've had a hit, all that effort's been a complete waste of time, I'll always be a junkie, might as well go the whole hog' – at which point lapse becomes full-scale relapse. Some even plan a 'controlled lapse' with the client so these feelings can be explored with greater force.

The basic planks of relapse prevention consist of predicting likely high-risk situations and planning in advance how to deal with them, increasing drug-free social contacts and avoiding the drug culture, reinforcing the negative memories of drug use as opposed to the positive, providing continuing support and help with problem solving, and perhaps urging membership of one of the many self-help groups. Sometimes, drug treatment may have a place. Long-term naltrexone, an opioid antagonist, will protect against impulsive scoring because it blocks the 'high', and certain antidepressants such as desipramine or sertraline have proved helpful in reducing craving in a proportion of compulsive cocaine users.

What are the more common causes of relapse? It is hardly surprising that low mood, feeling physically unwell or suffering drawn-out withdrawal symptoms, experiencing powerful craving, falling out with families or partners, and pressure from other drug users feature heavily in most surveys. A less obvious danger is feeling good: 'Life's so great I must snort a line to make it perfect!' Some people come a cropper when they decide to test their personal resolve, confident that enough time has passed to have cracked the problem.

For many people who have become seriously drug dependent, some sort of post-detoxification rehabilitation is essential if abstinence is to be maintained. Non-residential programmes usually consist of long-term counselling, individual or group psychotherapy of one sort or another, family or marital therapy, or more pragmatic approaches like help in moving to another district or finding work.

Self-help groups are made up of people with a common difficulty who meet regularly to provide mutual support, encouragement, and advice. Through regular attendance, people struggling to attain or retain abstinence may find the resolve to do so. Groups also exist for the families and partners of such people.

There are likely to be a number of self-help groups of one sort or another in any average health district, and they can generally be contacted through a GP or the local walk-in counselling clinic. Many individuals find that self-help groups are very effective in giving a sense of purpose and belonging, and provide a credible abstinence role-model for those who have got used to thinking that this is beyond their reach.

One of the better known drug self-help groups is Narcotics Anonymous (NA). This came into being in the 1950s, basing its philosophy on that of the better known Alcoholics Anonymous. Members meet very regularly, and anyone who is an ex-user or has a desire to stop taking drugs is welcome to attend. Complete honesty is required, and new attenders may be given an experienced 'sponsor' to whom they can turn for advice or support. At the heart of the meetings is the 'twelve steps philosophy' which requires each member:

(1)   to admit to powerlessness over his addiction, and concede that life has become unmanageable
(2)   to believe that a power greater than himself could restore him to sanity
(3)   to undertake to turn his will and life over to God 'as he understands Him'
(4)   to make a 'searching and fearless moral inventory' of himself
(5)   to admit to God, himself, and to another human being the exact nature of his wrongs
(6)   to be entirely ready to have God remove all these defects of character
(7)   to 'humbly ask Him to remove his shortcomings'
(8)   to make a list of all the persons he has harmed, and be willing to make amends to them all
(9)   to make direct amends to such people whenever possible, except when to do so would injure them or others
(10) to continue to take personal inventory, and when wrong promptly admit it
(11) to seek through prayer and meditation to improve conscious contact with God, 'praying only for knowledge of His will for us and the power to carry that out'
(12) having had a spiritual awakening as a result of these steps, to try to carry this message to other addicts and practise these principles in all his affairs.

Recognizing that the religious orientation would not appeal to everybody, it is stressed that the way of attaining that spiritual dimension which is central to the process is left entirely to the individual to determine. NA members are accustomed to concentrating on 'one day at a time' rather than trying to envisage a life without drugs stretching ahead interminably. This results in the rewards and satisfaction of success being experienced immediately rather than at some indeterminate point in the future.

Residential rehabilitation usually takes place in units practising the so-called 'Minnesota Method', or in therapeutic communities of one sort or another. The Minnesota method is a rather ill-defined, individually tailored package applied over a fixed time-span, usually between four and six weeks. It relies heavily on the 12-step approach, with a tightly structured timetable which includes education, individual and group therapy sessions, skills training, confidence building, and attention to physical health. Families may be involved in the process. After completing the programme, there is an expectation that most clients would continue to attend NA meetings regularly, or move into a hostel or some other sheltered environment.

Therapeutic communities aim to provide a safe, drug-free environment in which maladaptive ways of coping with life's challenges can be confronted by the peer group, and new ways explored. The organization of such communities varies from place to place, and it makes sense for an interested person to shop around in order to find a regime which seems acceptable. Most programmes last many months, and often involve long periods in which contact with family and friends is discouraged or banned. This sort of arrangement may not be appropriate or desirable for someone who retains a degree of social structure, such as an intact family or regular employment. In certain circumstances, the courts are prepared to consider placement in a suitable community as an alternative to a prison sentence.

Many therapeutic communities operate as 'concept houses'. This idea originated in 1959 with the Synanon organization of California. Daily life is highly structured with inmates organized in a very formal hierarchy based on seniority and progress through the system. Staff are generally recovered addicts or, more correctly, 'addicts who are not using at the moment' since this is not seen as a condition which can be cured, only put into remission. The aim is to provide a surrogate family in which a global change in life-view can be nurtured. All behaviour and interactions are closely scrutinized by other residents and subject to peer review through regular 'encounter' groups. These potentially harrowing and confrontational sessions may sometimes go on for several hours. Individuals are brought face to face with their behaviour or personal foibles in a very direct way, and exposed to a particularly vigorous form of peer pressure. Privileges and responsibilities have to be earned, and a system of rewards and punishment is stringently applied. To get into such a community, a number of hurdles must first be cleared, for example becoming drug-free and getting through a detailed assessment procedure. New admissions are accorded low status, and may be given a range of menial and unpleasant tasks in the service of the community. Shame, guilt, and public humiliation are sometimes used to enforce conformity. Serious transgression of the rules can result in expulsion and immediate cessation of all access to community members. If a person stays the distance, profound changes for the better are claimed but it is difficult to find concrete research evidence to prove this. Reintegration into the outside world after a long stay in a community of this sort can prove problematic.

A major difficulty for all these forms of rehabilitation is finding the money to pay for them. Provision in health and social service budgets is very limited, and this is partly because of the lack of bullet-proof evidence that they are effective. It is often up to the individual to raise the necessary cash. This problem is likely to become more pronounced as central protection of budgets for drug and alcohol rehabilitation disappears, and local purchasers of health care choose to deploy that provision into other budgets. It seems inevitable that a number of rehabilitation units will fold as a result of this process, further reducing the choice available to these most needy of clients.

chapter 15

drug policy – a time for change?

How are drugs controlled?

The signatory nations to the Single Convention on Narcotic Drugs (1961) and the Convention on Psychotropic Substances (1971) are required to 'limit to medical and scientific purposes the cultivation, production, manufacture, export, import, distribution of, trade in, use, and possession of [certain] drugs'. The list of drugs to be controlled includes raw opium and coca, opiates and opiate-like drugs, cocaine and cannabis in their various forms, brain stimulants, sedatives and sleeping pills, and hallucinogens. Draconian methods for the enforcement of these controls are justified because of the grave public health, social, and economic risks the drugs are said to pose. A licensing system enables the International Narcotics Control Board to monitor the worldwide trade in licit drugs.

The main policy-making organization for the international control of drugs is the Commission on Narcotic Drugs which has delegates from the member states of the United Nations (UN), along with representation from all those non-UN countries which signed the 1961 Convention. The Commission receives information and recommendations from a variety of interested organizations, and instigates surveys and research. Its role is to devise and monitor strategies aimed at the control of drug abuse and to advise governments on appropriate systems of legal restraint.

Regulation in the UK is through the Misuse of Drugs Act (1971) and Regulations (1985). The former divides drugs into three classes according to their perceived potential for causing harm, and the severity with which offenders are to be dealt. To illustrate these distinctions, a dealer in Class A drugs convicted of a first offence in the Crown Court is liable to maximum penalties of life imprisonment plus an unlimited fine, whereas a Class C dealer faces a maximum of up to two years' imprisonment plus an unlimited fine. Class A contains cocaine and coca leaf, the stronger opioids (opium, dextromoramide, dipipanone, fentanyl, diamorphine [heroin], levomethorphan, levomoramide, methadone, morphine, pethidine), the hallucinogens (LSD, psilocin, and related substances), tetrahydrocannabinol, and hash oil. Barbiturates and similar compounds including methaqualone, the stronger stimulants (amphetamine, dexamphetamine, methylamphetamine, and methylphenidate), the weaker opioids (codeine, dihydrocodeine, and pentazocine [not strictly an opioid, but a *partial opiate agonist* – see Chapter 12]), and cannabis in herbal and resin form make up Class B. Class C consists of dextropropoxyphene (Distalgesic), the weaker stimulants (diethylpropion, phentermine), the benzodiazepines and some other mild sedatives, pain killers, and sleeping pills.

The Misuse of Drugs Regulations allocates drugs into five schedules which define how they must be stored, prescribed, and documented. Schedule 1 is for substances which possess no recognized application in conventional medical practice, such as coca leaf, opium, cannabis, and LSD. Doctors cannot prescribe these under any circumstances, and a special licence from the Home Office is required for anybody who wishes to carry out research on them. This research would, in practice, be limited to animal studies since it seems unlikely in the current legal climate that any research ethics committee would give approval for a study involving administration to humans. Schedule 2 contains those drugs with important medical indications which are also seen as posing very great potential for misuse. These include the opioids, dexamphetamine, and cocaine. Because of the rather daunting list of rules, many doctors are unaware that with the exception of heroin, dipipanone (Diconal), and cocaine, any doctor can prescribe any opioid or stimulant to any addict. A special Home Office licence is required to prescribe the three named drugs to addicts, but any doctor can prescribe even these to non-addicts for medical indications. Schedule 3 is for drugs known to be abused, but to a less worrying degree than those in the previous category. These include barbiturate-like sedatives and sleeping pills, temazepam alone from the benzodiazepines, and a motley range of slimming tablets and milder painkillers. Schedule 4 entails only a modest level of control and includes the rest of the benzodiazepines, and Schedule 5 is reserved for concoctions which contain tiny amounts of substances from higher up the scale.

Alcohol and tobacco

In comparison with these stringent controls, governments collude with commercial interests which encourage maximal consumption of our two favourite recreational drugs by a combination of easy access and sophisticated advertising and promotional campaigns. Yet smoking is the largest single avoidable cause of death and ill health, killing around two and a half million people every year.

Strategies aimed at reducing smoking

Health education campaigns in schools and through the media seem reassuringly sensible, although there is little evidence that they influence behaviour very much. 'Quit clinics' and self-help clubs are useful, but are thin on the ground. However, there is no doubt that the most effective interventions depend on legislation and are therefore in the hands of governments. Laws can either be aimed at restricting access to tobacco or at changing the behaviour and attitudes of the public.

The most powerful measures in the first category are controls over advertising and promotion, and taxation. The tobacco industry would not spend $2 billion yearly on promotion if it did not believe it to be highly influential on sales. Countries such as Norway and Sweden which have imposed a total ban on advertising have seen sharp falls in consumption immediately following this. And tobacco is what is known as an 'elastic' commodity – if you make it more expensive, less people use it and those that do use it less. In both the UK and US, periodic boosts in the tax on cigarettes have been linked with downturns in consumption. Sales to minors can be reduced by high-profile prosecutions of shopkeepers and others who sell them cigarettes, and by banning vending machines from places they are likely to frequent. Restrictions on tar and nicotine content seem sensible on the face of it, but benefits may be neutralized by compensatory changes in smoking habits such as increased frequency or depth of puffing. Obliging companies to display tar and nicotine content on the packet at least lets the smoker make decisions about levels of risk.

Restricting smoking in public places and the workplace has a major impact upon consumption, but some believe this represents an unacceptable infringement on the personal freedom of the smoker. Since cigarettes are a perfectly legal commodity some sort of balance must be struck. However, this strategy is likely to have powerful knock-on effects if, as seems to be the case, it insidiously causes tobacco to become socially unacceptable in more and more places. Some see this as another dreadful example of creeping political correctness, but most pragmatists would welcome the guarantee of enjoying a meal without receiving facefuls of fumes from the next table, or avoiding 12 hours of passive smoking courtesy of their neighbour in a jumbo jet.

Strategies aimed at reducing drinking

Accepting that most people use alcohol in an entirely appropriate and life-enhancing way, most policy makers now have as their target the reduction of high-risk drinking rather than all drinking. Since alcohol, like tobacco, is an elastic commodity, increasing price through taxation undoubtedly reduces consumption in the general population, which in turn correlates with the prevalence of alcohol-related damage in that population. But many people find it hard to accept that what is for the majority a harmless pleasure should be manipulated excessively in this way, and it does produce sharp contrasts between prices in neighbouring countries which encourages smuggling and a black economy. Financial deterrence may in any case not work very well in the case of the heaviest dependent drinkers who are most at risk.

On the other hand, excessive or inappropriate drinking causes a mountain of harm and human misery, so what other strategies which have been shown to be productive can governments adopt? Clearly, these must be designed so as to be consistent with the customs and cultural values of the particular country. Limitations imposed upon advertising and promotion are undoubtedly effective. Educating the public about safe levels of drinking, encouraging employers and educators to instigate clear workplace policies on alcohol, restricting the number of licensed premises and points of sale, banning sale of alcohol to minors, and remorselessly pursuing and punishing drunk drivers are effective strategies adopted in most countries. Random, high-profile, roadside breath tests greatly enhance the impact of the latter. Compulsory rehabilitation programmes for drunk drivers have a modest effect in preventing reoffending.

Labelling drink containers with the alcohol content empowers the drinker to behave sensibly, and producing and promoting low-alcohol beverages means there is always an alternative to getting caned other than leaving your mates halfway through the evening. Putting pressure on retailers or bartenders not to supply more alcohol to people who are already drunk by holding them liable for damage caused by their customers is becoming more common in some countries. Warning labels drawing attention to the risks of drunk driving or drinking in pregnancy have been shown to stick in the mind, but whether they actually cause people to behave more prudently has yet to be demonstrated.

British policy on illegal drugs

Like most countries, the British response to illegal drugs has centred on three aims: to reduce the supply of drugs, to stifle demand for them, and to provide treatment for those who develop drug-related problems.

The harm-reduction approach (Chapter 14) has been well established in Britain since the mid-1980s, fuelled by fear of an HIV epidemic among injecting drug users, which appears at the time of writing to have been successfully prevented. By the early 1990s most health districts had adapted their response to drugs to this philosophy. Typically, arrangements were made for easy access to free needles and syringes on an exchange basis, with outreach workers providing help and support to those otherwise out of contact with services. User-friendly, walk-in agencies run by streetwise people in an accessible location were found to attract individuals who would not have dreamt of going to a doctor or social worker.

The statutory sector was expected to aim for a rapid and flexible response tailored to the individual's need. Education about HIV was to be a matter of routine along with easy access to testing for those who wished it, with counselling before and after the test and absolute confidentiality. Ideally, there was to be access to in-patient and out-patient detoxification facilities, prescribing services, community-based counselling and nursing, and more specialized psychological treatments when indicated. The usefulness of residential rehabilitation units and self-help groups was widely recognized.

Unfortunately, certain groups of people consistently did not get the help they required. Women, particularly those trying to care for small children, were often hesitant about making contact because services seemed intimidating and male orientated, or they feared that their children would be whisked away into care. People from ethnic minorities often felt disenfranchised. Users of drugs other than opioids, and younger people generally, found it difficult to imagine that anything on offer would have any relevance for them.

In 1994, the Conservative government launched a new initiative heralded by the White Paper 'Tackling drugs together'. The three objectives specified were to increase the safety of communities from drug-related crime, to reduce the acceptability and availability of drugs to young people, and to reduce the health and other risks caused by drug misuse.

The first was to be achieved by beefing up police, probation, and customs activity and improving communication between these organizations, and by targeting drug misuse in prisons by introducing mandatory drug testing of prisoners and improving security. The White Paper emphasized that the government had no plans even to discuss the possibility of legalizing or decriminalizing any drug. This position had already been put uncompromisingly by Tim Rathbone MP, Chairman of the All Party Drug Misuse Group of the House of Commons: 'Arguments for legalization are born of despair. Government actions and political leadership can tackle the awful problems of drug misuse.'

The need for better services for young people who had already developed drug-related problems was recognized, but the second objective was to be approached primarily by encouraging schools to mount drug education and prevention programmes. The problem here has been that the organizers of these programmes have paid insufficient attention to the evidence from America about what actually works. The research suggests that an effective prevention programme for schools would contain a number of ingredients. First it would be necessary to provide accurate information about the drugs; immediately we encounter problems. It is often the case that the trainers have less first-hand knowledge than the youngsters they are training. If an exaggerated account of the dangers of drugs familiar to the audience is given, all credibility will be lost. The trouble is that the true facts about a drug like cannabis might not seem deterrent enough, so there is a temptation to propagandize. But it is actually not necessary to invent risks to demonstrate convincingly that use of cannabis is likely to be counter-productive for people taking exams, learning new skills, playing sport, and so on. It is also essential that the educational package deals with alcohol and tobacco in the same terms as illegal drugs. Moralizing or scare-mongering is not merely useless but may actually increase the likelihood of experimentation.

Improving knowledge is not usually sufficient in itself to bring about changes in behaviour. Better results are achieved when relevant skills training is provided alongside the giving of information, with an emphasis on group discussions and student participation. Help in clarifying personal goals and ethical values, ambition raising, advice about managing stress, enhancing self-esteem and confidence, assertiveness training, rehearsing adaptive coping strategies, talking about ways of resisting peer pressure, and providing exciting alternatives to drug use are all important. Following a North American lead, several companies introduced workplace policies on drugs (and alcohol) which sometimes involved compulsory urine screening. Concern has been expressed that the results of such screening may reflect activity during leisure hours which has no bearing on work performance. For example, a single cannabis cigarette can result in a positive urine test for three weeks or more.

Reduction of the harmful effects of drug misuse was to be brought about by improving access to services, founding a national telephone helpline, and targeting particular groups such as people charged with drug-related offences who might be diverted from prison into treatment programmes. 'Drug action teams' consisting of senior representatives of all relevant statutory and non-statutory organizations were established in each health district to encourage a locally appropriate design and delivery of services and better communication and cooperation between agencies. The effectiveness of these arrangements has been limited by the fact that little in the way of new resources accompanied the organizational changes.

In April 1998, New Labour unveiled a 10-year cross-party strategy entitled '*Tackling drugs to build a better Britain*'. Much of this simply follows on from its predecessor, but it does contain one important new emphasis. As the author pointed out in the first edition of this book, tackling the social conditions which so obviously foster self-destructive indulgence in alcohol and drugs is an absolutely fundamental requirement. This means supporting deprived families whilst not further under-mining their self-respect and desire to become self-supporting, rehabilitating the decayed inner-city environment, providing something for the youth of our urban estates to do other than sniffing glue or trashing cars, and reintegrating the disenfranchised. How can one be surprised, the author asked, if people confronted with chronic boredom, discomfort, or despair seek an escape through a chemical numbing of the spirit or the hellish paradise of crack?

'Helping young people to resist drug misuse in order to achieve their potential in society' brings a very welcome new emphasis on attacking inequalities and social exclusion through programmes for training and employment, reforms of the welfare state, initiatives in education and health, and improvements in housing provision. A regeneration budget has been made available for improve-ment of amenities in run-down communities. The need to give young people easy access to help and advice, teach them practical skills and boost their confidence, and promote exciting alternatives to drugs also features prominently. It remains to be seen whether the resources to pursue these excellent ideas are made available.

The other three objectives more or less follow the line of the previous govern-ment: protecting communities from drug-related crime and antisocial behaviour, treatment to enable people to overcome drug-related problems, and 'stifling availability' of drugs. The strategies by which these are to be achieved are very much business as usual with an emphasis on rapid access to well-integrated services organized and coordinated by drug action teams according to local needs. There is an increased emphasis on treatment for offenders, engaging the interest and cooperation of local communities, energetically tackling drugs in clubs, the workplace and among road users, and cracking down hard on street dealers. An ex-policeman has been appointed 'drug czar' to develop national policy and oversee implementation, reporting back to government at ministerial level.

So, the British public can rest assured that its government shares the popular belief that 'the drug problem' poses a huge threat to society as a result of the vast criminal network which feeds off it, the risks posed to individual and public health, and the social disruption which stems from broken families and people stripped of hope and dignity. The policy outlined above is well thought out and in some ways progressive.

This government shares with a conviction equal to that of preceding administrations the view that there is no scope for 'thinking the unthinkable' and altering the legal status of any currently controlled drug. Prohibition is here to stay, and the central role in the battle against drugs remains in the hands of policemen, customs officers, and lawyers. Is this sensible?

The war on drugs

Drug prohibition requires the suppression by force of unauthorized cultivation, manufacture, transport across national frontiers, marketing, and personal use of controlled substances. This is the 'war on drugs' and it is an expensive undertaking. Of the £1.4 billion spent by the British government in combating drugs in 1997, 62% went to enforcement agencies and a further 13% went on international initiatives targeting cultivation and supply. US expenditure continues to spiral upwards: the federal drug control budget now exceeds $15 billion, representing a fourfold increase in expenditure over 10 years, and more than two-thirds of this is allocated to suppression of supply. Four hundred thousand people are languishing in American jails for violating drug laws. Whilst it is now standard practice for purchasers of treatment services to demand clear evidence of effectiveness, no such strictures are applied to enforcement agencies.

Can the taxpayer be confident that these vast sums are well spent? If the yardstick is price and availability of the drugs on the street, the answer would have to be 'no.' Despite heroic expenditure on enforcement over three decades, the real price of street drugs has fallen steadily while access, especially for young people in their teens, gets easier and easier. In 1993, the Chief Investigation Officer for Customs and Excise put on record his opinion that the British drug problem was worse than ever before, and surveys confirm the impression of many drug agencies that heroin and cocaine are even easier to obtain in 1999 than they were 10 years ago. Average purity of these two drugs has remained constant or increased. Drug seizures go up steeply every year, but clearly represent the tip of an iceberg. Sometimes even the isolated successes may turn out to be pyrrhic victories. In Australia, a reduction in the availability of cannabis was mirrored by an increase in availability of amphetamine. Temporary shortages of heroin on American streets have been associated with the development of 'designer' drugs, often of horrifying toxicity. Nature, and the drugs black market, abhor a vaccum.

The figures for worldwide production of street drugs are not particularly encouraging either. Illicit production of opium has increased year on year from 2242 tonnes in 1987 to 5000 tonnes in 1996, whilst that of coca leaves is thought to have doubled between 1985 and 1994. Customs and police officers in the developed world seem to accept that only 10% or so of illicit drugs entering a country are intercepted or seized on the street. The country with the world's most repressive drug policy – the United States – continues to struggle with the most devastating drug problem.

Far from being discouraged by such evidence which has convinced many observers that the war on drugs can never be won, its proponents remain fervently committed to the cause and tend to regard critics as defeatists. But there are those of polar opposite view who are equally convinced that the drug problem we now confront is self-inflicted, the product of a delusion. The psychiatrist Thomas Szasz (1985) has drawn a provocative parallel:

> 'Formerly, opium was a panacea; now it is the cause and symptom of countless maladies, medical and social, the world over. Formerly, masturbation was the cause and symptom of mental illness; now it is the cure for social inhibition and the practice ground for training in heterosexual athleticism... the danger of masturbation disappeared when we

ceased to believe in it: we then ceased to attribute danger
to the practice and to its practitioners; and ceased to call
it "self-abuse"'.

Spinoza held that those who try to restrain personal behaviour by force of law
are more likely to arouse vices than reform them. Does an emphasis on external
regulation undermine the processes of self-regulation that we all have to fall
back on in order to contain our pursuit of pleasurable activities within reasonable
limits?

Why stop adults from using drugs if they wish to?

The libertarian argument, as the author interprets it, would proceed along the
following lines: 'What I do to my body is my own affair, as long as I don't harm
anyone else. I may have risky habits, but it is up to me to decide whether the
benefits or pleasures of such habits justify these risks. There is some good
evidence that a diet rich in saturated fat carries a very significant risk to health,
but there are no suggestions that the intake of eggs should be regulated by law.
If I choose to devour an omelette and chips followed by chocolate truffles
with lashings of double cream every night, it's my lookout and nobody else's.
Surely I should be allowed to decide what I put into my own body? But if I grow
a few cannabis plants in my greenhouse for my own personal consumption, I face
a possible prison sentence and confiscation of my assets. It all boils down to an
arbitrary and conditioned concept of "good" and "bad" pleasures imposed on the
population by special interest groups, puritans, or do-gooders.'

It seems reasonable at least to debate the justification for maintaining the
current distinctions between the legal and illegal recreational drugs, founded as
they are upon quirks of history. It cannot be based upon a calculation of personal
risk or social disruption, since nobody could possibly doubt the awesome toxicity
of tobacco smoke, or the domestic and public devastation associated with
alcohol misuse. Neither can it relate to addictive potential, since nicotine is the
most addictive of all drugs in terms of capture rate among those who experiment
with a single exposure. Surely it can't be a taboo against intoxication, or loss of
personal control? Nothing could be more intimidating or depressing than a pack

of lager louts reeling toward you on a night-time city street, urinating against walls, smashing windows, and howling obscenities.

Anthropologists have argued that medical and sociological research, with its problem-orientated focus within non-representative pathological samples, exaggerates the risks of drug use. This perspective would suggest that doctors may not be the most appropriate people to guide policy makers. Many clinicians and other concerned parties have had little or no first-hand contact with the recreational, non-problematic use of drugs other than alcohol, tobacco, or caffeine. They find it hard to conceive that such use could exist, tending to equate 'drugs' with inevitable addiction and deviant behaviour, and forgetting that the illegal nature of drug use drives it underground and necessitates a whole new deviant lifestyle. Those using drugs without problems, like social drinkers, remain 'invisible'. Only the abusers and the non-copers surface in their clinics. Drug addicts presenting to the average general practitioner or drug dependency unit are no more representative of drug use in the community than skid-row alcoholics are of ordinary social drinking.

A whole industry has grown up around the treatment and control of drug use with large numbers of 'experts' producing a range of conflicting contributions to the legalization debate, which rarely progresses far beyond the sphere of vested interest. The predictions of these experts are very widely discrepant. There is an understandable reluctance amongst politicians to instigate change, with a preference for high-profile rhetoric along conventional lines rather than the risk of 'a step into the unknown'. This is to underestimate the parlous state of affairs that now confronts us: the tremendous opportunity that prohibition continues to provide to organized crime, and the viciousness and debauchery that is thus sustained; the crippling financial burden of keeping up the war on drugs; and the fact that the physical and social problems created by making drugs illegal may sometimes exceed the primary risks of the drugs themselves.

The legalization/decriminalization debate

The main arguments for and against decriminalizing street drugs are boringly familiar to most people. Those in favour propose that self-control driven by education and informal peer pressure is preferable to coercion by the state, and would bring drug policy into line with society's approach to other potentially unhealthy activities such as excessive drinking, overeating, or boxing. Prohibition has proved counter-productive. It has vastly increased the profitability and sophistication of organized crime, it costs billions of dollars in law enforcement worldwide, and it has not been conspicuously successful in its primary goal of reducing supply. There are more people in prison in North America than in any other democratic country at any time in history – and more than half are there for drug-related crimes. Price and availability of drugs are very similar in countries with harsh and liberal drug policies. When applied to alcohol in the US, it became evident after repeal that the social damage had greatly outweighed the health benefits. Demand for the more problematic drugs such as heroin and crack cocaine is relatively inelastic so that an increase in price has only a limited effect on consumption and is passed on to the public by an increase in street crime. Addicts will switch drugs rather than stop using if supplies are interrupted. Cannabis is bulky and the demand less inelastic so suppression may be more successful, but this may simply provide an impetus for criminals to market more profitable (and dangerous) drugs with greater vigour. Far from protecting individuals from themselves, the necessity of buying adulterated drugs from unscrupulous gangsters has made drug use infinitely more risky. Many pre-prohibition addicts were able to live full and productive lives, with some famous doctors among them. Problems which are primarily social or medical are being reclassified as forensic.

Relaxing the law would result in a large financial saving which could be channelled into drug treatment and education, and a reduction in the risks associated with drug use which would benefit both individual and public health. Addicts could lead more normal lives with the secondary bonus that the meaning and image of the 'junkie', which may seem glamorous and attractive to some, would be eliminated. The viability of criminal organizations would be damaged and one of the most important drives to street crime would be removed. Pressure marketing of drugs in deprived urban areas by criminals would become unprofitable. Anthropological studies and historical reviews suggest that abundant supply does not inevitably result in uncontrolled consumption.

Those opposed to changes in the law argue that this would be a dangerous and irresponsible social experiment which would take us into the unknown. These drugs are taken for no other reason than to induce intoxication, which is disruptive and not acceptable in our society. To relax the law would be to signal that intoxication is admissable, and would reduce the incentive to manage life without resorting to drugs. The psychopharmacology of drugs as powerful as heroin and cocaine is such that it would be quite inappropriate for them to be treated as ordinary consumer commodities. There is simply no way of knowing how many new users there might be, but if alcohol can be taken as a guide, it is apparent that levels of consumption within the population are proportional to availability, and that the prevalence of problem use relates to this general consumption. Cannabis may be less dangerous but all drugs carry risks, and we already have more than enough problems with alcohol and tobacco. A valid part of the duty of the state is to protect individuals from themselves. Even if it could be successfully argued that an adult must be allowed to take responsibility for his or her own actions, this is certainly not the case for children and adolescents and relaxation in the law would inevitably mean an increase in their use of drugs. Legal restraint is imperative to protect the public at large from the consequences and costs (for example to the NHS) of drug taking. The pursuit of pleasure for pleasure's sake is selfish and encourages people to avoid work and take advantage of the welfare state. Although not completely successful, the war on drugs must have delayed or deterred some potential users. Legalization would unleash entrepreneurial activity which would encourage drug use and because some restrictions would still be necessary you would still be stuck with a black market.

What can be learned from the Dutch approach to cannabis?

Is there anything to be learnt from examining the policies of other countries? 'Harm reduction' is a familiar concept in treatment these days (see Chapter 14), but in the Netherlands for more than two decades it has also been the guiding principle in defining how the drug laws should be implemented. Whilst still aiming to minimize supply and remain in step with other European countries, the Dutch have placed less emphasis on punishing personal possession and use. The police cooperate with a declared wish to keep addicts integrated in society rather than force them underground. There is an acknowledgement that the effects of repressive drug policy are often confused in the public mind with the effects of drugs themselves. According to a spokesman from the Ministry of Welfare, Health, and Cultural Affairs, the misuse of drugs is seen as '… a matter of social well-being and public health rather than as a problem for the police and the courts'.

A fundamental practical distinction in the Dutch approach is the differentiation of 'drugs presenting unacceptable risks' from 'hemp products'. In 1976, a formal policy of non-enforcement was adopted whereby possession or trade in small amounts (up to 30 grams) of cannabis would no longer be prosecuted, though such activity remained technically illegal. The reason given for this *de facto* decriminalization was to '…avoid a situation in which consumers of cannabis suffer more damage from the criminal proceedings than from the drug itself'. Unfortunately, the fact that the police continued to prosecute those who deal in amounts greater than 30 grams (in other words, the wholesalers) meant that the legitimate businessman continued to be excluded, leaving the field open to the criminal entrepreneur. This approach has not been popular with European neighbours, who have labelled Holland a 'narco-state'. International pressure led the Dutch government to lower the threshold for non-enforcement to 5 grams. Currently there are well over 1000 retail outlets for cannabis, usually 'brown' coffee shops. Advertising is not allowed, and sales to minors or hard drugs on the premises are rigorously prosecuted. One spin-off, desirable or not depending on your point of view, is that quality control has improved considerably as a result of customer discrimination; home-produced Dutch cannabis is now reckoned by some to be the best in the world.

Public opinion, interestingly, is often at odds with government policy: there is generally a more repressive attitude to drugs among Dutch people than, for example, in Southern France where the law against personal use is rigorously enforced. But what is known of the impact of such modifications of law enforcement?

This has been analysed by MacCoun and Reuter (1997). Between 1976 and 1983, depenalization resulted in 'little if any effect on levels of use' but between

1984 and 1996 prevalence of cannabis use 'increased sharply', particularly among young people aged between 18 and 20. But interpretation of this is complicated by the fact that prevalence rates increased equally rapidly in countries with rigorous prohibition between 1992 and 1996. Currently, prevalence and price of cannabis are very similar in Holland and the US. There is some evidence that the Dutch are having some success in separating 'hard' and 'soft' drugs: only 22% of Dutch cannabis smokers have tried cocaine, compared to 33% in the US.

The conclusion is that depenalization in Holland did not significantly increase consumption, a finding which has been replicated in a dozen or so US states, Italy, and Spain. The leap in prevalence between 1984 and 1996 is probably explained by increased commercialization, a factor which contributed to the harmful backlash following the American alcohol prohibition.

Should we think the unthinkable?

The starting point, the author would argue, is to accept that recreational drug taking by a substantial minority of the population is here to stay. The past is the best guide to the future, and there has never in the history of mankind been a tribe, race, or society which has not resorted to mind-altering drugs. It is difficult to see any reason why modern Britain should buck this trend. Secondly, the evidence suggests that for the large majority of these people no measurable detrimental effects will result from this, just as one finds in the case of alcohol. Of course, the casualties that do occur with alcohol and other drugs are highly visible and tragic, but so are those associated with a host of other risky yet enjoyable activities. Is taking a recreational drug a valid pleasure? Few would dispute that a glass of wine can be life-enhancing, yet some doctors and others at the end of the 19th century were arguing that alcohol was so inherently addictive that individuals simply could not be trusted to make decisions for themselves about whether to drink or not. Ardent prohibitionists discounted the moderation and harmless pleasure of the majority in a vain attempt to protect the vulnerable minority. Those reformed addicts who supported firm external control had found a comforting model of addiction which absolved the 'victim' from any personal responsibility for his state.

New Labour has instituted one of the two radical steps that were proposed in this book's first edition, namely to instigate a policy aimed at alleviating the social conditions which foster problem drug use. It will be a major triumph if these admirable sentiments are actually translated into an injection of capital into local housing budgets to eliminate Rachman-style bedsitters, more resources to give the inhabitants of dilapidated estates education and skills training relevant to modern economic realities, and access to leisure activities other than joyriding and dealing crack. How sad, then, that the necessary second step, namely a radical reappraisal of the vastly expensive and lamentably unsuccessful war on drugs, has been rejected so uncompromisingly by the Home Secretary. Even debating the issue was politically beyond the pale, and ministers who fleetingly raised their heads above the parapet have been humiliatingly slapped down.

Arguments for changes in the law do not in the least reflect a lack of concern about the undoubted risks that drugs pose, but rather an awareness that the present policy is simply not doing justice to our predicament. Availability and price of street drugs are moving in the wrong direction. Criminal domination of drug supply leads to adulterated and contaminated products being sold at vastly inflated prices to the terrible detriment of individual and public health, and preserves the most profitable felonious enterprise of all time. The illegal drugs market in Britain is now estimated to be worth up to £8.6 billion each year. Drug dealing is the biggest illegal economic enterprise of all time. Every man, woman, and child feels the wind of this evil in the ever-growing insecurity and violence that pervades all our lives. A government-funded study found that a sample of 1000 addicts committed a total of 70 728 crimes in a three-month period, at an overall cost to the public purse of £12.2 million. Burglary, street robbery, shoplifting, and vehicle theft carried out to raise money for street drugs cost its victims £7.5 million. Assuming, very conservatively, that there are 150 000 opiate addicts in the country, and that this sample is roughly representative of them, the British taxpayer is having to fork out over £7000 million, of which two-thirds is the cost of criminal behaviour. It is sheer complacency to argue that we are already doing all we can to resist this implacable erosion of the quality of life. Those who look for more constructive policies cannot sensibly be dismissed as defeatist; it is those who glumly or complacently insist that there are no alternatives who are more deserving of that label.

Few would dispute that some drugs carry far more risks than others. Injecting heroin is surely more worrying than smoking cannabis, yet the great majority of our police and customs time is focused on suppressing the latter. In 1995, a total of 54.69 tonnes of illegal drugs were seized, of which no less than 52 tonnes (95%) consisted of cannabis. Although many police forces have adopted a cautioning policy for first-time cannabis offenders, this is unevenly and arbitrarily applied. The ethnic minorities and those with unconventional appearances or lifestyles seem more likely to be busted. People still get custodial sentences for possession of a small lump of cannabis for personal use, and 82% of British people found guilty of drug offences in 1995 were charged in connection with cannabis. All this attention seems grossly out of proportion to the threat posed by the stuff. Similarly, the everyday experience of young people taking Ecstasy at raves is greatly at odds with the lurid accounts which appear in the tabloid newspapers. The dangers associated with the occasional use of pharmaceutically pure MDMA, though genuine and potentially tragic for a tiny proportion of users, must be kept in perspective. Every night such an event takes place, dozens of young people will have been crippled or killed as a result of alcohol-related trauma.

Cannabis has become quietly endemic in our society, and the experiences of the Dutch and others fully justify a depenalization approach. However, it is important that the law is changed rather than merely suspended, and that wholesaling becomes legitimate as well as retailing, otherwise domination of the market will remain in the hands of those with criminal connections. Release, the widely respected London-based drugs and legal advice agency, has called for the introduction of licensed premises such as cafes or clubs which could sell cannabis, Ecstasy, and 'poppers' to members with strict monitoring of quality control and the normal regulations concerning trading standards and consumer protection. Apart from the vast savings which would result from abandoning the impossible dream of stamping out cannabis, there would be a healthy taxation revenue to look forward to. Naturally, there would have to be strict limits imposed on the marketing of these drugs, and all the restrictions on use that are currently applied to alcohol. It would seem sensible alongside this development to curtail further the active promotion of alcohol and tobacco, bearing in mind that the latter is responsible for more deaths than heroin, cocaine, alcohol, road accidents, the

HIV virus, murder, and suicide all put together. The impact of this change of policy on volume of consumption and incidence of drug-related problems would have to be monitored closely.

An important spin-off would be the improved feasibility of controlled clinical trials examining the therapeutic potential of cannabis and its derivatives. A recent survey in the UK suggested that a clear majority of doctors think this drug should be available on prescription. Some people argue that the euphoric effect would be a contraindication, but a drug which can cheer up a person who is seriously ill should be welcomed, not banned. The lamentable ignorance about the human pharmacology and toxicology of both cannabis and Ecstasy could be remedied, in particular the effects of the former on short-term memory and the evidence of neurotoxicity in the latter.

As far as other drugs are concerned, it is a pity that such debate as has occurred has been polarized between the 'do-nothings' and the 'total legalizers'. There is surely potential for compromise and a cautious stepwise approach between these two extreme positions. Welcome changes in treatment philosophy have already taken place in this country, but the question of substitute prescribing of opioids to addicts has generated an acrimonious debate extenting over several decades. A complete spectrum of views still exists among doctors, ranging from those who argue against any form of substitute prescribing as collusive with dependency or ethically unacceptable to those who advocate that cocaine and heroin should be readily available to addicts in order to undercut the grotesquely overpriced black market.

The overriding need is to wrest control of the drugs market from the criminal. This necessitates a move further along the path of controlled availability of opioids and stimulants from doctors with the involvement and support of other interested parties locally, particularly the police. A drug habit would become much cheaper even if the addict had to bear the cost of the drugs to the NHS, so that a deviant career would no longer be inevitable. Reintegration of the drug user into normal society would restore peer pressure as a potent restraint on behaviour. It is certainly possible that such 'normalization' initiatives might result in increased numbers of people using harder drugs, some of whom are bound to become dependent. Although an addiction to pharmaceutical drugs is much less dangerous to health and welfare than a street drug habit, it is highly undesirable and still carries a number of risks for the individual and his or her social circle. For this reason, such initiatives should be organized as controlled trials in order that the effects can be monitored carefully by independent observers. Until this work has been done, all we have to go on is the rash speculations of the 'do nothings' and the 'total legalisers'. Whether some increase in individual risk is a price worth paying for the benefits to society of undermining organized crime and reducing the profits of drug dealing is a matter for public debate. Government-sponsored research of this sort would provide a more rational basis for this debate than presently exists.

The implications of the current total suppression of naturally occurring and milder forms of the main classes of drugs, such as opium and coca, is worthy of some consideration. Historically, these have proved to be containable within the fabric of mainstream society. Cracking down on them has resulted, in many countries, in an exploding use of the infinitely more powerful and destructive synthetic alternatives.

Every effort should be made to divert convicted drug misusers away from prison and into residential rehabilitation units. Many drug users continue to use drugs in prison and simply learn to be more deviant, while non-drug-using inmates are exposed to the temptation of taking up the habit to ease their boredom or distress.

There is scant political will for changes in drug policy at present, probably because it does not seem much of a vote winner. The momentum for change can only come from better informed and wider public discussion of the issues. The changes in policy which are feasible for individual nations acting independently are rather limited because of the possibility of 'drug tourism', although this is likely to be a negligible problem in the case of cannabis and other 'soft' drugs. The debate must clearly be conducted on an international stage.

We live in an age when consumers demand value for money, and custodians of the public purse rightly demand evidence of effectiveness before allocating funds to treatment providers. Why are such constraints not applied to the agencies implementing the war on drugs, for which no such evidence currently exists? Seizure figures and inflated estimates of street values are useless because we don't know what percentage of the total market this represents. There has been no discernable impact upon the price or availability of hard drugs. In contrast, the government study referred to above showed that for every £1 spent on treatment, £3 are saved by reduced crime costs alone. The financial emphasis should be steadily reoriented away from enforcement into the regeneration of communities, and into demonstrably effective programmes for treatment and prevention.

selected bibliography and references

Books

Abadinski, H. (1989). *Drug abuse: an introduction.* Nelson-Hall, Chicago.

Braun, S. (1996). *Buzz: the science and lore of alcohol and caffeine.* Oxford University Press, Oxford.

Burroughs, W. (1996). *Junkie.* The Olympia Press, London.

CIBA Foundation Symposium 166 (1992). *Cocaine: scientific and social dimensions.* John Wiley & Sons, Chichester.

Cocteau, J. (1957). *Opium: diary of a cure.* Owen, London.

Crowley, A. (1922). *Diary of a drug fiend.* Collins, London.

Davies, J. B. (1992). *The myth of addiction.* Harwood Academic Publications Gmbh, Switzerland.

Galizio, M., Maisto, S. A. (ed.) (1985). *Determinants of substance abuse: biological, psychological, and environmental factors.* Plenum Press, New York and London.

Gerstein, D. R., Green, I. W. (ed.) (1993). *Preventing drug abuse: what do we know?* National Academic Press, Washington, DC.

Ghodse, H. (1989). *Drugs and addictive behaviour – a guide to treatment.* Blackwell, Oxford.

Goodman, L. S., Gilman, A. (ed.) (1982). *The pharmacological basis of therapeutics.* Macmillan, New York.

Gossop, M. (1987). *Living with drugs* (2nd edn). Wildwood House Ltd, Aldershot.

Grahame-Smith, D., Aronson, J. (1992). *Oxford textbook of clinical pharmacology and drug therapy.* Oxford University Press, Oxford.

Grinspoon, L. (1975). *The speed culture.* Harvard University Press, Cambridge, MA.

Grinspoon, L. (1977). *Marihuana reconsidered* (2nd edn). Harvard University Press, Cambridge, MA.

Grinspoon, L., Bakalar, J. B. (1979). *Psychedelic drugs reconsidered.* Basic Books, New York.

Hoffer, A., Osmond, H. (1967). *The hallucinogens.* Academic Press, New York.

Huxley, A. (1959). *The doors of perception and heaven and hell.* Penguin Books, Harmondsworth.

Kerouac, J. (1976). *On the road.* Penguin Books, Harmondsworth.

Laurence, D. R., Bennett, P. N. (1992). *Clinical pharmacology* (7th edn). Churchill Livingstone, Edinburgh.

Laurie, P. (1967). *Drugs: medical, psychological, and social facts.* Penguin Books, Harmondsworth.

Leary, T. (1968). *The politics of Ecstasy.* G. P. Putnam, New York.

Lowinson, J. H., Ruiz, P., Millman, R. B., Langrod, J. G. (ed.) (1992). *Substance abuse.* Williams & Wilkins, Baltimore.

Miller, W. (ed.) (1985). *The addictive behaviours.* Pergamon, New York.

Orford, J. (1985). *Excessive appetites: a psychological view of addictions.* John Wiley & Sons, Chichester.

Plant, M., Plant, M. (1992). *Risk takers.* Routledge, London.

Plant, M., Single, E., Stockwell, T. (1997). *Alcohol: minimising the harm.* Free Association Books, London.

Russell, R. (1973). *Bird lives!* Quartet Books, London.

Shapiro, H. (1988). *Waiting for the man: the story of drugs and popular music.* Quartet Books, London.

Stockley, D. (1992). *Drug warning: an illustrated guide for parents, teachers, and employers* (2nd edn). Optima Books, London.

Szasz, T. S. (1985). *Ceremonial chemistry: the ritual persecution of drugs, addicts, and pushers.* (rev. edn). Learning Publications, Holmes Beach, Fl.

Szasz, T. S. (1992). *Our right to drugs: the case for a free market.* Praeger, New York.

Trocchi, A. (1966). *Cain's book*. Jupiter Books, Calder & Boyars Ltd, London.

Tyler, A. (1966). *Street drugs* (rev. edn). New English Library, London.

Watson, R. R. (ed.) (1990). *Drug and alcohol abuse prevention*. The Humana Press, Inc., New York.

Weil, A. (1973). *The natural mind*. Jonathan Cape, London.

Wolfe, T. (1969). *The electric kool-aid acid test*. Bantam Books, New York.

Reports

Action on Smoking and Health (1997). *Basic facts on smoking*. ASH, London.

Advisory Committee on Misuse of Drugs (1988). *AIDS and drug misuse, Part 1*. HMSO, London.

Chatlos, J. C. (1997). Substance use and abuse and the impact on academic difficulties. *Child and Adolescent Psychiatric Clinics of North America*, 6, 545–68.

European School Survey Project on Alcohol and Other Drugs (1997). *The 1995 ESPAD Report*. Council of Europe Pompidou Group, Stockholm.

Government Statistical Service (1991). *Statistics of drugs seizures and offenders dealt with, United Kingdom, 1991*. Research and Statistics Department, London.

Government Statistical Services (1998). *Drug misuse statistics for six months ending September 1996*. Department of Health Bulletin No. 5.

Health Education Authority (1997). *Results of the 1995 National Drugs Campaign Survey*. HEA, London.

Home Office Research and Statistics Directorate (1997). *Drug misuse declared in 1996: latest results from the British Crime Survey*. Home Office, London.

Home Office Statistical Bulletin (1996). *The 1996 British Crime Survey*. Research & Statistics Directorate, London.

House of Lords Select Committee on Science and Technology (1998). *Cannabis: the Scientific and Medical evidence*. HL Paper 151. The Stationery Office, London.

Institute for the Study of Drug Dependence (1997). *Drug misuse in Britain in 1996* ISDD, London.

International Narcotics Control Board (1992). *Report of the International Narcotics Control Board for 1992*. United Nations, Geneva.

New Internationalist (1991). *The crazy war on drugs.* Issue **224**, October 1991.

Office for National Statistics (1997). *Preliminary results from the 1996 General Household Survey.* HMSO, London.

Office of Population Censuses and Statistics (1996). *Living in Britain.* HMSO, London.

Royal College of Physicians (1992). *Smoking and the young,* RCP, London.

Royal Colleges of Physicians, Psychiatrists, and General Practitioners (1995). *Alcohol and the heart in perspective.* Report of a joint working group, Oxford.

Schools Health Education Unit (1993). *Young people in 1992.* School of Education, Exeter University.

Solowij, N., Lee, N. (1991). *Survey of Ecstasy (MDMA) users in Sydney.* Research Grant Report Series DAD 91–69. Drug and Alcohol Directorate, NSW health Department, Australia.

United Nations International Drug Control Programme (1997). *World Drug Report.* Oxford University Press, Oxford.

Wootton Committee (1968). *Cannabis: Report by the Advisory Committee on Drug Dependence.* HMSO, London.

Selected scientific papers

Chapter 1: Why use drugs?

Bolling, K. (1994). *Smoking among secondary school children in England in 1993.* HMSO, London.

Brook, J. S., Whiteman, M., Gordon, A. S. (1983). Stages of drug use in adolescence: personality, peer, and family correlates. *Development Psychology,* **19**, 269–277.

Brook, D. W., Brook, J. S. (1990). The etiology and consequences of adolescent drug use. In: *Drug and alcohol abuse prevention* (ed. R. R. Watson). The Humana Press, Inc., New York.

Brown, G. L., Linnoila, M. I. (1990). CSF serotonin metabolite studies in depression, impulsivity, and violence. *Journal of Clinical Psychiatry,* **51** (Suppl.), 31–43.

Coopersmith, S. (1967). *The antecedents of self-esteem.* W. H. Freeman, San Francisco.

Dembo, R., Shern, D. (1982). Relative deviance and the process(es) of drug involvement among inner-city youths. *International Journal of the Addictions*, **17**, 1373–99.

Galizio, M., Rosenthal, D., Stein, F. A. (1983). Sensation seeking, reinforcement, and student drug use. *Addictive Behaviours*, **8**, 243–52.

Gorsuch, R. L., Butler, M. C. (1976). Initial drug abuse: a review of predisposing social psychological factors. *Psychological Bulletin*, **83**, 120–37.

Hawkins, J. D., Catalano, R. F., Miller, J. Y. (1992). Risk and protective factors for alcohol and other drug problems in adolescence and early adulthood: implications for substance abuse prevention. *Psychological Bulletin*, **112**, 64–105.

Jaffe, L. T., Archer, R. P. (1987). The prediction of drug use among college students from MMPI, MCMI, and sensation-seeking scales. *Journal of Personality Assessment*, **51**, 243–53.

Jessor, R. (1976). Predicting time of onset of marijuana use: a developmental study of high school youth. *Journal of Consulting and Clinical Psychology*, **44**, 125–34.

Kandel, D. B. (1980). Drug and drinking behaviour among youth. *Annual Review Sociology*, **6**, 235–85.

Kandel, D. B., Kessler, R. C., Margulies, R. Z. (1978). Antecedents of adolescent initiation into stages of drug use: a developmental analysis. *Journal of Youth and Adolescence*, **7**, 13–40.

Kandel, D. B., Davies, M. (1996). High-school students who use crack and other drugs. *Archives of General Psychiatry*, **53**, 71–9.

Malhotra, M. K. (1983). Familial and personal correlates (risk factors) of drug consumption among German youth. *Acta Paedopsychiatrica*, **49**, 199–209.

Measham, F., Newcombe, R., Parker, H. (1993). The post-heroin generation. *Druglink*, **May/June**, 16–17.

Measham, F., Newcombe, R., Parker, H. (1994). The normalisation of recreational drug use among young people in North West England. *British Journal of Sociology*, **45**, 287–312.

Moore, S., Gullone, E. (1996). Predicting adolescent risk behaviour using a personalized cost–benefit analysis. *Journal of Youth and Adolescence*, **25**, 343–59.

Novacek, J., Raskin, R., Hogan, R. (1991). Why do adolescents use drugs? Age, sex, and user differences. *Journal of Youth and Adolescence*, **20**, 475–92.

Pritchard, C., Cotton, A., Cox, M. (1992). Truancy, illegal drug use, and knowledge of HIV infection in 932 14–16 year-old adolescents. *Journal of Adolescence*, **15**, 1–17.

Richardson, J. L., Radziszewska, B., Dent, C.D., Flay, B. R. (1993). Relationship between after-school care of adolescents and substance use, risk taking, depressed mood, and academic achievement. *Pediatrics*, **92**, 32–8.

Robson, P. (1988). Self-esteem – a psychiatrist's view. *British Journal of Psychiatry*, **153**, 6–15.

Robson, P. (1996). Young people and illegal drugs. In: *Adolescent medicine* (ed. A. Macfarlane). Royal College of Physicians, London.

Sadava, S. W., Forsyth, R. (1977). Person – environment interaction and college-student drug use: a multivariate longitudinal study. *Genetic Psychology Monographs*, **96**, 211–45.

Sell, L., Robson, P. (1998). Perceptions of college life, emotional well-being, and patterns of drug and alcohol use among Oxford undergraduates. *Oxford Review of Education*, **24**, 235–43.

Shedler, J., Block, J. (1990). Adolescent drug use and psychological health: a longitudinal survey. *American Psychologist*, **45**, 612–30.

Smith, G. M. (1974). Teenage drug use: a search for causes and consequences. *Personality and Social Psychology Bulletin*, **1**, 426–9.

Sutherland, I., Willner, P. (1998). Patterns of alcohol, cigarette, and illicit drug use in English adolescents. *Addiction*, **93**, 1199–208.

Teichman, M., Barnea, Z., Ravav, G. (1989). Personality and substance use among adolescents: a longitudinal study. *British Journal of Addiction*, **84**, 181–90.

Trad, P. V. (1994). Developmental vicissitudes that promote drug abuse in adolescents. *American Journal of Drug and Alcohol Abuse*, **20**, 459–81.

Wald, N., Nicolaides-Bouman, A. (ed.) (1991). *UK smoking statistics* (2nd edn). Oxford University Press, Oxford.

Webb, E., Ashton, H., Kelly, P., Kamali, F. (1997). Patterns of alcohol consumption, smoking, and illicit drug use in British university students: interfaculty comparisons. *Drug and Alcohol Dependence*, **47**, 145–53.

Zuckerman, M. (1979). *Sensation seeking: beyond the optimal level of arousal*. Wiley, New York.

Chapter 2: The consequences of drug use

Blackwell, J. S. (1983). Drifting, controlling, and overcoming: opiate users who avoid becoming chronically dependent. *Journal of Drug Issues*, **13**, 219–35.

Bradley, B. P., Phillips, G., Green, L., Gossop, M. (1989). Circumstances surrounding the initial lapse to opiate use following detoxification. *British Journal of Psychiatry*, **154**, 354–9.

Cottrell, D., Childs-Clarke, A., Ghodse, A. H. (1985). British opiate addicts: an 11-year follow-up. *British Journal of Psychiatry*, **146**, 448–50.

Edwards, J. G., Goldie, A. (1987). A ten-year follow-up study of Southampton opiate addicts. *British Journal of Psychiatry*, **151**, 679–83

Frischer, M., Goldberg, D., Rahman, M., Berney, L. (1997). Mortality and survival among a cohort of drug injectors in Glasgow, 1982–1994. *Addiction*, **92**, 419–27.

Gossop, M., Green, L., Phillips, G., Bradley, B. (1987). What happens to opiate addicts immediately after treatment: a prospective follow-up study. *British Medical Journal*, **294**, 1377–80.

Gossop, M., Green, L., Phillips, G., Bradley, B. (1989). Lapse, relapse, and survival among opiate addicts after treatment. *British Journal of Psychiatry*, **154**, 348–53.

Judson, B. A., Goldstein, A. (1982). Prediction of long-term outcome for heroin addicts admitted to a methadone maintenance programme. *Drug and Alcohol Dependence*, **10**, 383–91.

McLellan, A. T., Luborsky, L., Woody, G. E., O'Brien, C. P., Druley, K. A. (1983). Predicting response to alcohol and drug abuse treatments. *Archives of General Psychiatry*, **40**, 620–5.

McLellan, A. T., Luborsky, L., O'Brien, C. P., Woody, G. E., Druley, K. A. (1982). Is treatment for substance abuse effective? *Journal of the American Medical Association*, **247**, 1423–8.

Maddux, J. F., Desmond, D. P. (1982). Residence relocation inhibits opioid dependence. *Archives of General Psychiatry*, **39**, 1313–17.

Marshall, E. J., Edwards, G., Taylor C. (1994). Mortality in men with drinking problems: a 20 year follow-up. *Addiction*, **89**, 1293–1298.

Milby, J. B. (1988). Methadone maintenance to abstinence: how many make it? *Journal of Nervous and Mental Diseases*, **176**, 409–22.

Mulleady, G., Sherr, L. (1989). Lifestyle factors for drug users in relation to risks for HIV. *AIDS Care*, **1**, 45–50.

Newcomb, M. D., Scheier, L. M., Bentler, P. M. (1993). Effects of adolescent drug use on adult mental health: a prospective study of a community sample. *Experimental and Clinical Psychopharmacology*, **1**, 215–41.

Roberts, I., Barker, M., Li, L. (1997). Analysis of trends in deaths from accidental drug poisoning in teenagers. *British Medical Journal*, **315**, 289.

Robins, L. H. (1979). Addict careers. In: *Handbook on drug abuse* (ed. R. L. Dupont, A. Goldstein, J. O'Donnell), pp. 325–36. N.I.D.A., Washington.

Robson, P. (1996). Young people and illegal drugs. In: *Adolescent medicine* (ed. A. Macfarlane). Royal College of Physicians, London.

Robson, P., Bruce, M. (1997). A comparison of 'visible' and 'invisible' users of amphetamine, cocaine, and heroin: two distinct populations? *Addiction*, **92**, 1729–36.

Segest, E., Mygind, O., Bay, H. (1989). The allocation of drug addicts to different types of treatment. An evaluation and a two-year follow-up. *American Journal of Drug and Alcohol Abuse*, **15**, 41–53.

Simpson, D. D. (1979). The relation of time spent in drug abuse treatment to post-treatment outcome. *American Journal of Psychiatry*, **136**, 1449–53.

Simpson, D. D., Savage, J., Lloyd, M. R. (1979). Follow-up evaluation of treatment of drug abuse during 1969 to 1972. *Archives of General Psychiatry*, **36**, 772–80.

Stimson, G. V., Oppenheimer, E., Thorley, A. (1978). Seven-year follow-up of heroin addicts: drug use and outcome. *British Medical Journal*, **1**, 1190–2.

Thorley, A. (1981). Longitudinal studies of drug dependence. In: *Drug problems in Britain: a review of ten years* (ed. G. Edwards, C. Busch). Academic Press, London.

Torralba, L., Brugal, M. T.,Villalbi, J. R., Tortosa, A., Toribio, A., Valverda, J. L. (1996). Mortality due to adverse drug reactions: opiates and cocaine in Barcelona, 1989–93. *Addiction*, **91**, 419–26.

Vaillant, G. E. (1988). What can long-term follow-up teach us about relapse and prevention of relapse in addiction? *British Journal of Addiction*, **83**, 1147–57.

White, N. J. (1989). Prescribing in pregnancy. In: *Oxford textbook of medicine* (ed. D. J. Weatherall, J. G. G. Ledingham, D. A. Warrell). Oxford University Press, Oxford.

Zinberg, N. E., Jacobson, R. C. (1976). The natural history of 'chipping' (controlled use of opiates). *American Journal of Psychiatry*, **133**, 37–40.

Chapter 3: Alcohol

Anderson, P., Cremona, A., Paton, A. *et al.* (1993). The risk of alcohol. *Addiction*, **88**, 1493–508.

Andreasson, S., Romelsjo, A., Allebeck, P. (1988). Alcohol and mortality among young men: longitudinal study of Swedish conscripts. *British Medical Journal*, **296**, 1021–5.

Babor, T. (1986). *Alcohol: customs and rituals.* Burke Publishing Company Ltd, London.

Braun, S. (1996). *Buzz: the science and lore of alcohol and caffeine.* Oxford University Press, New York.

Edwards, G. (1987). *The treatment of drinking problems.* Blackwell Scientific Publications, Oxford.

Edwards, G., Anderson, P., Babor, T. F. *et al.* (1994). *Alcohol policy and the public good.* Oxford University Press, Oxford.

Fillmore, K. M., Golding, J. M., Graves, K. L. *et al.* (1998). Alcohol consumption and mortality. 1. Characteristics of drinking groups. *Addiction*, **93**, 183–97.

Leino, E. V., Romelsjo, A., Shoemaker, C. *et al.* (1998). Alcohol consumption and mortality. II. Studies of male populations. *Addiction*, **93**, 205–18.

McKeganey, N. (1998). Alcopops and young people: a suitable case for concern. *Addiction*, **93**, 471–3.

Marshall, E. J., Edwards, G., Taylor, C. (1994). Mortality in men with drinking problems: a 20-year follow-up. *Addiction*, **89**, 1293–8.

Mendelson, J. H., Mello, N. K. (1992). *Medical diagnosis and treatment of alcoholism.* McGraw-Hill, Inc., New York.

Porter, R. (1985). The drinking man's disease: the 'pre-history' of alcoholism in Georgian England. *British Journal of Addiction*, **80**, 385–96.

Rehm, J. Sempos, C. T. (1995). Alcohol consumption and all-cause mortality. *Addiction*, **90**, 471–80; commentaries. 481–8.

Robinson, J. (1988). *The demon drink*. Mitchell Beazley International Ltd, London.

Royal College of Physicians (1987). *A great and growing evil: the medical consequences of alcohol abuse*. Tavistock, London.

Spring, J. A., Buss, D. H. (1977). Three centuries of alcohol in the British diet. *Nature*, **270**, 567–72.

Vale, J. A., Meredith, T. J., Proudfoot, A. T. (1987). *Poisoning by alcohols and glycols*. In: *Oxford textbook of medicine* (2nd edn.) (ed. D. J. Weatherall, J. G. G. Ledingham, D. A. Warrell). Oxford University Press, Oxford.

Warner, J. (1997). Shifting categories of the social harms associated with alcohol: examples from late medieval and early modern England. *American Journal of Public Health*, **87**, 1788–97.

Warner, J. (1998). Historical perspectives on the shifting boundaries around youth and alcohol. The example of pre-industrial England, 1350–1750. *Addiction*, **93**, 641–57.

Chapter 4: Tobacco

Action on Smoking and Health (1997). Basic factsheets on tobacco and the tobacco industry. ASH, London.

Dyer, C. (1998). Confidential tobacco documents enter public domain. *British Medical Journal*, **316**, 1186.

Escobedo, L. G., Reddy, M., Giovino, G. A. (1998). The relationship between depressive symptoms and cigarette smoking. *Addiction*, **93**, 433–40.

Heishman, S. J. (1998). What aspects of human performance are truly enhanced by nicotine? *Addiction*, **93**, 317–20.

Henningfield, J. E. (1985). *Nicotine: an old-fashioned addiction*. Burke Publishing Company Ltd, London.

Laurence, D. R., Bennet, P. N. (1992). *Clinical pharmacology* (7th edn). Churchill Livingstone, Edinburgh.

Shiffman, S. (1989). Tobacco 'chippers' – individual differences in tobacco dependence. *Psychopharmacology*, **97**, 539–47.

Smee, C., Parsonage, M., Anderson, R., Duckworth, S. (1992). The effect of tobacco advertising on tobacco consumption. *Health Trends*, **24**, 111–2.

Wald, N., Nicolaides-Bouman, A. (1991). *UK smoking statistics*. Oxford University Press, Oxford.

Chapter 5: Cannabis

Adams, I. B., Martin, B. R. (1996). Cannabis: pharmacology and toxicology in animals and humans. *Addiction*, **91**, 1585–614.

British Medical Association (1997). *Therapeutic uses of cannabis*. Harwood Academic Publishers, Amsterdam.

Chait, L. D., Perry, J. L. (1992). Factors influencing self-administration of, and subjective response to, placebo marijuana. *Behavioural Pharmacology*, **3**, 545–52.

Culver, C. M., King, F. W. (1974). Neuropsychological assessment of undergraduate marijuana and LSD users. *Archives of General Psychiatry*, 31, 707–11.

Deahl, M. (1991). Cannabis and memory loss. *British Journal of Addiction*, **86**, 249–52.

de Fonseca, F. R., Carrera, M. R. A., Navarro, M., Koob, G. F., Weiss, F. (1997). Activation of corticotropin-releasing factor in the limbic system during cannabinoid withdrawal. *Science*, **276**, 2050–3.

Dittrich, A., Battig, K., von Zeppelin, I. (1973). Effects of delta 9 THC on memory, attention, and subjective state. *Psychopharmacologia*, **33**, 369–76.

English, D. R., Hulse, G. K., Milne, E., Holman, C. D. J., Bower, C. I. (1997). Maternal cannabis use and birth weight: a meta-analysis. *Addiction*, **92**, 1553–60.

Erinoff, L. (1990). Neurobiology of drug abuse: learning and memory. *N.I.D.A. Research Monograph 97*.

Feeney, D. M. (1976). Marijuana use among epileptics [letter]. *Journal of the American Medical Association*, **235**, 1105.

Grant, I., Rochford, J., Fleming, T., Stunkard, A. (1973). A neuropsychological assessment of the effects of moderate marijuana use. *Journal of Nervous and Mental Disease*, **156**, 278–80.

Hall, W., Solowij, N., Lemon, J. (ed.) (1994). *The health and psychological consequences of cannabis use*, National Drug Strategy Monograph Series No. 25, Australian Government Publishing Service, Canberra.

Howlett, A. C., Bidaut-Russell, M., Devane, W. A., Melvin, L. S., Johnson, M. R., Herkenham, M. (1990). The cannabinoid receptor: biochemical, anatomical and behavioural characterization. *Trends in Neurosciences*, 13, 421–3.

Mechoulam, R. (1986). The pharmacohistory of *Cannabis sativa*. In: *Cannabinoids as therapeutic agents* (ed. R. Mechoulam). CRC Press, Boca Raton, FL.

Mendhiratta, S. S., Wig, N. N., Verma, S. K. (1978). Some psychological correlates of long-term heavy cannabis users. *British Journal of Psychiatry*, 132, 482–6.

O'Shaugnessy, W. B. (1843). On the *Cannabis indica* or Indian hemp. *Pharmacology Journal*, 2, 594.

Pertwee, R. (1995). Pharmacological, physiological , and clinical implications of the discovery of cannabinoid receptors: an overview. In: *Cannabinoid receptors* (ed. R. Pertwee). Harcourt Brace, London.

Reynolds, J. R. (1890). Therapeutic uses and toxic effects of *Cannabis indica*. *Lancet*. 1, 637–8.

Robson, P. (1997). Cannabis. *Archives of Diseases in Childhood*, 77, 164–6.

Robson, P. (1998). Cannabis as medicine: time for the phoenix to arise? *British Medical Journal*, 316, 1034–5.

Rochford, J., Grant, I., LaVigne, G. (1977). Medical students and drugs: further neuropsychological and use pattern considerations. *International Journal of the Addictions*, 12, 1057–65.

Schwartz, R. H., Gruenewald, P. J., Klitzner, M., Ferdio, P. (1989). Short-term memory impairment in cannabis-dependent adolescents. *American Journal of Diseases of Childhood*, 143, 1214–19.

Tashkin, D. P. (1991). Marijuana and lung function. In: *Biochemistry and physiology of substance abuse*, Vol. 3 (ed. R. R. Watson). CRC Press, Boca Raton, FL.

Thomas, H. (1993). Psychiatric symptoms in cannabis users. *British Journal of Psychiatry*, 163, 141–9.

Varma, V. K., Malhotra, A. K., Dang, R., Das, K., Nehra, R. (1988). Cannabis and cognitive functions: a prospective study. *Drug and Alcohol Dependence*, 21, 147–52.

Wert, R. C., Raulin, M. L. (1986). The chronic cerebral effects of cannabis use. 1. Methodological issues and neurological findings. *International Journal of the Addictions*, **21**, 605–28.

Chapter 6: Cocaine, amphetamines, and other stimulants

Bateman, D. A., Ng, S. K. C., Hansen, C. A., Heagarty, M. C. (1993). The effects of intrauterine cocaine exposure in newborns. *American Journal of Public Health*, **83**, 190–3.

Chen, K., Scheier, L. M., Kandel, D. B. (1996). Effects of chronic cocaine use on physical health: a prospective study in a general population sample. *Drug and Alcohol Dependence*, **43**, 23–7.

Chiarello, R. J., Cole, J. O. (1987). The use of psychostimulants in general psychiatry. *Archives of General Psychiatry*, **44**, 288–95.

Connell, P. H. (1958). Amphetamine psychosis. *Maudsley Monograph No. 5*. Oxford University Press, Oxford.

Gawin, F. H. (1991). Cocaine addiction: psychology and neurophysiology. *Science*, **251**, 1580–6.

Gawin, F. H., Kleber, H. D. (1986). Abstinence symptomatology and psychiatric diagnosis in cocaine abusers. *Archives of General Psychiatry*, **43**, 107–13.

Gawin, F. H., Ellinwood, E. H. (1988). Cocaine and other stimulants. *New England Journal of Medicine*, **318**, 1173–82.

Gawin, F. H., Kleber, H. D., Byck, R., Rounsaville, B. J., Kosten, T. R., Jatlow, P. I., *et al.* (1989). Desipramine facilitation of initial cocaine abstinence. *Archives of General Psychiatry*, **46**, 117–21.

Gossop, M., Griffiths, P., Powis, B., Strang, J. (1994). Cocaine: patterns of use, route of administration, and severity of dependence. *British Journal of Psychiatry*, **164**, 660–4.

Griffin, M. L., Weiss, R. D., Mirin, S. M., Lange, U. (1989). A comparison of male and female cocaine abusers. *Archives of General Psychiatry*, **46**, 122–5.

Griffiths, P., Gossop, M., Wickenden, S., Dunworth, J., Harris, K., Lloyd, C. (1997). A transcultural pattern of drug use: qat (khat) in the UK. *British Journal of Psychiatry*, **170**, 281–4.

Hall, W., Hando, J., Darke, S., Ross, J. (1996). Psychological morbidity and route of administration among amphetamine users in Sydney, Australia. *Addiction*, **91**, 81–7.

Hando, J., Flaherty, B., Rutter, S. (1997). An Australian profile on the use of cocaine. *Addiction*, **92**, 173–82.

Hulse, G. K., English, D. R., Milne, E., Holman, C. J. D., Bower, C. I. (1997). Maternal cocaine use and low-birth-weight newborns: a meta-analysis. *Addiction*, **92**, 1561–70.

Hulse, G. K., Milne, E., English, D. R., Holman, C. J. D. (1997). Assessing the relationship between maternal cocaine use and abruptio placentae. *Addiction*, **92**, 1547–51.

Kleber, H. D. (1988). Epidemic cocaine abuse: America's present, Britain's future? *British Journal of Addiction*, **83**, 1359–71.

Klee, H. (1997). (ed.) *Amphetamine misuse*. Harwood Academy Publishers, The Netherlands.

Musto, D. F. (1973). Sherock Holmes and Sigmund Freud: a study in cocaine, *History of Medicine*, **5**, 16–20.

Musto, D. F. (1991). Opium, cocaine, and marijuana in American history. *Scientific American*, **July**, 40–7.

Newcomb, M. D., Bentler, P. M. (1986). Cocaine use among adolescents: longitudinal associations with social context, psychopathology, and use of other substances. *Addictive Behaviours*, **11**, 263–73.

Robson, P., Bruce, M. (1997). A comparison of 'visible' and 'invisible' users of amphetamine, cocaine, and heroin: two distinct populations? *Addiction*, **92**, 1729–36.

Shapiro, H. (1989). Crack: a briefing from the Institute for the Study of Drug Dependence. *Druglink*, **Sept/Oct**, 8–11.

Strang, J., Edwards, G. (1989). Cocaine and crack: the drug and the hype are both dangerous. *British Medical Journal*, **299**, 337–8.

Strang, J., Griffiths, P., Gossop, M. (1990). Crack and cocaine use in South London drug addicts: 1987–1989. *British Journal of Addiction*, **85**, 193–6.

Swerdlow, N. R., Hauger, R., Irwin, M., Koob, G. F., Britton, K. T., Pulvirenti, L. (1991). Endocrine, immune, and neurochemical changes in rats during withdrawal from chronic amphetamine intoxication. *Neuropsychopharmacology*, **5**, 23–31.

Chapter 7: Psychedelics and hallucinogens

Abraham, H. D., Aldridge, A. M. (1993). Adverse consequences of lysergic acid diethylamide. *Addiction*, **88**, 1327–34.

Abraham, H. D., Aldridge, A. M., Gogia, P. (1996). The psychopharmacology of hallucinogens. *Neuropsychopharmacology*, **14**, 285–98.

Abramson, H. A., Jarvik, M. E., Kaufman, M. R., Kronetsky, C., Levine, A., Wagner, M. (1955). Lysergic acid diethylamide (LSD–25): 1. Physiological and perceptual responses. *Journal of Physiology*, **39**, 3–62.

Bowers, M. B. (1977). Psychoses precipitated by psychotomimetic drugs: a follow-up study. *Archives of General Psychiatry*, **34**, 832–5.

Budd, R. D., Lindstrom, D. M. (1982). Characteristics of victims of PCP-related deaths in Los Angeles County, *Journal of Toxicology and Clinical Toxicology*, **19**, 997–1004.

Eisner, B. G., Cohen, S. (1958). Psychotherapy with lysergic acid diethylamide. *Journal of Nervous and Mental Diseases*, **127**, 528–39.

Grinspoon, L. (1979). The major psychedelic drugs: sources and effects *and* psychedelic drugs in the twentieth century. *Psychedelic drugs reconsidered*. Basic Books, Inc. New York.

Hofmann, A. (1980). *LSD: my problem child*. McGraw-Hill, New York.

Javitt, D. C., Zukin, S. R. (1991). Recent advances in the phencyclidine model of schizophrenia. *American Journal of Psychiatry*, **148**, 1301–8.

Isbell, H., Belleville, R. E., Fraser, H. F., Wikler, A., Logan, C. R. (1956). Studies on lysergic acid diethylamide (LSD–25). *Archives of Neurology and Psychiatry*, **76**, 468–78.

Matefy, R. E. (1978). Psychedelic drug flashbacks. *Addictive Behaviour*, **3**, 165–78.

Milhorn, H. T. (1991). Diagnosis and management of phencyclidine intoxication. *American Family Physician*, **43**, 1293–302.

Pierce, P. A., Peroutka, S. J. (1990). Antagonist properties of d-LSD at 5-hydroxytryptamine$_2$ receptors *Neuropsychopharmacology*, **3**, 503–8.

Rudgley, R. (1995). The archaic use of hallucinogens in Europe: an archaeology of altered states. *Addiction*, **90**, 163–4.

Sanders-Bush, E., Burris, K. D., Knoth, K. (1988). Lysergic acid diethylamide and 2,5-dimethoxy-4-methylamphetamine are partial agonists at serotonin receptors linked to phosphoinositide hydrolysis. *Journal of Pharmacology and Experimental Therapeutics*, **246**, 924–8.

Yesavage, J. A., Freeman, A. M. (1978). Acute phencyclidine (PCP) intoxication: psychopathology and prognosis. *Journal of Clinical Psychiatry*, **44**, 664–5.

Weil, A. T. (1977). Observations on consciousness alteration: some notes on Datura. *Journal of Psychedelic Drugs*, **9**, 165–9.

Chapter 8: The inhalants

Anderson, H. R. (1990). Increase in deaths from deliberate inhalation of fuel gases and pressurised aerosols [letter]. *British Medical Journal.* **301**, 41.

Chadwick, O., Anderson, R., Bland, M., Ramsey, J. (1989). Neuropsychological consequences of volatile substance abuse: a population-based study of secondary school pupils. *British Medical Journal*, **298**, 1679–84.

Cooke, B. R. B., Evans, D. A., Farrow, S. C. (1988). Solvent misuse in secondary school children: a prevalence study. *Community Medicine*, **10**, 8–13.

Davies, B., Thorley, A., O'Connor, D. (1985). Progression of addiction careers in young adult solvent misusers. *British Medical Journal*, **290**, 109–10.

Dinwiddie, S. H. (1994). Abuse of inhalants: a review. *Addiction*, **89**, 925–39.

Editorial (1990) Solvent abuse: little progress after 20 years. *British Medical Journal*, **300**, 135–6.

Ives, R. (1990). Helping the sniffers. *Druglink*, **5** (5), 10–12.

Ives, R. (1990). The fad that refuses to fade. *Druglink*, **5** (5), 12–13.

King, M. D., Day, R. E., Oliver, J. S., Lush, M., Watson, J. M. (1981). Solvent encephalopathy. *British Medical Journal*, **283**, 663–5.

Nicholi, A. M. (1983). The inhalants: an overview. *Psychosomatics*, **24**, 914–21.

Lynn, E. J., Walter, R. G., Harris, L. A., Dendy, R., James, M. (1972). Nitrous oxide: it's a gas. *Journal of Psychedelic Drugs*, **5**, 1–7.

Ramsey, J., Bloor, K., Anderson, R. (1990). 'Dangerous games: UK solvent deaths 1983–1988. *Druglink*, **5** (5), 8–9.

Richardson, H. (1989). Volatile substance abuse: evaluation and treatment. *Human Toxicology*, **8**, 319–22.

Ron, M. A. (1986). Volatile substance abuse: a review of possible long-term neurological, intellectual, and psychiatric sequelae. *British Journal of Psychiatry*, **148**, 235–46.

Schwartz, R. H., Peary, P. (1986). Abuse of isobutyl nitrite inhalation (Rush) by adolescents. *Clinical Pediatrics*, **25**, 308–10.

Westermeyer, J. (1987). The psychiatrist and solvent inhalant abuse: recognition, assessment, and treatment. *American Journal of Psychiatry*, **144**, 903–7.

Chapter 9: Ecstasy and other 'party drugs'

Barnes, D. M. (1988). New data intensify the agony over Ecstasy. *Science*, **239**, 864–6.

Chadwick, I. S., Linsey, A., Freemont, A. J., Doran, B., Curry, P. D. (1991). Ecstasy, a fatality associated with coagulopathy and hyperthermia. *Journal of the Royal Society of Medicine*, **84**, 371.

Creighton, F. J., Black, D. L., Hyde, C. E. (1991). Ecstasy psychosis and flashbacks. *British Journal of Psychiatry*, **159**, 713–15.

Curran, H. V., Travill, R. A. (1997). Mood and cognitive effects of MDMA: weekend 'high' followed by mid-week low. *Addiction*, **92**, 821–31.

Dorn, N., Murji, K., South, N. (1991). Abby, the Ecstasy dealer. *Druglink*, **6** (6), 14–15.

Forsyth, A. J. M. (1996). Places and patterns of drug use in the Scottish dance scene. *Addiction*, **91**, 511–21.

Galloway, G. P., Frederick, S. L., Staggers, F. E., Gonzales, M., Stalcup, A., Smith, D. E. (1997). Gamma-hydroxybutyrate: an emerging drug of abuse that causes physical dependence. *Addiction*, **92**, 89–96.

Greer, B., Tolbert, R. (1986). Subjective reports of the effects of MDMA in a clinical setting. *Journal of Psychoactive Drugs*, **18**, 319–27.

Hayner, G. N., Mckinney, H. (1986). MDMA: the darker side of Ecstasy. *Journal of Psychoactive Drugs*, **18**, 341–7.

Henry, J. A. (1992). Toxicity and deaths from Ecstasy. *Lancet*, **340**, 384–7.

Lenton, S. Boys, A., Norcross, K. (1997). Raves, drugs, and experience: drug use by a sample of people who attend raves in Western Australia. *Addiction*, **92**, 1327–37.

Mcguire, P., Fahy, T. (1991). Chronic paranoid psychosis after misuse of MDMA (Ecstasy). *British Medical Journal*, **302**, 697.

Molliver, M. E., Berger, U. V., Mamounas, L. A., Molliver, D. C., O'Hearn, E., Wilson, M. A. (1990). Neurotoxicity of MDMA and related compounds: anatomic studies. *Annals of the New York Academy of Sciences*, **600**, 640–64.

Pearson, G., Ditton, J., Newcombe, R., Gilman, M. (1991). An introduction to Ecstasy use by young people in Britain. *Druglink*, **6** (6), 10–11.

Price, L. H., Ricaurte, G. A., Krystal, J. H., Heninger, G. R. (1989). Neurendocrine and mood responses to intravenous L-tryptophan in MDMA users. *Archives of General Psychiatry*, **46**, 20–2.

Shapiro, H. (1989). The speed trip: MDMA in perspective. *Druglink*, **4** (2), 14–15.

Solowij, N., Hall, W., Lee, N. (1992). Recreational MDMA use in Sydney: a profile of Ecstasy users and their experiences with the drug. *British Journal of Addiction*, **87**, 1161–72.

Steele, T. D., McCann, U.D., Ricaurte, G. A. (1994). 3, 4-Methylenedioxymethamphetamine (MDMA, 'Ecstasy'): pharmacology and toxicology in animals and humans. *Addiction*, **89**, 539–50.

Whitaker-Azmitia, P. M., Aronson, T. A. (1989). Ecstasy-induced panic [letter]. *American Journal of Psychiatry*, **146**, 119.

Chapter 10: Anabolic steroids

Korkia, P. (1994) Anabolic steroid use in Britain. *Drug Policy*, 5, 6–10.

Korkia, P. (1997). Anabolic– androgenic steroids and their uses in sport and recreation. *Journal of Substance Misuse*, 2, 131–5.

Williamson, D. (1994). The psychological effects of anabolic steorids. *Drug Policy*, 5, 18–22.

Chapter 11: Tranquillizers and sleeping pills

Busto, U. E., Sellers, E. M., (1991). Anxiolytics and sedative/hypnotics dependence. *British Journal of Addiction*, **86**, 1647–52.

Darke, S. (1994). Benzodiazepine use among injecting drug users: problems and implications. *Addiction*, **89**, 379–82.

Darke, S., Ross, J., Cohen, J. (1994). The use of benzodiazepines among regular amphetamine users. *Addiction*, **89**, 1683–90.

Higgit, A. C., Lader, M. H., Fonagy, P. (1985). Clinical management of benzodiazepine dependence. *British Medical Journal*, **291**, 688–90.

Klee, H., Faugier, J., Hayes, C., Boulton, T., Morris, J. (1990). AIDS-related risk behaviour, polydrug use, and temazepam. *British Journal of Addiction*, **85**, 1125–32.

Lader, M., File, S. (1987). The biological basis of benzodiazepine dependence. *Psychological Medicine*, **17**, 539–47.

Lader, M., Morton, S. (1991). Benzodiazepine problems. *British Journal of Addiction*, **86**, 823–8.

Leonard, B. E. (1989). Are all benzodiazepines the same? An assessment of the similarities and differences in pharmacological properties. *Psychiatry in Practice*, (Special Issue), **April**, 9–12.

Livingston, M. G. (1991). Benzodiazepine dependence: avoidance, detection, and management. *Prescribers Journal*, **31**, 149–56.

Lynch, S., Priest, R. (1992). Insomnia: who suffers, when, and why? *Prescriber*, **5th March**, 37–44.

Nutt, D. (1991). Actions of classic and alternative anxiolytics. *Prescriber*, **19th May**, 31–4.

Perera, K. M. H., Tulley, M., Jenner, F. A. (1987). The use of benzodiazepines among drug addicts. *British Journal of Addiction*, **82**, 511–15.

Petersson, H., Lader, M. (1984). Dependence on tranquillizers. *Maudsley Monograph No. 28*. Oxford University Press, Oxford.

Rickels, K., Schweizer, E., Case, W. G., Greenblatt, D. J. (1990). Long-term therapeutic use of benzodiazepines: effects of abrupt discontinuation. *Archives of General Psychiatry*, **47**, 899–907.

Schweizer, E., Rickels, K., Case, G., Greenblatt, D. J. (1990). Long-term therapeutic use of benzodiazepines: effect of gradual taper. *Archives of General Psychiatry*, **47**, 908–15.

Seivewright, N., Donmall, M., Daly, C. (1993). Benzodiazepines in the illicit drugs scene: the UK picture and some treatment dilemmas. *International Journal of Drug Policy*, **4**, 42–8.

Warneke, L. B. (1991). Benzodiazepines: abuse and new use. *Canadian Journal of Psychiatry*, **36**, 194–204.

Chapter 12: Heroin and the opioids

Ball, J. C., Lange, W. R., Myers, C. P., Friedman, S. R. (1988). Reducing the risk of AIDS through methadone maintenance treatment. *Journal of Health and Social Behaviour*, **29**, 214–26.

Bennett, T., Wright, R. (1986). The impact of prescribing on the crimes of opioid users. *British Journal of Addiction*, **81**, 265–73.

Blackwell, J. S. (1983). Drifting, controlling, and overcoming: opiate users who avoid becoming chronically dependent. *Journal of Drug Issues*, **13**, 219–35.

Caviston, P. (1987). Pregnancy and opiate addiction. *British Medical Journal*, **295**, 285.

Darke, S., Zador, D. (1996). Fatal heroin overdose: a review. *Addiction*, **91**, 1765–72.

Farrell, M., Neeleman, J., Griffiths, P., Strang, J. (1996). Suicide and overdose among opiate addicts. *Addiction*, **91**, 321–3.

Kalant, H. (1997). Opium revisited: a brief review of its nature, composition, non-medical use, and relative risks. *Addiction*, **92**, 267–77.

Kramer, J. C. (1980). The opiates: two centuries of scientific study. *Journal of Psychedelic Drugs.*, **12**, 89–103.

Levinthal, C. F. (1985). Milk of paradise, milk of hell: the history of ideas about opium. *Perspectives in Biology and Medicine*, **28**, 561–77.

Martindale Pharmacopoeia (29th edn). Chlorpromazine – use in neonates withdrawing from opiates. p. 724.

Musto, D. F. (1991). Opium, cocaine, and marijuana in American history. *Scientific American*, **July**, 40–7.

Porter, J., Jick, H. (1980). Addiction rare in patients treated with narcotics [letter]. *New England Journal of Medicine*, **302**, 123.

Rounsaville, B. J., Weissman, M. M., Crits-Christoph, K., Wilber, C., Kleber, H. (1982). Diagnosis and symptoms of depression in opiate addicts. *Archives of General Psychiatry*, **39**, 151–6.

Skidmore, C. A., Robertson, J. R., Roberts, J. J. K. (1989). Changes in HIV risk-taking behaviour in intravenous drug users: a second follow-up.*British Journal of Addiction*, **84**, 695–6.

Sternbach, G. I., Varon, J. (1992). Designer drugs. *Postgraduate Medicine*, **91**, 169–76.

Strang, J., Griffiths, P., Gossop, M. (1997). Heroin smoking by 'chasing the dragon': origins and history. *Addiction*, **92**, 673–83.

Swift, W., Williams, G., Neill, O., Grenyer, B. (1990). The prevalence of minor psychopathology in opioid users seeking treatment. *British Journal of Addiction*, **85**, 629–34.

Tagliaro, F., De Battisti, Z., Smith, F. P., Marigo, M. (1998). Death from heroin over-dose: findings from hair analysis. *Lancet*, **351**, 1923–5.

Thomson, J. W. (1984). Opioid peptides. *British Medical Journal*, **288**, 259–60.

Wood, P. L. (1982). Multiple opiate receptors: support for unique mu, delta, and kappa sites. *Neuropharmacology*, **21**, 487–97.

Zinberg, N. E. (1979). Non-addictive opiate use. In: *Handbook on drug abuse* (ed. R. L. Dupont, A. Goldstein, and J. O'Donnell), pp. 303–14. N.I.D.A., Washington.

Zinberg, N. E., Jacobson, R. C. (1976). The natural history of 'chipping' (controlled use of opiates). *American Journal of Psychiatry*, **133**, 37–40.

Chapter 13: The nature of addiction

Babor, T. F., Cooney, N. L., Lauerman, R. J. (1987). The dependence syndrome concept as a psychological theory of relapse behaviour: an empirical evaluation of alcoholic and opiate addicts. *British Journal of Addiction*, **82**, 393–405.

Childress, A. R., McLellan, A. T., O'Brien, C. P. (1986). Conditioned responses in a methadone population: a comparison of laboratory, clinic, and natural settings. *Journal of Substance Abuse Treatment*, **3**, 173–9.

Dimond, S. J. (1980). Consciousness. In: *Neuropsychology: a textbook of systems and psychological functions of the human brain* (ed. S. J. Dimond). Butterworths, London.

Epping-Jordan, M. P., Watkins, S. S., Koob, G. F., Markou, A. (1998). Dramatic decreases in brain reward function during nicotine withdrawal. *Nature*, **393**, 76–9.

Glassman, A. H., Koob, G. F. (1996). Psychoactive smoke. *Nature*, **379**, 677–8.

Gossop, M. (1976). Drug dependence and self-esteem. *International Journal of the Addictions*, **11**, 741–53.

Lart, R. (1992). Changing images of the addict and addiction. *International Journal of Drug Policy*, **3**, 118–25.

Legarda, J. J., Bradley, B. P., Sartory, G. (1987). Subjective and psychophysiological effects of drug-related cues in drug users. *Journal of Psychophysiology*, **4**, 393–400.

McAuliffe, W. E., Rohman, M., Felman, B., Launer, E. K. (1985). The role of euphoric effects in the opiate addictions of heroin addicts, medical patients, and impaired health professionals. *Journal of Drug Issues*, **Spring**, 203–24.

Pidoplichko, V. I., DeBiasi, M., Williams, J. T., Dani, J. A. (1997). Nicotine activates and desensitizes midbrain dopamine neurons. *Nature*, **390**, 401–4.

Room, R. (1989). Drugs, consciousness, and self-control: popular and medical conceptions. *International Review of Psychiatry*, **1**, 63–70.

Saunders, B., Allsop, S. (1987). Relapse: a psychological perspective. *British Journal of Addiction*, **82**, 417–29.

Stewart, J., de Wit, H., and Eikelboom, R. (1984). Role of unconditioned and conditioned drug effects in the self-administration of opiates and stimulants. *Psychological Review*, **91**, 251–68.

West, R. (1989). The psychological basis of addiction. *International Review of Psychiatry*, **1**, 71–80.

Wikler, A., Pescor, F. T. (1967). Classical conditioning of a morphine abstinence phenomenon, reinforcement of opioid-drinking behaviour, and 'relapse' in morphine-addicted rats. *Psychopharmacologia*, **10**, 255–84.

Wilson, G. T. (1987). Cognitive processes in addiction. *British Journal of Addiction*, **82**, 343–53.

Wise, R. A. (1988). The neurobiology of craving: implications for the understanding and treatment of addiction. *Journal of Abnormal Psychology*, **97**, 118–32.

Chapter 14: Helping problem drug users

Bennett, T., Wright, R. (1986). The impact of prescribing on the crimes of opioid users. *British Journal of Addiction*, **81**, 265–73.

Bradley, B. P., Phillips, G., Green, L., Gossop, M. (1989). Circumstances surrounding the initial lapse to opiate use following detoxification. *British Journal of Psychiatry*, **154**, 354–9.

Brettle, R. P., Bisset, K., Burns, S., Davidson, J., Davidson, S. J., Gray, J. M. N., *et al.* (1987). Human immunodeficiency virus and drug misuse: the Edinburgh experience. *British Medical Journal*, **295**, 421–4.

Charney, D. S., Heringer, G. R., Kleber, H. D. (1986). Combined use of clonidine and naltrexone as a rapid, safe, and effective treatment of abrupt withdrawal from methadone. *American Journal of Psychiatry*, **143**, 831–7.

Drummond, D. C. (1997). Alcohol interventions: do the best things come in small packages? *Addiction*, **92**, 375–9.

Gossop, M. (1978). A review of the evidence for methadone maintenance as a treatment for narcotic addiction. *Lancet*, **1**, 812–15.

Gossop, M., Green, L., Phillips, G., Bradley, B. (1989). Lapse, relapse, and survival among opiate addicts after treatment – a prospective follow-up study. *British Journal of Psychiatry*, **154**, 348–53.

Gossop, M., Griffiths, P., Bradley, B., Strang, J. (1989). Opiate withdrawal symptoms in response to 10-day and 21-day methadone withdrawal programmes.*British Journal of Psychiatry*, **154**, 360–3.

Hajek, P., West, R. (1998). Treating nicotine dependence: the case for specialist smokers' clinics. *Addiction*, **93**, 637–40.

Hartnoll, L., Mitcheson, M. C., Battersby, A., Brown, G., Ellis, M., Fleming, P., *et al.* (1980). Evaluation of heroin maintenance in controlled trial. *Archives of General Psychiatry*, **37**, 877–84.

Hughes, J. R. *et al.* (1996). Practice guidelines for the treatment of patients with nicotine dependence. *American Journal of Psychiatry*, **153**, 1–31.

Joe, G. W., Simpson, D. D. (1975). Retention in treatment of drug abusers: 1971–72 DARP admissions. *American Journal of Drug and Alcohol Abuse*, **2**, 63–71.

Joe, G. W., Simpson, D. D., Broome, K. M. (1998). Effects of readiness for drug abuse treatment on client retention and assessment of process. *Addiction*, **93**, 1177–90.

Judson, B. A., Goldstein, A. (1982). Prediction of long-term outcome for heroin addicts admitted to a methadone maintenance program. *Drug and Alcohol Dependence*, **10**, 383–91.

Kleber, H. D. (1989). Treatment of drug dependence: what works. *International Review of Psychiatry*, **1**, 81–100.

Kreek, M. J. (1979). Methadone in treatment: physiological and pharmacological issues. In: *Handbook on drug abuse* (ed. R. L. Dupont, A. Goldstein, and J. O'Donnell), pp. 57–86, N.I.D.A., Washington.

McCrady, B. S., Langenbucher, J. W. (1996). Alcohol treatment and health care system reform. *Archives of General Psychiatry*, **53**, 737–46.

McLellan, A. T. Luborsky, L., Woody, G. E., O'Brien, C. P., Druley, K. A. (1982). Is treatment for substance abuse effective? *Journal of the American Medical Association*, **247**, 1423–8.

McLellan, A. T., Luborsky, L., O'Brien, W. G. E., Druley, K. A. (1983). Predicting response to alcohol and drug abuse treatments. *Archives of General Psychiatry*, **40**, 620–5.

McLellan, A. T., Woody, G. E., Luborsky, L., Geohl, L. (1988). Is the counsellor an 'active ingredient' in substance abuse rehabilitation? (An examination of treatment success among four counsellors.) *Journal of Nervous and Mental Disease*, **176**, 423–30.

Maddux, J. F., Desmond, D. P. (1982). Residence relocation inhibits opioid dependence. *Archives of General Psychiatry*, **39**, 1313–17.

Marks, I. (1990). Behavioural (non-chemical) addictions. *British Journal of Addiction*, **85**, 1389–94.

Marks, J. (1987). State-rationed drugs. *Druglink*, **2**, 14.

Marlatt, G. A., George, W. H. (1984). Relapse prevention: introduction and overview of the model. *British Journal of Addiction*, **79**, 261–73.

Marsch, L. A. (1998). The efficacy of methadone maintenance interventions in reducing illicit opiate use, HIV risk behaviour, and criminality: a meta-analysis. *Addiction*, **88**, 515–32.

Miller, W. R. (1983). Motivational interviewing with problem drinkers. *Behavioural Psychotherapy*, **11**, 147–72.

Perneger, T. V., Giner, F., del Rio, M., Mino, A. (1998). Randomised trial of heroin maintenance programme for addicts who fail in conventional drug treatments. *British Medical Journal*, **317**, 13–18.

Polkinghorne, J. (1996). *Task force to review services for drug misusers: a final report.* Department of Health Publications, London.

Prochaska, J. O., DiClemente, C. C. (1983). Stages and processes of self-change of smoking: toward an integrative model of change. *Journal of Consulting and Clinical Psychology*, **51**, 390–5.

Rathod, N. (1987). Substitution is not a solution. *Druglink*, **2**, 16.

Riley, D. (1987). The management of the pregnant drug addict. *Bulletin of the Royal College of Psychiatrist*, **11**, 362–5.

Robertson, J. R., Bucknall, A. B. V., Welsby, P. D., Roberts, J. J. K., Inglis, J. M., Peutherer, J. F. *et al.* (1986). Epidemic of AIDS-related virus infection among intravenous drug abusers. *British Medical Journal*, **292**, 527–9.

Robson, P. (1992). Opiate misusers: are treatments effective? In: *Practical problems in clinical psychiatry* (ed. K. Hawton and P. Cowen). Oxford University Press, Oxford.

Rounsaville, B. J., Glazer, W., Wiber, C. H., Weissman, M. M., Kleber, H. D. (1983). Short-term interpersonal psychotherapy in methadone-maintained opiate addicts. *Archives of General Psychiatry*, **40**, 629–36.

Russell, M. A., Stapleton, J. A., Jackson, P. H., Hajek, P., Belcher, M. (1987). District programme to reduce smoking: effect of clinic-supported brief intervention by general practitioners. *British Medical Journal*, **295**, 1240–4.

Schuckit, M. A. (1996). Recent developments in the pharmacotherapy of alcohol dependence. *Journal of Consulting and Clinical Psychology*, **64**, 669–76.

Simpson, D. (1979). The relation of time spent in drug-abuse treatment to post-treatment outcome. *American Journal of Psychiatry*, **136**, 1449–53.

Skidmore, C.A., Robertson, J. R., Roberts, J. J. K. (1989). Changes in HIV risk-taking behaviour in intravenous drug users: a second follow-up. *British Journal of Addiction*, **84**, 695–6.

Stewart, J., de Wit, H., Eikelboom, R. (1984). Role of unconditioned and conditioned drug effects in the self-administration of opiates and stimulants. *Psychological Review*, **91**, 251–68.

Stimson, G. V., Alldritt, I. J., Dolan, K. A., Donoghue, M. C., Lart, R. A. (1988). *Injecting equipment exchange schemes: final report.* Monitoring Research Group, Sociology Department, Goldsmiths' College, London SE14 6NW.

Swift, W., Williams, G., Neill, O., Grenyer, B. (1990). The prevalence of minor psychopathology in opioid users seeking treatment. *British Journal of Addiction*, **85**, 629–34.

Wolk, J., Wodak, A., Guinan, J. J., Macaskill, P., Simpson, J. M. (1990). The effect of a needle and syringe exchange on a methadone maintenance unit. *British Journal of Addiction*, **85**, 1445–50.

Woody, G.E., Luborsky, L., McLellan, A. T., O'Brien, C. P., Beek, A. T., Blaine, J., *et al.* (1983). Psychotherapy for opiate addicts – does it help? *Archives of General Psychiatry*, **40**, 639–45.

Chapter 15: Drug policy – a time for change?

Advisory Council on Misuse of Drugs (1988). *AIDS and drug misuse.* DHSS, HMSO, London.

Alexander, B. K. (1990). Alternatives to the war on drugs. *Journal of Drug Issues*, **20**, 1–27.

Berridge, V. (1984). Drugs and social policy: the establishment of drug control in Britain 1900–1930. *British Journal of Addiction*, **79**, 17–29.

Berridge, V., Rawson, N. S. B. (1979). Opiate use and legislative control: a nineteenth-century case study. *Social Science and Medicine*, 13, 351–63.

Clark, A. (1993). Adding up the pros and cons of legalization. *International Journal of Drug Policy*, **4**, 116–21.

Editorial (1987). Management of drug addicts: hostility, humanity, and pragmatism. *Lancet*, **May 9**, i, 1068–9.

Engelsman, E. L. (1989). Dutch policy on the management of drug-related problems. *British Journal of Addiction*, **84**, 211–18.

Engelsman, E. L. (1991). Drug misuse and the Dutch. *British Medical Journal*, **302**, 484–5.

Farrell, M., Strang, J. (1990). The lure of masterstrokes: drug legalization. *British Journal of Addiction*, **85**, 5–7.

Gerada, C., Orgel, M., Strang, J. (1992). Health clinics for problem drug misusers. *Health Trends*, **24**, 68–9.

Glanz, A. (1986). Findings of a national survey of the role of general practitioners in the treatment of opiate misuse: views on treatment. *British Medical Journal*, **293**, 543–5.

Home Office (1986). *Tackling drug misuse: a summary of the government's strategy* (2nd Edn). Home Office, London SW1H 9AT.

Lemmens, P. H. H. M., Garretson, H. F. L. (1998). Unstable pragmatism: Dutch policy under national and international pressure. *Addiction*, **93**, 157–62.

MacCoun, R., Reuter, P. (1997). Interpreting Dutch cannabis policy: reasoning by analogy in the legalization debate. *Science*, **278** 47–52.

Marks, J. (1985). Opium, the religion of the people. *Lancet*, 2, 1439–40.

Nadelman, E.(1992). Legalization or harm reduction: the debate continues. *International Journal of Drug Policy*, **3**, 76–82.

Plant, M., Single, E., Stockwell, T. (1997). *Alcohol: minimising the harm*. Free Association Books, London.

Robson, P. (1992). Illegal drugs: time to change the law? *Oxford Medical School Gazette*, **43**, 20–3.

Roemer, R. (1991). Public health and the law. In: *Oxford textbook of public health*, Vol. 1. (Ed. W. W. Holland, G. Knox, R. Detels) Oxford University Press, Oxford.

Ruttenber, A. J. (1991). Stalking the elusive designer drugs: techniques for monitoring new problems in drug abuse. *Journal of Addictive Diseases*, **11**, 71–7.

Saunders, J. B. (1990). The great legalization debate [editorial]. *Drug and Alcohol Review*, **9**, 3–5.

Smee, C., Parsonage, M., Anderson, R., Duckworth, S. (1992). The effect of tobacco advertising on tobacco consumption. *Health Trends*, **24**, 111–16.

Stevenson, R. (1991). The case for legalizing drugs. *Economic Affairs*, **11**, 14–17.

Smart, C. (1984). Social policy and drug addiction: a critical study of policy development. *British Journal of Addiction*, **79**, 31–9.

Strang, J. (1987). The prescribing debate. *Druglink*, **2** (4), 10–12.

Strang, J., Ghodse, H., Johns, A. (1987). Responding flexibly but not gullibly to drug addiction. *British Medical Journal*, **295**, 1364.

van de Wijngaart, G. J. (1989). What lessons from the Dutch experience can be applied? *British Journal of Addiction*, **84**, 990–2.

Willis, J. H. (1987). Reflection [editorial]. *British Journal of Addictions*, **82**, 1181–2.

index